W9-DGT-217

CONTEMPORARY ANALYSIS IN EDUCATION SERIES
General Editor: Philip Taylor

Contemporary Analysis in Education Series

The Aims of Primary Education and the National Curriculum

Edited by
Nigel Proctor

The Falmer Press
(A member of the Taylor & Francis Group)
London ● Philadelphia ● New York

UK   The Falmer Press, Rankine Road, Basingstoke, Hampshire
RG24 0PR

USA   The Falmer Press, Taylor & Francis Inc., 1900 Frost Road,
Suite 101, Bristol PA 19007

© Nigel Proctor 1990

*All rights reserved. No part of this publication may be reproduced, stored
in a retrieval system, or transmitted, in any form or by any means, electronic,
mechanical, photocopying, recording, or otherwise, without permission in
writing from the Publisher.*

First published 1990

British Library Cataloguing in Publication Data
The aims of primary education and the National Curriculum.
(Contemporary analysis in education series).
1. Great Britain. Primary education. Aims
I. Proctor, Nigel   II. Series
372.941
ISBN 1-85000-599-1
ISBN 1-85000-560-5 pbk

Library of Congress Cataloging-in-Publication Data
Proctor, Nigel.
The aims of primary education and the national curriculum/ed. by
Nigel Proctor.
Includes bibliographical references.
ISBN 1-85000-559-1. ISBN 1-85000-560-5 (pbk.)
1. Education, Elementary — Great Britain. 2 Education, Elementary
— Great Britain — Aims and objectives. 3. Curriculum planning —
Great Britain. I. Title.
LA633.P77 1990
372.941 — dc20

DISCARDED
WIDENER UNIVERSITY

Jacket design by Caroline Archer

Typeset in 10½/13 point Bembo by
Bramley Typesetting Limited, 12 Campbell Court, Bramley,
Basingstoke, Hants.

*Printed in Great Britain by
Taylor & Francis (Printers) Ltd, Basingstoke*

WIDENER UNIVERSITY
WOLFGRAM
LIBRARY
CHESTER PA.

Contents

Contents

General Editor's Preface

Education is a millennial pursuit. It is about betterment, the betterment of the young of today for their life in the future of tomorrow. In order to give the pursuit of education direction and its purpose meaning, some idea of what its aims are is essential. It is with this 'essential' in primary education that this book concerns itself. It is, of course, a concern circumscribed, at least for now, by the 1988 Education Reform Act and the National Curriculum.

It is the achievement of this book, its contributors and its editor, Nigel Proctor, to place the aims of primary education in both its social as well as its educational context. The history of the changing aims of primary education is not neglected nor are the influences of the major social and cultural changes of the twentieth century on them. Moreover, there is clear focus on the practicalities: on how aims can be and are managed in the day to day realities of the primary school.

The Aims of Primary Education and the National Curriculum is a timely book. National Curriculum or not, there remains the moral issue of how the primary school teacher justifies the claim that what they teach and how they teach it is for the betterment of the children whom they teach. It will not be education, but merely training, if questions of aims and purpose in primary education go by default; if teachers do not, even within the constraints of the present, ask: 'With what end in view do I teach?' If this book does nothing more than bring this question forcibly to the minds of primary school teachers in a way that informs their teaching, it will have served its purpose.

Philip Taylor
June, 1989

Preface

Primary education in this country is currently undergoing something of a revolution. This has been caused almost exclusively by the introduction of the National Curriculum and assessment, together with a number of administrative changes brought in by the 1988 Education Reform Act. More than ever before, attention is being paid to the aims and purposes of education, and to the type of curriculum which can best meet these aims.

John Dewey, writing about American education some fifty years ago, complained that:

> The traditional school could get along without any consistently developed philosophy of education. About all that was required in that time was a set of abstract words like culture, discipline, our great cultural heritage etc., actual guidance being derived not from them but from custom and established routines.

We could probably say the same about some traditional British primary schools until very recently, despite the international reputation held by our primary — and particularly infant — school system. The 'custom and established routines' mentioned by Dewey are commonly of the very highest order. This quality, experience and expertise must be the lynch-pin on which to establish a new set of goals for primary education which will raise still further the standards of our schools.

Some of the goals have already been set by the Government in the 1988 Education Reform Act. The two aims of education included in the Act use Dewey's 'set of abstract words like culture . . .' but the Act builds in an extremely tight structure with National Curriculum subjects following detailed programmes of study and standardized tests, which the Government considers will enable schools to meet these goals. But individual primary schools, governors, heads and teachers, will still have the responsibility to plan the curriculum and to justify the 'why', the 'how' and the 'what' of their teaching programmes to parents, advisers and inspectors. This book should help them to perform these duties.

This is therefore not a traditional book on the philosophy of primary education. It does not deal *per se* with child development, the concept and theory of play, experience and culture. Phrases such as 'whole personality', 'happy atmosphere', 'full and satisfying life', 'full development of powers' were rejected by the Plowden Report (CACE, 1967) and, although the words may be mentioned by individual contributors and are included in many curriculum statements, they do not form the basis of the book. Nor does the book represent a collection of research reports, though again it draws on evidence from empirical enquiry.

Instead, the book adopts an approach which has been termed 'liberal pragmatism' (Richards, 1987). This sees the primary curriculum as a set of learning experiences, usually determined by teachers, which shape and refine children's existing knowledge, interests and experiences; it is 'liberal' in giving a broad range of experience through a variety of teaching and learning styles, and 'pragmatic' in building on, and extending, much current practice through careful planning of aims and content. Richards argues that: 'The last 10 years have witnessed the gradual formulation, refinement and public expression of this view of primary education; the perspective has set, and continues to set, the agenda for discussion and policy-making in English primary education.'

It is hoped that this book will help to promote and develop this discussion. It is organized into five parts, each with a brief editorial introduction. Part 1 sets the scene by providing a historical perspective on the aims of primary education and considers when and how the new aims of the National Curriculum emerged. The second part focuses on the various roles and views of those most directly involved in teaching and learning: teachers and heads, children and parents. We then consider, in Part 3, some pragmatic ideas on how the aims can be implemented in primary schools, through curriculum coordinators, through cross-curricular work, and through adopting a 'whole-school' approach. Part 4 considers some of the attendant factors involved in primary education, such as to what extent environment and society influence the aims of primary education. Finally we examine what is happening in some other countries; is Britain alone in rethinking the aims of schools?

All the chapters have been written especially for this book by contributors drawn from all fields of our educational system, including four practising primary school teachers. This blend of experience ensures a range of comment on primary education which should be of interest and value to students on teacher-education courses and to practising teachers, heads and local authorities currently wrestling with the problems of replanning their curricula.

My sincere thanks are extended to Philip Taylor, who invited me to edit this book, and to Colin Richards, HMI, who provided considerable help and guidance in the early planning stages. I am also greatly indebted to the contributors for their interest, involvement and patience, and to Hogarth Press for permission to use the extract on page 171 from *Cider with Rosie* by Laurie Lee.

References

CENTRAL ADVISORY COUNCIL FOR EDUCATION (1967) *Children and Their Primary Schools: The Plowden Report*, London, HMSO.
DEWEY, J. (1938) *Experience and Education*, New York, Collier.
RICHARDS, C. (1987) 'Primary Education in England: An analysis of some recent issues and developments', *Curriculum* 8, 1, 6–12.

Part 1 The Changing Nature of Primary Education

Introduction

In this introductory part of the book we consider changes in the ways education aims have been stated between the 1944 and 1988 Education Acts, arguably the two most significant legislative actions affecting schools this century. The two acts have many similarities. Both included clauses which went against the principles of education espoused by educationists. For instance, by introducing selection in the secondary phase, the 1944 Act influenced the aims of primary schools, many of which introduced streaming and teaching methods aimed at examination success. This became a totally discredited policy in subsequent decades. The most recent legislation, by introducing standardized assessment, moderation across schools, parental choice and teacher appraisal, is again encouraging teachers to place 'examination' success as an essential teaching aim.

This must call into question whether government should have the key role in laying down educational aims. White (1989) suggests that, in theory, there is a strong case for government control, since aims must be publicly determined, with no single section — parents, teachers, unions, or industrialists — dominating the issue. He goes on to argue that, in a liberal-democratic society, the proper task of government is to promote the well-being of all citizens by equipping them with the necessary conditions of an autonomous life; any national curriculum committed to democratic principles must include in its goals preparing all young people to become equal citizens of a democracy. Neither the 1944 Act nor the 1988 seems to do this. So what *have* been the aims of primary education in the intervening period?

In Chapter 1 Peter Cunningham examines the rather elusive and vague aims of primary schools in the three decades following the Second World War. He pays particular attention to the work of three sectors of the educational world — HM Inspectorate, especially the contribution to the

Plowden Report; the influential body of teacher educators, especially the role of the Froebel movement; and the teacher unions, through their committees and reports. All of these diverse sectors placed the emphasis on a child-centred view of primary education, with 'creativity', 'experience', 'individual learning' and 'discovery' as the watch-words over the whole period. Little attention was paid to the detail of a curriculum which would meet these aims; this discussion was left to the period after 1977.

Chapter 2 considers this period — the so-called Great Education Debate — which led up to recent legislation. The changes from the first period are dramatic; instead of being vague and tenuous, the aims are specific and detailed, with quite different key words. Indeed cynics might want to amend some famous dictums: 'At the heart of the education process lies the subject'; 'the curriculum is to be thought of in terms of knowledge to be acquired and facts to be stored ready for assessment'. At the start of the debate the DES identified a number of Aims of Schools, but we are unable to determine whether these aims can ever be achieved through the subjects and assessment of the National Curriculum. As with the 1944 Act, the National Curriculum of the 1988 Act does not appear to be a consensus curriculum; it does not properly reflect the collated views of teachers, parents, industrialists or the community. So where does that leave us now?

This question is considered in Chapter 3 by Philip Gammage, a member of the National Curriculum Council. He takes the stance of a visitor to the primary school of the late 1980s, observing the changes schools are undergoing and reflecting on how these match, or conflict with, current philosophy on the purpose of primary education. Enjoyment of learning is still regarded by most teachers as a fundamental aim, yet among the profession itself there is a ground-swell of anxiety and low morale which has, in part, been caused by the increased prescription and centralization in organization introduced by the 1988 Act. We can only hope that the very best practice will survive.

References

WHITE, J. (1989) 'Two national curricula — Baker's and Stalin's: Towards a liberal alternative', *British Journal of Educational Studies*, 36, 3, 218–31.

Chapter 1

The Nature of Primary Education: Early Perspectives 1944–1977

Peter Cunningham

Introduction

Why open a book on the nature of primary education, which is essentially forward-looking, with a backward glance? One answer is that the historical canvas enables us to examine relationships between the popular, the political and the professional expressions of aims and purposes, contrasting positions which are frequently in a state of dynamic tension. Another answer lies not simply in learning lessons from history, but in heightening awareness of the length of a teacher's career and the pace of social and political change. Those who underwent initial training in the 1950s, with the social conditions and educational assumptions then prevailing, were in mid-career during the 1970s; student teachers of the 1970s will reach their mid-career at the turn of the century, and those of the 1980s can hope to be highly experienced and senior teachers during the first decade of the next millenium. At the same time the pace of change affecting the practice of primary education over the period 1944–1977 seems to have accelerated; birthrate most obviously affected the size of the clientele, but different family structures also had an impact on children's learning environment, whilst immigration from the 'old Commonwealth' enriched the variety of cultural backgrounds which primary schoolchildren enjoyed; a changing economic climate impinged on primary schools not only through the loosening and tightening by turns of the public purse-strings but also in altering the personal and domestic circumstances of children, and the world of employment for which most of them were ultimately being prepared.

Political and Popular Aims

Hardly more than three generations ago, it was clear from debates surrounding the introduction and early development of universal compulsory elementary schooling that considerations about aims included the basic skills of the labour force, safeguarding the political order, the achievement of public health, and the development of child care with its impact on the labour market. None of these broader aims and purposes have disappeared, although they may now be overtaken by debates on the finer points of curriculum and teaching method, teaching styles, pupil progress and school effectiveness.

Forty years on, in the 1944 Act, the aims of primary education were in every respect elusive and vague, contrasting sharply with the detailed National Curriculum of the 1988 Education Reform Act. The Act of 1944 did no more than define primary education as 'that suitable to the requirements of junior pupils', those children aged between five and eleven. Given the implementation of a selective system of secondary education, which was one outcome of the 1944 Act, it was inevitable that one purpose of primary education would be to begin the necessary process of streaming, and a force for change in primary school practice during subsequent decades was the gradual discrediting of that process.

Beyond the definition of the 1944 Act, which was legalistic in the extreme, lay the purposes and aims of professional educationists, in particular the idealism of Percy Nunn, whose principles of 'individuality', 'freedom' and 'growth' were known through his influential book *Education, Its Data and First Principles*, published in 1920 and still in print in 1945. Its thinking had been reflected in the 1927 Board of Education *Handbook of Suggestions for Teachers*.

The report of the Hadow Committee of 1931, a Consultative Committee of the Board of Education on the Primary School, had given official approval to the principles of activity and discovery learning epitomized in the work of Susan Isaacs, psychologist and psychoanalyst, who had published her observations of children at the experimental Malting House School in books on intellectual and emotional growth. Later, the Act of 1944 facilitated in a practical way the advance of these principles by promising to remove all children over the age of eleven from the former all-age elementary schools, thus leaving the new institution of the universal primary school to concentrate on development of the pre-adolescent child.

The 1944 Education Act attracted great admiration, and subsequently nostalgia, as a key element in the legislation for social reconstruction following the Second World War and as the dawn of a new era in education, although later reappraisal in critical perspectives may have modified that judgement (Green *et al.*, 1981; Aldrich and Leighton, 1985; Simon, 1986). Yet a question put to the *Brains Trust* panel in 1946 asked: 'Has the advance of education in the last fifty years added to human happiness?' Put sceptically in a period of optimistic social reform, this question at least suggested that human happiness might be a fundamental aim of education. Another radio series of the same year, *Teachers in the Witness Box*, featured a parent observing that

> The poor oppressed taxpayer sees daily ... wandering about up and down the various towns and cities, boys and girls who seem to be a pack of sheep ... in the attendance of one or two school teachers. Is this the new educational craze 'Local Study'? Why are you spending money on this kind of thing?

Here the question of public cost was broached, in addition to doubts about the freer organization of curriculum.

Such glimpses of public opinion, an ill-documented aspect of the educational past, are introduced as a reminder that the aims of education are not the exclusive preserve either of professionals or of the state. Parents may be simply bowing to the weight of the law in sending their children to school, but they also have their own individual aims and aspirations, and as any class teacher can relate after parent interviews, these are often various and conflicting.

One key factor in the 1980s is populist politics. In 1944 a wartime coalition government had drafted a statute intended to improve educational opportunity relative to 'age, ability and aptitude'; in 1988, responding to the growth of consumerism, the government made considerable show of responding to popular concern and sought to apply the principle of market forces to the provision of education, ostensibly 'rolling back the frontiers' of the state, though introducing at the same time a National Curriculum.

Politically, the changes from 1944 to 1977 might be recorded simply in terms of General Election results, but more complex shifts have to be recorded where educational policy is concerned, shifts which do not necessarily follow party lines. Certainly educational policies became more polarized in the 1970s between Labour and Conservative parties, but more significant still was the move from consensus on expansion and about the acceptance of professional autonomy in curriculum matters, to a concern shown by both major parties for centralizing educational decision-making and for giving the lay voice more of a say. In addition, social change in the post-war period, increasingly analyzed by the ubiquitous social sciences, appeared to underline the role of the teacher as an important and powerful agent of social change, a development which turned sour in the later years of the period, as sociological thought came to see the function of schools as reproducing hierarchies, the teacher's role as a repressive one, and education as ineffectual in improving the life-chances of its clients.

Economic growth in the 1950s facilitated the expansion and improvement of teacher education, whilst economic recession from 1973 soon pinched the improved salaries and conditions which the Plowden generation of teachers had anticipated and enjoyed. 1977, the end year of this study, was distinguished in educational politics for its 'Great Debate', the Labour government's brave attempt to create a platform for the views of parents and employers in the field of education, where for too long, it was implied, professional opinion had held sway. It is not difficult to see the populist appeal of the Conservative government's educational policies in the later 1980s as the natural progression of this event, the justifications for which were identified in social and economic circumstances.

Professional Perspectives

Beyond this broad indication of changing perspectives from the public and political viewpoint, the professional response now becomes the main focus of our attention. Professional aims and purposes are sometimes over-simplified by reference to one or other single report, and the progress of primary schooling in particular has sometimes been reduced to an inspirational lineage followed back through the Plowden Report of 1967 to the Hadow Report of 1931, the experiments of Susan Isaacs, the philosophy of John Dewey and observations of Edmond Holmes in the first decades of the twentieth century, and further back still to Pestalozzi, Froebel and Rousseau, representing the impact on education of the Enlightenment.

For a picture of professional opinion during the period 1944–77, it may be helpful to examine a number of professional agencies concerned with primary education which disseminated their views through a variety of media. Three such agencies will be considered: Her Majesty's Inspectorate, teacher educators and professional development and teacher unions. In doing this, some selectivity will be necessary as well as a departure from a strictly chronological approach (see Cunningham, 1988; Selleck, 1972).

Her Majesty's Inspectorate

Ever since the establishment of an inspectorate in 1839, HMI has had an ambiguous role; having been devised to safeguard value for money in public expenditure, its function was soon redefined by the enlightened Civil Servant, Kay-Shuttleworth, as required 'to contribute . . . to the improvement of the work' in schools (cited by Browne, 1979). Residential courses for teachers of the primary age range were organized by the Inspectorate from the 1930s onwards, and after 1945 this form of provision expanded steadily from sixty-four courses in 1954 to 175 in 1968–69. The International Bureau of

Education in the late 1950s defined the role of inspection as a service to interpret to teachers and public alike the educational policies of the authorities, and also to interpret to the competent authorities, the experiences, needs and aspirations of teachers (International Bureau of Education, 1956). A two-way process of interaction was clearly envisaged, and implemented not only through courses, but also through the publication of pamphlets, through an official handbook on primary education in 1959, and through the researches and enquiries which were undertaken for the Committee of the Central Advisory Council chaired by Lady Plowden from 1964–1967.

The Staff Inspector for Junior Education from 1946 to 1955 was Schiller, whose own professional background had been as a teacher at the progressive public school, Rendcomb, followed by a year's course under Nunn at the London Day Training College (later the London University Institute of Education) (Schiller, 1979). A number of pamphlets published by the Ministry of Education (MoE) with advice from HMI in the immediate post-war years illustrated the practical implementation of Nunn's and Schiller's ideals, in particular *Story of a School* (MoE, 1949) which described the achievements of A.L. Stone, a Birmingham headteacher whom Schiller had seen at work. Steward Street Junior School was described in words and pictures, with a heavy emphasis on the expressive and performing arts (even arithmetic was linked with music). The 'three Rs' were to take second place to the development of the child's personality, and the practice of the arts was to encourage this by cultivating the child's interest and extending concentration and self-discipline; through the arts, too, children were to find their own personalities. Such pamphlets outlined aims and purposes for the interested public as well as for the profession.

More specifically aimed at the professionals, however, was the Ministry of Education's book *Primary Education*, published in 1959 (MoE, 1959). The text of this book claimed to spring from the experience of HM Inspectors gained during their visits to schools and in discussion with teachers at various courses and conferences. It was therefore not to be a *Handbook of Suggestions* as its pre-war antecedents had been, but a description of practices to be found in the more successful schools discussed in the light of current knowledge and experience of children's capacities and reactions. This 'child-centred' approach came across in the book's structure, which described the developing child and the appropriate teaching methods to be used in school, before going on to deal with the curriculum as 'fields of learning' related to the whole child:

> One salient feature of primary education today is the ever deepening concern with children as children which has gradually spread from nursery and infant schools to the junior schools. This concern shows itself especially in the awareness of the child as a whole with inter-dependent spiritual, emotional, intellectual and physical needs, and

in the appreciation of the wide range of aptitudes, abilities and temperaments which any class of children presents. (MoE, 1959: 10)

Primary Education quoted approvingly the Hadow Consultative Committee Report of 1931 which had talked of the educational process as a 'coherent whole'; it also quoted Hadow's best remembered statement, but at rather greater length than is usual:

> The curriculum is to be thought of in terms of activity and experience rather than of knowledge to be acquired and facts to be stored. Its aims should be to develop in a child the fundamental interests of civilised life so far as these powers and interests lie within the compass of childhood, to encourage him (sic) to attain gradually to that control and orderly management of his energies, impulses and emotions, which is the essence of moral and intellectual discipline, and to help him to discover the idea of duty and to ensue it, and to open out his imagination and his sympathies in such a way that he may be prepared to understand and to follow in later years the highest examples of excellence in life and conduct. (MoE, 1959: 7–8)

Cited in this context, it is clear that the 'child-centredness' was far from a licence for 'free expression', an accusation often levelled against progressive educationists. Indeed, as with A.L. Stone's views, there is a strong element of education as a means to an end: self-discipline *and* social discipline.

The curriculum section of *Primary Education* gave considerable attention to art, craft and needlework, dealt with immediately after language and mathematics and accorded as much space as the latter. It was the work specifically of HMI Robin Tanner, himself a practising etcher committed to the ideals of the Arts and Crafts movement. He and Schiller ran courses for teachers, encouraging their own personal involvement in making art. Dartington Hall, home of art patrons, Leonard and Dorothy Elmhirst, and of their progressive boarding school, was one location for these courses, at which teachers met practitioners of craft and developed their own sensibilities and skills in an aesthetic environment. Tanner's views reiterated the individualism already noted:

> The essence of the artist is his (sic) uniqueness: no two children are alike. Within any group there will be some who, by virtue of their innate sensibility, will see far further and work with much greater expressiveness than others; while some, and especially those with a meagre background, will respond only haltingly to what is offered them. But, undoubtedly, the experience of an education in learning to see must be provided for all children — not as an isolated 'subject' or as a set of skills to be practised, but as a very means of learning and living. (MoE, 1959: 221)

Tanner also voiced a Ruskinian emphasis on the crafts, which embodied suggestions of undoubted educational value, but which, carried to its extremes, sometimes succeeded in imbuing progressive primary practice with a distinctly anti-modern tone:

> The foolish separation between Art and Craft in our present day life which has led to the making of so much that is ugly to look at and unpleasant to use should be a warning. . . The education of children should surely aim at fulfilling their creative powers as both artists and craftsmen; and at the same time it should foster their growth as discerning people, able to choose and select, to discriminate between the true and the counterfeit, to reject the shoddy and false. . .
> (MoE, 1959: 218)

The high point of articulated purpose in primary education during these years was undoubtedly the publication of the Plowden Report in 1967, the origin, nature and impact of which deserve special attention.

The 1944 Education Act had seen the setting up of two Central Advisory Councils for Education (one for England, and one for Wales), the duties of which were 'to advise the Minister upon such matters connected with educational theory and practice as they think fit, and upon any questions referred to them by him'. In fact the Councils seem never to have exercised the degree of independent initiative implied by this form of words, and it was not until 1963 that it began to consider, on the request of the then Minister of Education Sir Edward Boyle, the subject of 'primary education in all its aspects, and the transition to secondary education'. The terms of reference reflected not only the sense of considerable development in the theory and practice of primary schooling over the previous decade during which government policy had been preoccupied with the organization of secondary schooling, but also the growing professional and public unease at the system of selection at 11+ which had tended to dominate the curriculum in the later years of primary schooling.

This enquiry, the last to be undertaken by the Central Advisory Council which, after a further nineteen years during which it was never reconvened, was eventually abolished by legislation in 1986, was a substantial event. It lasted more than three years and its report was finally published in two volumes of more than 500 pages each at a cost of £120,000. It was of major significance in highlighting the impact of social disadvantage on educational opportunity and advocating a policy of positive discrimination in the redistribution of educational resources to compensate for social and economic deprivation. Such conclusions were derived in part from a major research project which it commissioned, which revealed that parental attitudes exerted the greatest influence on educational achievement. These findings were also consistent with the promotion of a more child-centred pedagogy, one which sought more parental involvement in the child's education and a freer, more individualistic approach to classroom activity, with an emphasis on creativity and discovery learning. Incidental to the curriculum, but of crucial significance, was its proposal that corporal punishment should be banned, though there was no legislative response, and it took European legislation twenty years later to secure this. The enquiry was well publicized both in the professional press and more widely through the media, and following its publication acquired a totemic status amongst advocates of a child-centred view of primary education. Though it was relatively cautious on the details of curriculum and teaching method, it was widely represented, by friend and foe alike, as setting the official seal on a more informal and progressive approach to primary schooling.

Plowden's multi-faceted significance has yet to be subjected to full historical analysis, but a look at the mechanics of the enquiry sheds some light on the aims and purposes which it eventually proposed. The selected chairperson was Lady Plowden, whose previous associations with primary education were minimal, but the role of John Blackie HMI, Chief Inspector for Primary Education 1963–66 and Assessor to the Committee, clearly influenced the educational assumptions on which the committee worked, and the direction which the enquiry took. His own educational philosophy had been expressed in a collection of writings published in 1963 where he summarized his values as 'Christian, progressive, and founded in art, literature, music and craftsmanship as the highest achievement of the human imagination' and his view of teachers as 'guardians and transmitters of culture' (Blackie, 1963).

The list of witnesses giving evidence also reveals a distinctive bias. Former HMIs included Schiller and Tanner, whilst from the world of teacher education came Dietrich Hanff (Tanner's adopted son), Elizabeth Lawrence, former Director of the National Froebel Foundation, and Elizabeth Hitchfield, lecturer at the Froebel Educational Institute. Nathan Isaacs, widower of Susan and a widely read interpreter of Piaget in Britain, also had associations with the Froebel movement, and Dorothy Gardner, biographer of Susan Isaacs and her successor as Reader in Child Development at the London Institute of Education, also gave evidence. Both Alec Clegg and Stuart Mason, Chief Education Officers of Yorkshire's West Riding and of Leicestershire respectively, represented the personal interest in progressive education shown by both of these notable administrators and reflected in the practice within their authorities. Another notably progressive LEA, Oxfordshire, was represented amongst witnesses by its chief Primary Adviser, Edith Moorhouse, two primary headteachers and one former headteacher (one Oxfordshire headteacher was already a member of the Plowden Committee);

John Coe, who was to succeed Edith Moorhouse and had enjoyed strong links with Schiller, and with the West Riding, also submitted evidence.

Thus a network of individuals with shared ideals was drawn together which gave a great sense of conviction and unanimity to the report, in which little dissent on approaches to curriculum and method is recorded. Its priorities were encapsulated in its title: *Children and Their Primary Schools* and by its most famous statement of philosophy which opened the first substantial chapter, 'The Children: Their Growth and Development':

> At the heart of the educational process lies the child. No advances in policy, no acquisitions of new equipment have their desired effect unless they are in harmony with the nature of the child, unless they are fundamentally acceptable to him.

So it was that a few individual HMIs, through their publications and in-service training had a significant impact on the professional definition of aims and purposes in primary education during the 1950s. Their role in shaping the Plowden Report and the wide publicity given to the latter promoted this progressive view of primary education for a wider public. Given the popular and media interest in the 1960s, their principles gained wide acceptance.

Teacher Education and Professional Development

As long ago as 1905 the official *Handbook of Suggestions* (BoE, 1905) had stated that

> The only uniformity of practice that the Board of Education desire to see in the teaching of the Public Elementary Schools is that each teacher shall think for himself, and work out for himself such methods of teaching as may use his powers to the best advantage and be best suited to the particular needs and conditions of the school.

Given this well-established tradition of teacher autonomy in matters of curriculum and teaching method, training institutions were in a powerful position to influence the character of primary education. The aims and purposes of primary education should thus be understood also through their mediation in programmes of teacher education and training.

The years 1944–1977 saw continuous and considerable growth in the teacher education sector. Fifty-five new colleges were founded in the period 1945–60, more than half as many again as those pre-existing the war. Numbers of students almost doubled from 25,000 to 48,000 between 1952 and 1960, and almost doubled again to reach 95,000 by 1968. At the same time the content of teacher education expanded with the extension to three years of the Teacher's Certificate course in 1960 and the introduction of BEd degree courses from 1965. Thus there was scope for new emphases within courses of initial training for primary teachers, and a profitable market for new textbooks.

The wider discovery of Piaget in Britain coincided with the lengthening of initial training from two to three years, the third year regarded very much as for additional academic work. Degree courses demanded elaboration of more theoretical elements. Closer study of child development was ideally suited to a more academic but still professionally relevant course. Piaget's account of child development was seen as providing useful theoretical support for progressive primary practices already established, such as activity-based learning. Digests of Piagetian theories, one by Brearley and Hitchfield, and another by Beard, became very common as course textbooks, providing a common core of principles through which many young primary teachers now interpreted their task (Brearley and Hitchfield, 1966; Beard, R. 1969).

The expansion of educational publishing also provided attractively illustrated books which conveyed the spirit and atmosphere of the child-centred classroom. Brown and Precious (1968) *The Integrated Day in the Primary School*, Leonard Marsh's (1970) *Alongside the Child in the Primary School* and Ridgway and Lawton's (1968) *Family Grouping in the Primary School*, are notable examples of the genre. Such titles appeared widely on reading lists for primary teachers in training. A series of well illustrated small pamphlets under the general title *British Primary Schools Today* was produced by the Schools Council (Anglo-American Primary Education Project, 1971/2), and provided a brief but vivid introduction to aspects of progressive practice for students and others.

A variety of innovations in in-service training facilitated the dissemination of innovatory practice. Teachers' Centres developed in the second half of this period as locations at which teachers could come together and share ideas, and the growth of personal mobility through car ownership had a profound impact on professional development in enabling teachers to attend such centres and to visit other schools. Another technology of service to education was television, providing an appropriate medium by which to convey the colour and movement characteristic of progressive primary classrooms.

One amongst many themes worthy of attention in the development of professional perspectives is the influence of the Froebel movement during these years. Pedagogical developments for the primary age range in the years under review have sometimes been defined as an extension of the kindergarten principle into the whole of the primary school age range, and to this extent the role of the Froebel movement in teacher education is of interest. Amongst the relatively few professional organizations for primary teachers in the early post-war period, the National Froebel Foundation was prominent. It had emerged in the later nineteenth century amongst educationists interested in kindergarten principles, and in marked contrast with the Montessori equivalent, had received official recognition from the Board of Education for its teaching qualification.

The colleges recognized for internal examination after 1945 included the Froebel Educational Institute at Roehampton, Rachel McMillan College in Deptford, Maria Grey in Twickenham, and Westhill in Birmingham, and the early 1950s saw a surge in demand for places at these institutions. Significantly, the Froebel Certificate course required three years' study at a time when the usual Training College Certificate involved only a two year course. However, the 1950s following the McNair Report (1944) saw a gradual transfer of responsibility to University Institutes of Education for the validation of teacher qualification, which led the Froebel Foundation to concentrate its specific efforts on in-service courses. From pre-war years, an increasing number of qualified teachers had been seeking the Froebel Certificate (one year full-time or two years part-time) as an additional qualification (Froebel Foundation Minutes, 1950, 1952, 1959).

The Froebel Institute continued to play a leading role in the initial training of primary teachers through the considerable influence of Molly Brearley, its Principal from 1955 to 1970, whose numerous writings give an insight into the ideals of teacher education as reflected in her own, and other progressive colleges. Describing initial training courses she laid stress on the growth of the individual student as an independent professional, eschewing dependence on textbooks in preference for first-hand observation of children, and learning the professional role by doing, with school attachments carefully phased, and students working in schools in pairs with joint responsibility for classes. Not only did this pattern reflect the very principles of individual learning and discovery learning advocated for children in the primary school, but it also seemed the most effective way of preparing a teacher who would be flexible, resourceful and understanding of the principles underlying a more open approach to primary teaching (Brearley *et al.*, 1972).

Brearley chaired a group of lecturers from the Froebel Institute in compiling *Fundamentals in the First School* (1969), which became a widely-read text. It affirmed six 'generalizations from psychological knowledge and professional experience':

(i) children are unique persons and their individuality is to be acknowledged and respected;

(ii) each person constructs his own mind (sic) as a result of interaction with things and people in his environment;

(iii) learning is continuous and knowledge cumulative;

(iv) the concept of 'stages' in intellectual development is useful in helping to understand some distinguishable phases of development in a child's thought;

(v) children encouraged in cooperative efforts with other children and with teachers will collaborate in the search for and sharing of knowledge;

(vi) the mental processes involved in the search for knowledge and understanding contain their own self-expanding and extending propulsion.

The underlying precepts were not simply liberal, humane, creative and cooperative, but were grounded too in the psychological insights provided by the work of Piaget, whose ideas the National Froebel Foundation did a great deal to propagate in Britain through pamphlets and digests published for teachers. Piaget's theories were important in giving scientific legitimacy to certain aims and purposes at a time when greater academic rigour was being demanded of initial training courses, extended to three years, validated by universities and eventually given degree status. 'New mathematics' particularly seemed to implement a recognition of the child's transition from the stage of concrete operations to that of formal operations, which was seen to occur during the primary school career. In 1954, in a Froebel pamphlet on *Number in the Primary School*, Brearley expounded the following principles:

(1) We must teach at the rate at which the child learns;

(2) A child must see sense in what he learns;

(3) The child's activities and the purposes of arithmetic must harmonize;

(4) Meanings must precede symbols; understanding must precede drill;

(5) We must present arithmetic as an object of natural interest;

(6) We must ensure orderly development of quantitative thinking;

(7) The way children think of numbers is as important as is the result of their thinking. (Brearley, 1954)

Amongst the early introductions to Piagetian theory were two other Froebel pamphlets written by Nathan Isaacs: *Some Aspects of Piaget's Work* (1955) (8th edn. 1965), and *Piaget: Some Answers to Teachers' Questions* (1965).

The influence of the Froebelians both through their colleges and through their publications and in-service work made a significant contribution to the dissemination of child-centred ideals and 'informal' practice. Other colleges can be identified as sources of teachers committed to such ideals and practices, and a notable example for its national significance was

Goldsmiths' College. As well as the National Froebel Foundation, teacher associations also played a role in disseminating new ideas and practices, the most important of which was the National Union of Teachers.

Teacher Unions: The National Union of Teachers

Among its membership, the National Union of Teachers represented a considerable proportion of primary teachers in the period 1944–1977, and its contribution to professional discourse on the aims and purposes of primary education deserves attention. At its Annual Conference in 1944, the Union adopted a programme of education developments in line with its standing as a professional body with a professed concern for the welfare of children in schools. The Union Executive claimed a tradition of high idealism in education, helping to foster favourable public opinion and lobbying for improved conditions, such that it now held a position of 'prestige and power in the life of the nation' (NUT, 1944). Resolutions were passed at annual conferences before the war calling for the establishment of a research and educational bureau, and the question as the Executive saw it was what modification could be made in Union machinery to enable it to undertake educational work closely associated with the actual professional duties of the teacher.

One cog in the machine was the Primary Schools Advisory Committee. Its early discussions concentrated on such practical difficulties as the shortage of equipment for schools. In 1946 however the 'Content and Method of Education' appeared on the agenda, with statements prepared for discussion concerning infant/nursery and junior schools.

The child's realization of its own individual place in society and the need to foster a sense of social responsibility was given a high priority, but the child was also to be respected as a person, the teacher should work alongside, and be prepared to learn from, as well as to teach the child. At the same time, there was reference to 'definite class lessons' starting at about the age of six. For the junior school, large classes were considered the chief adversity, and the need felt by most teachers to stress 'arithmetic' in preparation for the common entrance examination: 'That has set a standard characteristic of the junior school'. However, the child's 'tremendous enthusiasm for life' at this age was noted, so that 'many teachers would like to work alongside their interests and not to oppose them' (NUT, 1946). Another indicator of the committee's approach to the task of primary education was a short article by its Vice-Chairman, T.E. Newell, published anonymously in the Union's journal *The Schoolmaster* and circulated for discussion at a committee meeting in 1947. Under the heading of 'Primary School Problems', the continuing large classes, insufficient freedom for the teacher in the classroom, lack of visual aids and facilities, and the narrowing of classwork to meet the curriculum of the Special Place Exam were enumerated. Many of the answers were seen to lie in improved provision, although Newell advocated such improvements as curriculum integration and abolition of the timetable in favour of project work for at least one week or fortnight each term (NUT, 1948).

A lengthy discussion in committee was continued from March 1956 to November 1957 under an agenda item entitled 'The Threat to the Primary School'. This dramatic topic concerned problems of the status of the primary school and its teachers, in relation to the secondary sector; 'manpower, materials and money' were the salient aspects of the debate when reduced to its basics, but in discussing such issues as the quality of teacher training, methods of promotion (especially the tendency to confer primary headships on displaced secondary heads) amenities and equipment, it was ultimately the quality of the younger children's education which was at stake. One committee member accused not only the government but the Union's National Executive of ignoring the primary schools 'which had improved out of all knowledge, in spite of the difficulties' (NUT, 1956).

The committee's report was submitted to the Executive which was in the process of preparing a pamphlet, *Fair Play for Primary Schools*, eventually published in 1960. Whilst this document did not in itself advocate any particular philosophy of primary education, in the conditions of the later 1950s (when priorities in resourcing for the secondary sector, adopted immediately after the war, appeared to have been indefinitely prolonged) the Union nevertheless contributed to raising public awareness about the importance of the primary stage of education. So much official attention had been given during the 1950s to the new secondary sector, that the primary school was beginning to be described as the 'Cinderella' of the system.

At about the same time, the Union also published its own Consultative Committee report on *The Curriculum of the Junior School*. The establishment of such a committee had been another of the NUT's 'educational developments' in the post-war period (perhaps intended to reflect the Ministry of Education's own Central Advisory Council established under the 1944 Act), and its first and second reports, both published in 1949, had been concerned with processes of transfer from primary to secondary schools, and with nursery-infant education. The NUT junior school curriculum report (1959) has been overlooked by van der Eyken (1973) and Hyndman (1978) among others, as one of the key documents of the period, appearing in the long gap between the official reports of Hadow (1931) and Plowden (1967). It made strong reference to contemporary practice *as it was*, quoting the opinions of teachers who had given evidence.

Indeed most of the eight male and four female committee members were from primary schools, although the chair was occupied by Dorothy Dymond, Principal of the City of Portsmouth Training College, and former lecturer in history at the progressive Goldsmith's College. The Secretary to the committee was Evan Owens, Head of a Worcestershire Primary School and a man of high professional and academic standing. Witnesses to the committee included four from the City of Portsmouth Training College, three from Worcestershire, and five others from committee members' own institutions, but a broader constituency was also reflected amongst the list of witnesses: Charlotte Fleming from the London Institute of Education, and Alfred Yates, Senior Research Officer at the National Foundation for Educational Research both furnished the committee with up-to-date information on psychological research, whilst two others came from BBC School Broadcasting service; amongst the six HMIs was Ruth Foster, responsible for the new Ministry handbooks encouraging a developmental and creative approach to physical education; Mary Crowley from the Ministry of Education represented the innovatory work in primary school planning of the Architects and Building Branch. Other witnesses included: H.A.T. Child, former Senior Educational Psychologist to the London County Council, and chronicler of progressive education (Child and Child 1969); Miss E. Pike, former head of Childeric Road Junior Demonstration School, a well-known experimental school in London that had been made use of both by Goldsmiths' College and by the BBC; and Eric Briault, Deputy Education Officer of the London County Council.

The declared aim of the report was to stress two principles especially: the importance of learning through direct experience, and the importance of giving children access to excellence 'in all the rich implications of the phrase', that learning should 'follow the growing maturity of the child' but should also be 'purposive' (NUT, 1959). It stressed the radically changed atmosphere of the junior school, especially in the more natural relations between teacher and pupil, and noted that the greater freedom and informality had been learned from the good practice of infant schools. Though it acknowledged that recent psychological research had cast doubt on the principles of intellectual classification, some form of streaming was felt to be advisable in circumstances of restricted staffing and accommodation. The core of the report dealt with curriculum. This was treated under subject headings (with a rather less liberal approach to integration than that reflected in the contemporary volume published by the Ministry of Education and discussed above), but the 'subject chapters' did at least include one on 'The Library' and another about 'Visual and Aural Aids', and were prefaced by a chapter entitled 'The Seamless Robe of Knowledge'. A.N. Whitehead's (1966) assertion of the 'seamless robe of learning' was acknowledged and the Herbartian principle of 'correlation', which had been misinterpreted and distorted into some notorious practices, was carefully distinguished from Dewey's 'pragmatism' which had engendered 'projects' and 'topics'. The practical consequences, the Report argued, were that a rigid syllabus and timetable of short periods had become obsolete (NUT, 1959). As far as teaching method was concerned however, the report deplored a negative and wasteful divergence that seemed to range teachers and schools into two irreconcilable camps under the banners of 'formal' or 'subject-centred' teaching and 'activity' or 'child-centred' teaching. Certainly the process of maturing was a more acceptable notion than preparation for maturity, but the practice of skills was also necessary for 'mastery and subsequent economy of effort'. The answer was seen to lie in a judicious blend of drill and Dewey.

Conclusion

A divergence of camps within the profession regarding curriculum approaches, noted in the 1959 NUT report, adumbrated what was to become a more public and political debate in the 1970s. The Plowden Report, though widely welcomed, soon became the object of professional criticism for its lack of philosophical rigour. An economic and political climate in the early 1970s radically changed by monetary inflation, industrial unrest and domestic terrorism engendered a cultural backlash which associated progressive primary schooling with liberal excess. The impact on aims and purposes of this changed climate in the years after 1977 will be examined in later chapters.

To give a comprehensive description of the nature of primary education prevailing at any given period would be an impossible task. There are significant regional and local variations in practice, there are contrasts between neighbouring schools and sometimes quite stark differences between one class and another within the same school. Educational debate, especially in the political and popular arena, is frequently marred by unwarranted generalizations from particular instances, and a National Curriculum will iron out only some aspects of the diversity. A retrospective view of educational principles and practices maintains our awareness of this diversity as we strive to identify prevailing trends. In addition, historical study enables us to recognize the agencies which shape the nature of primary education, to consider their interaction and the impact which they have on schooling as experienced by children. The choice of agencies in the foregoing chapter is necessarily selective. The inspectorate, teacher educators and teacher unions have all had considerable impact on practice and their influence merits close attention. By this means as teachers and educationists in the 1990s, we can sharpen our understanding of the forces which continue to modify the practice in our classrooms.

References

ALDRICH, R. and LEIGHTON, P. (1985) *Education: Time for a New Act?* Bedford Way Papers No. 23, London, University of London Institute of Education.

ANGLO-AMERICAN PRIMARY EDUCATION PROJECT (1971/2) *British Primary Schools Today*, London, Macmillan, for the Schools Council.

BEARD, R. (1969) *An Outline of Piaget's Developmental Psychology for Students and Teachers*, London, Routledge and Kegan Paul.

BLACKIE, J. (1963) *Good Enough for the Children?*, London, Faber.

BOARD OF EDUCATION (BoE) (1905) *Handbook of Suggestions for the Consideration of Teachers and Others Concerned with the Work of the Public Elementary Schools*, London, HMSO.

BOARD OF EDUCATION (1927) *Handbook of Suggestions for Teachers*, London, HMSO.

BOARD OF EDUCATION (1931) *Report of the Consultative Committee on the Primary School (Hadow Committee)*, London, HMSO.

BOARD OF EDUCATION (1944) *Teachers and Youth Leaders: McNair Report*, London, HMSO.

Brains Trust, BBC Written Archive Home Service 12.3.46.

BREARLEY, M. (1954) *Number in the Primary School*, 3rd edn. 1960, London, National Froebel Foundation.

BREARLEY, M. and HITCHFIELD, R. (1966) *A Teacher's Guide to Reading Piaget*, London, Routledge and Kegan Paul.

BREARLEY, M. et al. (1969) *Fundamentals in the First School*, Oxford, Blackwell.

BREARLEY, M., GODDARD, N., BROWSE, B. and KALLET, T. (1972) *Educating Teachers: British Primary Schools Today*, London, Macmillan for the Schools Council.

BROWN, M. and PRECIOUS, N. (1968) *The Integrated Day in the Primary School*, London, Ward Lock.

BROWNE, S. (1979) 'The accountability of Her Majesty's Inspectorate', in LELLO, J. (Ed) *Accountability in Education*, London, Ward Lock Educational, p. 35.

CENTRAL ADVISORY COUNCIL FOR EDUCATION (1967) *Children and Their Primary Schools: The Plowden Report*, London, HMSO.

CENTRE FOR CONTEMPORARY CULTURAL STUDIES (1981) *Unpopular Education: Schooling and Social Democracy in England Since 1944*, London, Hutchinson.

CHILD, H.A.T. and CHILD, L.A. (1969) 'A retrospective view of progressive education', in ASH, M. (Ed) (1969) *Who Are the Progressives Now?*, London, Routledge and Kegan Paul.

CUNNINGHAM, P. (1988) *Curriculum Change in the Primary School Since 1945*, Lewes, Falmer.

GRIFFIN-BEALE, C. (Ed) (1979) *Christian Schiller in His Own Words*, London, A. and C. Black.

HYNDMAN, M. (1978) *Schools and Schooling in England and Wales: A Documentary History*, London, Harper and Row.

INTERNATIONAL BUREAU OF EDUCATION (1956) *Bulletin 120*, Geneva, UNESCO.

ISAACS, S. (1930) *Intellectual Growth in Young Children*, London, George Routledge.

ISAACS, N. (1955) *Some Aspects of Piaget's Work*, London, National Froebel Foundation.

ISAACS, N. (n.d.[1965]) *Piaget: Some Answers to Teachers' Questions*, London, National Froebel Foundation.

MARSH, L. (1970) *Alongside the Child in the Primary School*, London, A. and C. Black.

MINISTRY OF EDUCATION (MoE) (1949) *Story of a School: A Headmaster's Experiences with Children aged Seven to Eleven* (Pamphlet No. 14), London, HMSO.

MINISTRY OF EDUCATION (1959) *Primary Education: Suggestions for the Consideration of Teachers and Others Concerned with the Work of Primary Schools*, London, HMSO.

NATIONAL FROEBEL FOUNDATION EDUCATION COMMITTEE MINUTES, 24 February 1950.

NATIONAL FROEBEL FOUNDATION EDUCATION COMMITTEE MINUTES, 17 October 1952.

NATIONAL FROEBEL FOUNDATION EDUCATION COMMITTEE MINUTES, 20 November 1959.

NUNN, P. (1945) *Education: Its Data and First Principles*, 3rd edn., London, Edward Arnold.

NUT (1944) *Educational developments of the National Union of Teachers, statement by the Executive for presentation to the Easter Conference 1944*.

NUT ARCHIVE, Primary Schools Advisory Committee Minutes 1946–59, 3 December 1946.

NUT ARCHIVE, Primary Schools Advisory Committee Minutes 1946–59, 4 May 1948.

NUT ARCHIVE, Primary Schools Advisory Committee Minutes 1946–59, 3 May 1956.

NUT (1959) *The Curriculum of the Junior School: Report of a Consultative Committee*, London, Schoolmaster Publishing Co. Ltd.

RIDGWAY, L. and LAWTON, I. (1968) *Family Grouping in the Primary School*, London, Ward Lock. (Originally published 1965 as *Family Grouping in the Infant School*).

The Schoolmaster (1947) 'Primary School Problems', by A Correspondent (T.E.N.), 24 July, p. 79.

SELLECK, R. (1972) *English Primary Education and the Progressives, 1914–1939*, London, Routledge and Kegan Paul.

SIMON, B. (1980) 'The Primary School Revolution: Myth or Reality?' in FEARN, E. and SIMON, B. (Eds) (1980) *Education in the Nineteen Sixties*, London, History of Education Society, 24–6.

SIMON, B. (1986) 'The 1944 Education Act: A Conservative Measure?' *History of Education*, 15, 1, 24–32.

Teachers in the Witness Box, BBC Written Archive, Scripts 4.11.46.

VAN DER EYKEN, W. (Ed) (1973) *Education, the Child and Society: A Documentary History 1900–1973*, Harmondsworth, Penguin.

WHITEHEAD, A.N. (1966) *The Aims of Education*, London, Benn. (Originally published 1929).

Chapter 2

Government Action: The Great Education Debate 1977–1986

Nigel Proctor

Introduction

It could be argued that 1977 represents a turning point in the history of education in this country, for it marks a new political initiative in determining the purpose and aims of the nation's schools (Proctor, 1988a). Prior to 1977, as we have seen in the first chapter, schools and individual teachers had great freedom to choose their own curriculum. Despite having arguably the most able civil servants in government (Van Straubenzee, 1987) the DES seemed to have neither the interest nor the expertise to dictate curriculum affairs. This view is supported by the statements of some politicians, from the rather caustic comment by George Tomlinson, Minister of Education after the war, that 'Minister knows nowt about curriculum' to a more considered, but equally cautious view of the civil servants that:

> It is a basic weakness that the Department of Education and Science is not manned by persons with educational experience. Among comparable countries, our Department of Education is the only one devoid of educationists. I know that, when challenged, the Department point out that there is the Inspectorate, but the Department always makes a virtue of the independence of the Inspectorate, and the plain fact is that the Inspectorate remains isolated from the administrative processes and decisions of the Department. (Willey, 1971)

Despite this apparent lack of expertise, the DES expressed interest in the curriculum in 1974 when the Permanent Secretary at the Department of Education and Science 'wondered' aloud to an OECD examining panel 'whether the Government could continue to debar itself from what has been termed "the secret garden of the curriculum"'. The intervention by the DES represents a backlash to the Plowden Report (CACE, 1967) which — though its key words had been 'equality' and 'community' — was seen by some to over-emphasize a child-centred education ('at the heart of the education process lies the child') and more progressive methods of teaching. The publication of the so-called 'black papers' and of Neville Bennett's (1976) research (which suggested that formal teaching methods might be most successful) gained great national media coverage, and the alarm was intensified following the outcry over the curriculum taught at William Tyndale Primary School, London, in 1975 (Auld, 1976).

The publicity finally required Government action, and the 'Great Education Debate' was heralded by James Callaghan's Ruskin College speech in 1976. Although introduced by a Labour Government, the debate was continued as part of Conservative party policy and culminated in the 1988 Education Reform Act (ERA). The period was marked by the publication of a series of reports and documents, particularly by the DES and HMI (Figure 2.1).

Introductory Moves: The Four Subjects for Debate

The period began with a series of regional conferences arranged by the DES during February and March 1977 and attended by invited educationists and others from industry and commerce. Although four subjects for debate were identified in the conference paper (DES, 1977a), investigation reveals two surprises. First, no detailed criteria for a school curriculum were ever introduced to guide debate about the purpose and aims of schools. The principle of establishing criteria has been adopted in later debates — on, for instance, the content of teacher education courses (the so-called CATE criteria) and of GCSE subject syllabi — and it is perhaps surprising that the curriculum debate did not start with a number of criteria which would have to be met by subsequent proposals. A set of ten criteria for a common curriculum has been published elsewhere (Proctor, 1984a). Such a strategy could have eliminated some of the problems the debate encountered and created a better basis for discussion by schools and local authorities.

The second surprise is that conference papers were not published to guide subsequent debate. Cynics might argue that the 'debate', and indeed the 'consultation process', were a smokescreen, for while educationists — including HMI — debated the purpose and arrangement of the curriculum, the DES focused the whole of attention and action on preparing legislation which would make their first four 'subjects for debate' the cornerstone of the Education Act. Only now can we reflect and analyze the importance of the four subjects, which were:

Figure 2.1 Curriculum Statements and Reports: 1977–1986

	DES statements	Reports	HMI statements and surveys
1977	*Educating Our Children* (conference paper) *Education in Schools* (The Green Paper) A Consultative Paper, HMSO		*Curriculum 11–16* (The Red Book), HMSO
1978		DES, *Special Education Needs* (The Warnock Report), HMSO	*Primary Education in England* (The Primary Survey), HMSO
1979	(FEU) *A Basis for Choice* (The Mansell Report), DES		*Aspects of Secondary Education in England* (The Secondary Survey), HMSO
1980	*A Framework for the School Curriculum*, HMSO		*A View of the Curriculum*, HMI Matters for Discussion Series, 11, HMSO
1981	*The School Curriculum*, HMSO Circular 6/81 (October)	Schools Council, *The Practical Curriculum*	
1982	(FEU) *Basic Skills* (DES)	DES, *Mathematics Counts* (The Cockcroft Report), HMSO House of Commons Educ. Sc. Arts Committee, *The Secondary School Curriculum and Examinations*, HMSO Gulbenkian Foundation, *The Arts in Schools*	*The New Teacher in School*, HMI Matters for Discussion Series, 15, HMSO *Bullock Revisited*, Discussion Paper, DES
1983	*Teaching Quality* (The White Paper), HMSO		*Curriculum 11–16: towards a statement of entitlement*, HMSO
1984	*The Organization and Content of the 5 to 16 Curriculum*, HMSO		*English from 5 to 16*, Curriculum Matters, 1, HMSO
1985	*Better Schools* (The White Paper), HMSO	House of Commons Educ. Sc. Arts Committee, *Achievement in Primary Schools*, HMSO	*The Curriculum from 5 to 16*, Curriculum Matters 2, HMSO
1986	*LEA Policies for the School Curriculum* (report on review), DES *The Education Act*		Five other Curriculum Matters publications — Mathematics, Music, Home Economics, Health Education, Geography

(1) *The aims and content of the school curriculum* How can a 'core curriculum' be established to meet the needs and aspirations of pupils and the needs of the country? (Paras 2.1–2.18).

Many believed that this would result in a loose and flexible arrangement of the curriculum — similar to the HMI's Areas of Experience (HMI, 1977) — for Baroness Young (1979) insisted that 'We do not believe in laying down a detailed curriculum in any context', and this was translated in *The School Curriculum* (DES, 1981) into the statement 'Neither the Government nor the local authorities should specify in detail what the schools should teach'. HMI (1977) were even more adamant:

> We repeat that it is not the intention to advocate a standard curriculum, not least because that would be educationally naive. One of the greatest assets of our educational arrangements is the freedom of schools to respond to differing circumstances in their localities and to encourage the enterprise and strength of their teachers.

However, we now have a *National* Curriculum with all schools following distinct programmes of study for three core and seven foundation subjects. How study of these subjects will 'meet the needs of pupils and the country' is still unclear.

(2) *The assessment of standards* How can we check that pupils are progressing in the acquisition of essential knowledge and basic skills? (Paras 3.1–3.27).

At the time few educationists would have considered standardized tests, for all the evidence from America showed the problems of test reliability and validity, and how difficult it was to define competency levels. However we now have Standard Assessment Tasks (SATs) and reporting and monitoring stages for primary school children at seven and eleven (DES, 1987b).

3. *The education and training of teachers* How can we ensure an improvement in school education unless the teachers are committed to what needs to be done and equipped with the necessary skills? (Paras 4.1–4.11).

Many teacher educators were pleased to see that their area was considered of vital importance in improving educational standards throughout the country and that proper emphasis was being placed on the acquisition of the necessary skills which had already been identified by HMI (Proctor, 1984b). However, in all the subsequent legislation, the emphasis has shifted from the acquisition of professional skills to the accumulation of academic, subject knowledge. Now half of the time of B.Ed primary courses is spent on studying academic subjects (DES, 1983) and the consequences of this for the primary school could be dramatic. This issue is discussed in greater detail later in this chapter.

(4) *School and working life* How can pupils be made aware of our industrial society and what contribution can industry make to education? (Paras 5.1–5.10).

This issue for 'debate' was eventually to find an echo in *The National Curriculum: A Consultation Document* (DES, 1987a). Schools 'should equip every pupil with the knowledge, skills, understanding and aptitudes to meet the responsibilities of adult life and *employment*'; there seems a preoccupation with the acquisition of vocational skills and knowledge about industry and commerce. The other item — industry's contribution to education — has evolved into the contentious issue of City Technology Colleges sponsored in part by commercial and industrial firms. Fortunately the whole of this 'subject for debate' is of only marginal importance to the country's primary schools, but later documents have helped shape the new curriculum of primary schools.

The Department of Education and the Aims of Schools

In the same year as the regional conferences of the 'Great Debate' the DES published its consultative paper *Education in Schools* (DES, 1977b) which identified eight 'Aims of Schools',

(i) to help children develop lively, enquiring minds; giving them the ability to question and to argue rationally, and to apply themselves to tasks;

(ii) to instil respect for moral values, for other people and for oneself, and tolerance of other races, religions, and ways of life;

(iii) to help children understand the world in which we live, and the interdependence of nations;

(iv) to help children to use language effectively and imaginatively in reading, writing and speaking;

(v) to help children to appreciate how the nation earns and maintains its standard of living and properly to esteem the essential role of industry and commerce in this process;

(vi) to provide a basis of mathematical, scientific and technical knowledge, enabling boys and girls to learn the essential skills needed in a fast-changing world of work;

(vii) to teach children about human achievement and aspirations in the arts and sciences, in religion, and in the search for a more just social order;

(viii) to encourage and foster the development of the children whose social or environmental disadvantages cripple their capacity to learn, if necessary by making additional resources available to them.

These were amended in *Framework for the School Curriculum* (DES, 1984) in which the policy of recognizing compulsory 'core' subjects was proposed. A year later *The School Curriculum* (DES, 1981) outlined the Government's intentions: English, mathematics, science, modern languages, the humanities, physical education and religious studies were seen as being of vital importance in the curriculum for all pupils throughout the period of compulsory education.

The 'Aims of Schools' represent an important change in stating educational intentions. Traditionally official documents and statements had begun with an outline of 'educational' aims, defined in one curriculum paper as 'broad statements of intent by which the curriculum is guided' rather than an indication of what pupils will learn (Scottish Central Committee, 1976).

The 'Aims of Schools' were quite different, although they were simplified in 1980 (see Figure 2.2). Some of the 1980 aims were less cluttered and there were some important omissions; for instance, 'the search for a more just social order' was omitted from the last aim of 1980, as was the necessity to provide additional resources for disadvantaged children (the last of the 1977 aims). It should be remembered that the 1977 list was compiled under a Labour Government while those of 1980 and 1981 were compiled under a Conservative Government.

Schools and LEAs have commonly included these lists of aims in their curriculum statements, but there are a number of problems. First, the aims appear more appropriate for secondary rather than for primary — or, for that matter, special schools but nowhere is this indicated. But this uniformity of aims for ages five–sixteen is consistent with the DES policy for the teaching and assessment of ten foundation subjects throughout the period of compulsory education — not just in secondary schools.

Second, in moving from broad, abstract aims to more detailed checklists, the aims have become so specific as to be analogous to objectives. Classifications of objectives range from Bloom's *Taxonomy* to more practical arrangements such as concepts, skills, values and attitudes, and if the DES aims are juxtaposed with either classification, their limitations become apparent. But, more important, if behavioural objectives *are* stated it is clear that they should guide curriculum content if learning outcomes are to be

Figure 2.2 Aims of Schools (DES)

The eight aims of Education in Schools (1977)	The six aims of the Framework document (1980) and The School Curriculum (1981)
(i) to help children develop lively, enquiring minds; giving them the ability to question and to argue rationally, and to apply themselves to tasks;	(i) To help pupils to develop lively, enquiring minds, the ability to question and argue rationally and to apply themselves to tasks, and physical skills;
(ii) to instil respect for moral values, for other people and for oneself, and tolerance of other races, religions, and ways of life;	(ii) to help pupils to acquire knowledge and skills relevant to adult life and employment in a fast-changing world;
(iii) to help children understand the world in which we live, and the interdependence of nations;	(iii) to help pupils to use language and number effectively;
(iv) to help children to use language effectively and imaginatively in reading, writing and speaking;	(iv) to instil respect for religious and moral values, and tolerance of other races, religions and way of life;
(v) to help children to appreciate how the nation earns and maintains its standard of living and properly to esteem the essential role of industry and commerce in this process;	(v) to help pupils to understand the world in which they live, and the interdependence of individuals, groups and nations;
(vi) to provide a basis of mathematical, scientific and technical knowledge, enabling boys and girls to learn the essential skills needed in a fast-changing world of work;	(vi) to help pupils to appreciate human achievements and aspirations.
(vii) to teach children about human achievement and aspirations in the arts and sciences, in religion, and in the search for a more just social order;	
(viii) to encourage and foster the development of the children whose social or environmental disadvantages cripple their capacity to learn, if necessary by making additional resources available to them.	

achieved. Indeed the *Framework* document (DES, 1980) insists that 'schools should *ensure* that where groups of pupils follow a common curriculum it is well matched to aims and objectives'. How well the full package of programmes of study in the National Curriculum subjects measure up to the Aims of Schools cannot be determined at the time of writing.

Third, many of the aims appear naive and inadequate and also virtually impossible to implement in the classroom (see Proctor, 1986). Can primary school teachers honestly say that they provide children with the knowledge necessary to meet all the aims? A personal opinion is that it would need an economics graduate to teach Aim (v) of the 1977 list, though, even then, I would not particularly want children to 'esteem' the essential role of industry in appreciating 'how the nation earns and maintains its standard of living.' Again, why is 'listening' omitted from the forms of language included in Aim (iv) when we know, from American and British research (e.g. Barnes, 1976), how teacher talk dominates classroom activities, with the children as listeners? It is beyond the scope of this chapter to go through each of the Aims of Schools (see instead White *et al.*, 1981) but elsewhere Proctor (1988b) provides a closer examination.

HM Inspectorate's Areas of Experience

At the start of the Great Debate on the aims of education HMI produced the 'Red Book' as their initial contribution to the curriculum debate at the same time as the DES's Green Paper. They began by commenting on an approach using only subjects (as advocated by the DES):

> It is not proposed that schools should plan and construct a common curriculum in terms of subject labels only: that would be to risk becoming trapped in discussions about the relative importance of this subject or that. Rather, it is necessary to look through the subject or discipline to the areas of experience and knowledge to which it may provide access, and to the skills and attitudes which it may assist to develop. (HMI, 1977)

HMI recognized eight 'areas of experience' arguing that the curriculum, during the period of compulsory education, should be concerned with introducing pupils to the aesthetic and creative, the ethical, the linguistic, the mathematical, the physical, the scientific, the social and political, and the spiritual. (See Figure 2.3) The list was followed by descriptions of a number of subjects in which the applicability of these 'areas' was demonstrated.

In a later document, *The Curriculum from 5–16*, HMI (1985a) added a

Figure 2.3 HMI Areas of Experience and Skills

Areas of Experience (1977)	Areas of Experience (1985)	Skills (1985)
aesthetic and creative	aesthetic and creative	creative and imagination
linguistic	linguistic and literacy	communication
mathematical	mathematical	numerical
physical	physical	physical
social and political	human and social	personal and social
scientific	scientific	problem-solving
ethical	moral	study
spiritual	spiritual	observation
	technological	

Sources: Curriculum 11–16 (HMI, 1977) The Curriculum from 5 to 16 (HMI, 1985a)

ninth area, the technological, and changed some of the titles of other areas for instance the term 'political' was acceptable under a Labour Government in 1977 but not under a Conservative Government in 1985. Apart from naming the areas of experience the document also provided guidance on structuring a curriculum with the breadth, balance, relevance differentiation, continuity and progression required by the DES. But the document has been criticized by Morrison (1987) for starting with the curriculum rather than the child. He argues that, 'delivering' the curriculum (Paragraph 8) adopts a 'transmission' model which fails to recognize current ideas on active learning. Moreover, the document neglects pedagogy, management and organization, the classroom environment, parental involvement children as decision-makers and their friendships and motivation.

In general, however, the areas of experience themselves have been fairly well received, and the House of Commons Select Committee (1982) considered them 'probably the most coherent proposal so far and a more hopeful framework for development.' Nevertheless there are a number of issues which should be considered by primary schools intending to use the 'areas' as a framework to help them teach the National Curriculum.

First, the HMI's method of approaching curriculum design is not new, and there are well-founded reservations about the whole process of classification (see Lloyd, 1976). Examples of ideas for structuring the curriculum are illustrated in Figure 2.4, ranging from only two types of 'worthwhile experience' in Aristotle's day to the ten subjects of the current National Curriculum. This diversity of approach is a major weakness. No one scheme is 'better' than the other. Indeed with the current vogue for conservation, ecology and the environment we should surely see 'the environmental' as one of the key 'areas', as in the Australian scheme. One Staff Inspector, Colin Richards (1989: 9), suggests that, in addition to the areas of experience, aspects of health education, education for family life, world studies, industry education, and multi-cultural education 'are pressing their claims as offering worthwhile, particularly relevant, experience to children at an age when their attitudes are being formed and basic views of the physical and social world established'. The problem is that any group of educationists could come up with such a scheme which they could defend and justify. An alternative framework, based on more scientific evidence, is proposed in Chapter 9.

Another issue is that HMI believe that equal importance should be attached to each of the areas throughout the period of compulsory education (5–16). Young children, particularly those with learning difficulties, will find it extremely difficult to appreciate all the areas; even teachers will need much greater guidance to ensure that they cover the full range of activities involved in an area such as 'the aesthetic and creative'. The practical problem of

Figure 2.4 Schemes for Structuring the Curriculum

Author	Date	Number of areas	FOCUS	DETAIL
Aristotle	300 BC	2	worthwhile activities	mechanical (slave) skills; aesthetic (liberal) education
Schwab	1962	3	kinds of discipline	investigative; appreciative; decisive
Peterson	1960	4	modes of thinking or modes of experiences	the logical; the empirical; the moral, the aesthetic
Lawton	1973	5	subject groupings	humanities and social sciences; moral education; mathematics; physical and biological sciences; expressive and creative arts
Phenix	1964	6	areas of knowledge	symbolics; empirics; aesthetics; synnoctics; ethics; synoptics
Hirst and Peters	1970	7	areas of knowledge	human studies; philosophy; moral judgement and awareness; religious understanding; formal logic and mathematics; physical sciences; aesthetic experience
HMI	1977	8	areas of experience	the aesthetic and creative; the ethical; the linguistic; the mathematical; the physical; the scientific; the social and political; the spiritual
Australian Curriculum Development Centre	1980	9	areas of knowledge and experience	arts and crafts; environmental studies; mathematics; social, cultural and civic studies; health education; science and technology; communication; moral reasoning and values; work leisure and lifestyle
DES	1988	10	subjects	English; mathematics; science; geography; history; technology; music; art; physical education and (for secondary) modern languages

equipping teachers with the skills necessary to teach 'the scientific' and 'the technological', particularly with so few subject specialists, is not considered. Perhaps the primary school should merely introduce children informally to each of the areas, leaving secondary schools to systematically cover each of them in depth, but this notion needs further explication and clarification.

Some educationists complain that they cannot understand what the areas actually mean (see Holt, 1983) or how they can be implemented in schools. Morrison (1987) critically points out that they represent 'a mixture of content, process, pedagogy, organization and exhortation, but with no evenness of treatment within and across the nine areas'. For me, the problem was exacerbated when HMI (1985a) published a list of eight skills, while revising the original list of areas. Figure 2.3 compares these three lists. It is clear that most of the skills repeat or resemble areas, such as numerical/mathematical and linguistic/communication, but there appear to be no 'associated' moral, spiritual or technological skills. Most of the eight skills are indivisible; for instance, many 'physical' skills are used 'creatively and imaginatively' in 'personal and social' 'communication'. Again, study, observation and problem-solving skills have no direct link with areas; Dearden writing about the primary school curriculum, asks:

> Can there be such general skills as skill in noticing, observing skill, thinking skill, comprehensive skills or listening skill? [Problem-solving skill is later added] If there cannot be, then effort will be mis-directed in trying to improve primary education in pursuit of such skills and related inservice training will be wrongly focused. The question is, therefore, no 'merely academic' one or a matter 'just of semantics'. (Dearden, 1980: 23)

While totally agreeing with Dearden's main line of argument, I would defend the use of 'listening'; the oral element of English is overwhelmingly and undeniably its most important component and considerable work has been done in developing children's listening skills in language and music.

Relatively few primary schools have adopted and implemented the 'areas' and HMI (1983a), concluded from a survey of five local authorities that 'even after five years of work in the enquiry, much remains to be done to reach agreement on the nature of the curriculum'. It went on to argue that 'certainly a consensus about the concepts and knowledge to be taught, as well as the skills and attitudes to be developed, will be needed if the entitlement curriculum is to be realized'. The DES may have been encouraged by this suggestion, for the National Curriculum announced a few years later comprised core and foundation subjects, for which clear programmes of study were to be identified.

Other Contributions to the Debate

Apart from documents and statements from HMI and the DES there were a number of important contributions from interest groups such as teachers' unions, parent-teacher bodies, subject associations and publishers, all hoping to influence the DES. Some of the most important contributions came from local education authorities (LEAs) which established working parties from among their teachers to write curriculum statements and teaching programmes for use in local schools. This action had been required of LEAs by the DES in October 1981 (Circular 6/81) and two years later (Circular 8/83) LEAs were asked to continually evaluate and review the curricula and teaching programmes in subsequent years. Of the hundred or so documents resulting from this requirement probably the best known is that produced by the Inner London Education Authority (Thomas, 1985); with a national figure as Chairman, the committee provided excellent advice to heads and teachers. Other important contributions were made by educationists, concerned that their ideas should be given some consideration during a period of national debate about the curriculum.

Two national bodies produced publications on the aims and content of education which had wide circulation and influence. The first was the Schools Council, established in 1964 by the Minister of Education to encourage and promote curriculum development in English and Welsh schools. It did this by giving financial grants totalling over £6 million to project teams, over 160 before the Schools Council was replaced by the School Curriculum Development Committee in 1983; the SCDC was itself replaced by the School Curriculum Council in 1988. Although most of the project teams produced material for teaching secondary school subjects, there were a number of important and influential projects on primary themes, such as *Place Time and Society* (Blyth *et al.*, 1976). Apart from Pat Ashton's project on the aims of school teachers (see Chapter 4) only a few considered the whole-school curriculum and the general aims of primary education (Schools Council, 1983). One contribution, *The Practical Curriculum* (1981), was, however, distributed by the School Council to all schools in England and Wales and therefore gained considerable attention. This included a discussion on the purpose of primary education and provided a list of more specific aims, viz:

   (i) to read fluently and accurately, with understanding, feeling and discrimination;

   (ii) to develop a legible style of handwriting and satisfactory standards of spelling, syntax, punctuation and usage;

   (iii) to communicate clearly and confidently in speech and writing, in ways appropriate for various occasions and purposes;

(iv) to listen attentively and with understanding;

(v) to learn how to acquire information from various sources, and to record information and findings in various ways;

(vi) to apply computational skills with speed and accuracy;

(vii) to understand the applications of mathematical ideas in various situations in home, classroom, school and local area;

(viii) to observe living and inanimate things, and to recognize characteristics such as pattern and order;

(ix) to master basic scientific ideas;

(x) to investigate solutions and interpret evidence, to analyze and to solve problems;

(xi) to develop awareness of self and sensitivity to others, acquire a set of moral values and the confidence to make and hold to moral judgements, and develop habits of self-discipline and acceptable behaviour;

(xii) to be aware of the geographical, historical and social aspects of the local environment and the national heritage, and to be aware of other times and places;

(xiii) to acquire sufficient control of self or of tools, equipment and instruments to be able to use music, drama and several forms of arts and crafts as means of expression;

(xiv) to develop agility and physical coordination, confidence in and through physical activity, and the ability to express feeling through movement.

Clearly, these aims are much more child-centred than the DES Aims of Schools and many primary schools may prefer to use them as a basis for staffroom debate about the curriculum.

The other national body whose publications on the curriculum are worthy of consideration is the Gulbenkian Foundation. Its main publication, *The Arts in Schools* (1982), was purchased by many local authorities for distribution to all their schools. It argued strongly for the inclusion of expressive arts in the curriculum, but such claims should have been unnecessary had the DES appreciated the meaning of the title of its original Green Paper, *Education in Schools* (DES, 1976b). The term 'education' is derived from the Latin 'educere' meaning to 'lead out' and places emphasis on the growth or development of individual potentialities, a basic principle of aesthetic education. The ancient Greek word for leisure (*skhole*) is the original of our word 'school'; Artistotle, reacting against the emphasis on the development of skills, which he allied to the practice of slavery, argued that 'free men' should have a 'liberal' education in order to provide a basis for the most fruitful use of leisure time; he included in education 'only such knowledge as does not make the learner mechanical' (Proctor, 1985).

Moreover, the Maud Report (1976) had urged a 'revolution' in educational policy to bring the arts 'nearer to the heart of the curriculum' while, two years later, the Conservative paper *The Arts – the Way Forward* (1978) argued that 'In any core of subjects laid down by central Government, the arts should have a guaranteed place'. Despite such pressure, the response had been disappointing and the Gulbenkian Foundation felt it necessary to publish its report since 'In the widespread discussions which have been taking place about the school curriculum, the arts — dance, drama, music, visual arts, literature — have been given little attention. We consider any neglect of the arts in education to be a serious matter.'

Further justification for the inclusion of aesthetic education in the National Curriculum was produced by the House of Commons Education, Science and Arts Committee (1982) which criticized such statements in *The School Curriculum* (DES, 1981) as

> Subjects like art, music and drama are needed to develop sensibilities without which the pupil will not be able to avail himself of many opportunities for enriching his personal experience. Such subjects as physical education, home economics and craft design and technology make a particular contribution to the acquisition of physical and practical skills which are an essential complement of the pupils' intellectual and personal development.

The Committee looked at this paragraph in detail and stated, 'We suggest that it is not necessary to be a strong proponent of creative aspects of the curriculum to consider this description of their potential role as essentially dismissive and lacking in any sympathetic awareness either of the schools or of pupils' personal development.' The committee had also received evidence from such bodies as the Royal Society of Arts arguing that 'the distinction between "physical and practical" on the one hand and "intellectual and personal" on the other was dangerous and fallacious, and moreover that the continuing maintenance of such distinctions was one of the most serious shortcomings in our educational system.'

Pressure for the inclusion of the expressive arts in the curriculum was so strong that the DES relented and included two of the arts subjects, music and art, among its foundation subjects in the National Curriculum. Just how the breadth of the expressive arts is to be experienced by all children through these two subjects is not explained, but one proposal is considered in Chapter 9.

Academic Subjects, Teacher Education and the Aims of Primary Education

The DES strongly believes that the aims of primary education can best be achieved through the teaching of academic subjects, for which programmes of study and Standard Assessment Tasks (SATs) are now being prepared. Not only should children be taught by subject specialists for part of the time, but the school's subject syllabi and schemes of work should be the responsibility of a subject consultant. (See Chapter 8 for a description of the role of the consultant.)

Such steps could be extremely damaging (Proctor, 1986). For instance, the Welsh HMI recently warmly commended the great effectiveness of the class teacher, with 'virtues which cannot lightly be discounted', even though there was a need to prevent children's under-achievement. 'It does not, however, follow that this need is best met by increasing specialization among primary teachers. It may be that there is potential within the present system which, properly used, could achieve this aim' (HMI, 1984b).

The greatest danger of introducing subject teaching and assessment is that emphasis may be placed on the acquisition of factual knowledge, even though such practice was condemned some fifty years ago. Hadow's often quoted dictum that 'the curriculum is to be thought of in terms of activity and experience rather than of knowledge to be acquired and facts to be stored' (Board of Education, 1931) appeared shortly before A.N. Whitehead (1932) warned that factual knowledge is inert because it performs no function or purpose in relation to the educational development of the learner: 'The merely well-informed man (sic) is the most useless bore on God's earth'.

Evidence from HMI surveys of schools does not support the DES stance on the value of academic subjects (Proctor, 1987). For instance, the survey of primary schools (HMI, 1978) was a far more encouraging document than that of secondary schools (HMI, 1979) and the notion of changing the former to match the latter seems totally illogical (Kelly, 1984). The primary survey identified some weaknesses in teachers' subject knowledge and the DES has used this 'evidence' to require all teacher training institutions to increase subject study to half of the B.Ed course; but the majority of teachers in the survey *must* have followed the old B.Ed subject route or its predecessor, the main subject Certificate, not the new professionally oriented courses. The DES appears to want to re-introduce the type of course which it, through its HMI, had previously condemned. Surveys have also shown that the vast majority of primary teachers — particularly women — have an arts/humanities background, and an HMI Welsh Survey (HMI, 1984) found only four out of 114 teachers questioned had a qualification in mathematics beyond GCE O-level. If subject expertise equals teaching quality, we should expect arts/humanities to be the best taught, and mathematics the worst taught, subject on the curriculum. The opposite is commonly the case. The Middle Schools Survey (HMI, 1985b), for instance, identifies the greatest need for improving in RE, geography, home studies and CDT, with history faring little better — yet *every* school had teachers qualified in history and geography.

Apart from their surveys of schools, HMI has published a number of excellent papers advising teacher training institutions on appropriate course content; in all of these, emphasis has been placed on increasing the amount of time spent on curriculum and professional courses (Proctor, 1984b) *not* on acquiring further subject knowledge. The last of these contributions, the *Content* paper (HMI, 1983), concluded that 'the professional skills which initial training can give to an intending teacher lie *at the heart of the* training process'.

Despite all the evidence to the contrary, the DES (1983) has insisted that nursery, infant and junior B.Ed courses must include two years of subject study 'at a level appropriate to higher education'. The Council for the Accreditation of Teacher Education (CATE) was established in 1984 partly to ensure and oversee the implementation of this requirement, using evidence drawn from HMI survey reports of each of the teacher training institutions. The changes currently taking place in teacher education will have profound effects not only on classroom practice but on the very aims of primary education for many years to come.

And so to the Education Reform Act (ERA)

Although the current scene in primary education is reviewed in the next chapter it would be remiss not to finish this chapter by referring briefly to the major components of the 1988 ERA since, as we have already seen, they mark the fruition of ideas which germinated in the four 'subjects for debate' in the DES regional conferences of 1977. Assessment and the National Curriculum will dominate changes in the aims of primary schools but aims will also be affected by two other administrative changes. If 'Open Enrolment' is extended to primary schools, they will be legally obliged to accept pupils up to an admission limit which may not be set lower than the number of pupils admitted in 1979. Parents will exercise their choice for the most popular school in the area. Teachers will therefore be under pressure to ensure that *their* school remains 'popular'. The main aim of the school may well be to improve success in national assessments; other 'educational' aims may disappear through the window. A major area of contention, highlighted by the recent case of the Dewsbury parents who were refusing to send their children to a mainly Asian school, is whether open enrolment will lead to an increase in the number of racially segregated schools. This will have profound effects in terms of aims of the schools affected.

A parallel administrative change is to devolve vastly increased powers of financial management to the governing bodies of individual schools —

powers previously discharged by the local authorities. Schools will have to consider if the quality of educational provision is a more important aim than mere cost-efficiency. They will also have to consider incentives to compete for pupils — the source of extra income. This part of the ERA increases the amount of competition which schools will have to endure.

But competition will also enter the lives of the children through new arrangements for assessment, no matter how well teachers might 'hide' the actual Standard Assessment Tasks (SATs) and how well-intentioned were the proposals made by the Task Group chaired by Paul Black, which moderated the worst excesses many feared. But there are other fears. One concerns failure labelling and that some pupils could be disadvantaged. There is the fear that some teachers will teach for the tests and ignore other important aspects of a child's education; there is the fear that relations between teachers, pupils and parents may be soured; there is the fear that schools may be damaged by appearing in 'League Tables' which would be used as the basis of judgements by parents on where they send their children. Equally important, the whole aim and purpose of assessment can be questioned; the response to the consultation document (DES, 1987a) made by Hertfordshire County Council stated:

> The desire to quicken the pace of raising standards to at least those of our 'competitor countries' might lead us . . . to inquire whether any of our competitors considers it necessary or effective to set up national examinations, controlled and monitored by organizations outside the schools, at the age of 16. To do so at 7, 11 and 14 as well is to adopt an approach not thought to be necessary in any major western industrial nation.

The National Curriculum is the most important outcome of the ERA. Its aim is to bring coherence to the system and so raise standards in school. This is a laudable aim, yet there has been an extremely hostile reaction from bodies on both left and right in their responses during the consultation process prior to the passage of the Bill through Parliament. Here I am indebted to Haviland for his excellent book *Take Care, Mr Baker* (1988) which is a compilation of 'the advice on education reform which the Government collected but withheld'. An eclectic group of sources include:

> The Royal Society of Arts '. . . does not believe that such a curriculum can be described in terms of particular subjects'.

> The NAS/UWT complained that 'a curriculum defined in terms of traditional subjects will make it more difficult to promote the development of cross-curricular themes. Important minority subjects . . . will be squeezed out'.

The Institute of Economic Affairs stated that 'the most effective National Curriculum is that set by the market. Uniformity between schools it not only unnecessary, it is potentially damaging'.

The CBI criticized 'the narrow confines of the traditional subject disciplines'.

The Derbyshire County Council was scathing: 'The document proposes a system designed to make rapid response to changing circumstances impossible so that tomorrow's need will be met by yesterday's vision'.

The Conservative Education Association was concerned that 'the curriculum should not . . . become narrow and prescriptive, which we fear could easily happen under the proposals'.

The National Association of Inspectors and Educational Advisers stated: 'At primary level there is overwhelming evidence that the basic skills are most successfully learnt when applied across the whole curriculum. We therefore find it hard to accept that "the majority of curriculum time at primary level should be devoted to the core subjects"'.

What is clear from the foregoing is that the National Curriculum is not a consensus curriculum; it is *not* the edited highlights of the views of teachers, educators, parents, industry or the community. It takes no cognizance of all the work on curriculum organization done by educationists illustrated in Figure 2.4; all of these proposals advocated skills and understanding or knowledge or experience *across* subject boundaries. The National Curriculum is a scheme produced by civil servants for politicians, and will constrain future educational development because of its formal and bureaucratic structure.

I end this chapter by quoting at length from the Reverend Charles Lutwidge Dodgson — Lewis Carroll — who, in 1865, conceived a national curriculum with prescribed syllabi and many familiar names, as you will discover:

> . . . before Alice could speak again, the Mock Turtle went on
> 'We had the best of educations — in fact, we went to school every day —'
> *I've* been to a day-school, too,' said Alice; 'you needn't be so proud as all that.'
> 'With extras?' asked the Mock Turtle a little anxiously.
> 'Yes,' said Alice, 'we learned French and music.'
> 'And washing?' said the Mock Turtle.
> 'Certainly not!' said Alice indignantly.

'Ah! then yours wasn't a really good school,' said the Mock Turtle in a tone of great relief. 'Now at *ours* they had at the end of the bill, "French, music, *and washing* — extra."' [washing = science and technology?]

'You couldn't have wanted it much,' said Alice; 'living at the bottom of the sea.'

'I couldn't afford to learn it,' said the Mock Turtle with a sigh. 'I only took the regular course.'

'What was that?' inquired Alice.

'Reeling and Writhing, of course, to begin with,' the Mock Turtle replied; 'and then the different branches of Arithmetic — Ambition, Distraction, Uglification, and Derision.'...

Alice ... turned to the Mock Turtle, and said 'What else had you to learn?'

'Well, there was Mystery,' the Mock Turtle replied, counting off the subjects on his flappers, '— Mystery, ancient and modern, with Seaography: then Drawling — the Drawling-master was an old conger-eel, that used to come once a week: *he* taught us Drawling, Stretching, and Fainting in Coils.' [is this physical education?]

These are the ten subjects of the National Curriculum. The final words in Lewis Carroll's book are:

In a Wonderland they lie,
Dreaming as the days go by,
Dreaming as the summers die:

Ever drifting down the stream —
Lingering in the golden gleam —
Life, what is it but a dream?

What more needs to be said?

References

ASHTON, P. (1975) *Aims of Primary Education*. Research Studies Series, London, Schools Council.

AULD, R. (1976) *William Tyndale Infant and Junior School: Report of a Public Inquiry*. London, ILEA.

BARNES, D. (1976) *From Communication to Curriculum*. London, Penguin.

BENNETT, N. (1976) *Teaching Styles and Pupil Progress*. Milton Keynes, Open Books.

BLYTH, A. *et al.* (1976) *Curriculum Planning in History, Geography and Social Science*. London, Collins.

BOARD OF EDUCATION (1931) *The Primary School: The Hadow Report*. London, HMSO.

CARROLL, L. (1865) *Alice's Adventures in Wonderland* and *Through the Looking Glass.* (combined volumes), Harmondsworth, Puffin Books, (1987).

CENTRAL ADVISORY COUNCIL FOR EDUCATION (1967) *Children and Their Primary School: The Plowden Report.* London, HMSO.

CONSERVATIVE PARTY (1978) *The Arts: The Way Forward.* London, Conservative Party.

DEARDEN, R. (1980) 'The primary survey: an assessment', in RICHARDS, C. *op. cit.*

DES (1977a) *Educating Our Children: Conference Paper.* London, DES.

DES (1977b) *Education in Schools: The Green Paper.* London, DES.

DES (1978) *Special Education Needs: The Warnock Report.* London, HMSO.

DES (1980) *A Framework for the School Curriculum.* London, HMSO.

DES (1981) *The School Curriculum.* London, HMSO.

DES (1983) *Teaching Quality: White Paper.* London, HMSO.

DES (1984) *The Organisation and Content of the 5 to 16 Curriculum.* London, HMSO.

DES (1987a) *The National Curriculum 5–16: A Consultative Document.* London, HMSO.

DES (1987b) *National Curriculum: Taskforce on Assessment and Testing.* London, DES.

FAIRHALL, J. (1987) Comment in *The Guardian.* 12 March.

THE GULBENKIAN FOUNDATION (1982) *The Arts in Schools.* London, Calouste Gulbenkian Foundation.

HAVILAND, J. (1988) *Take Care, Mr. Baker.* London, Fourth Estate.

HMI (1977) *Curriculum 11–16: The Red Book.* London, HMSO.

HMI (1978) *Primary Education in England: The Primary Survey.* London, HMSO.

HMI (1979) *Aspects of Secondary Education in England: The Secondary Survey.* London, HMSO.

HMI (1983a) *Curriculum 11–16: Towards a Statement of Entitlement.* London, HMSO.

HMI (1983b) *Teaching in Schools: The Content of Initial Training.* London, DES.

HMI (1984) *Curriculum and Organisation of Primary Schools in Wales: Education Issues.* 7, London, HMSO.

HMI (1985a) *The Curriculum from 5 to 16: Curriculum Matters.* 2, London, HMSO.

HMI (1985b) *Education 8 to 12 in Combined and Middle School: An HMI Survey.* London, HMSO.

HOLT, M. (1983) *Curriculum Workshop: An Introduction to Whole Curriculum Planning.* London, Routledge and Kegan Paul.

HOUSE OF COMMONS: EDUCATION SELECT COMMITTEE (1982) *The Secondary School Curriculum and Examinations.* London, HMSO.

KELLY, A.V. (1984) 'The danger of tampering', *Times Educational Supplement.* 15 June.

LLOYD, D. (Ed) (1976) *Philosophy and the Teacher.* London, Routledge and Kegan Paul.

MAUD, R. (1976) *Support for the Arts in England and Wales: The Maud Report.* London, Calouste Gulbenkian Foundation.

MORRISON, K. (1987) 'The curriculum from 5–16: A primary response', *Curriculum,* 8, 2, 37–44.

PROCTOR, N. (1984a) 'Criteria for a common curriculum', *Curriculum,* 5, 1, 10–17.

PROCTOR, N. (1984b) 'Professional studies and the QTS review', *Journal of Education for Teaching,* 10, 1, 61–72.

PROCTOR, N. (1985) 'From basics to aesthetics in the curriculum', *British Journal of Aesthetics,* 25, 1, 57–65.

PROCTOR, N. (1986) 'Rethinking your primary curriculum statement', *Education,* 3–13, 14, 1, 9–16.

PROCTOR, N. (1987) 'Academic subjects in the B.Ed (primary) course: Some worrying evidence', *Journal of Further and Higher Education*, 11, 3, 35–44.

PROCTOR, N. (1988a) 'Government control of the curriculum: Some evidence', *British Education Research Journal*, 14, 2, 155–66.

PROCTOR, N. (1988b) 'Developing lively, enquiring minds: Some considerations for curriculum planning', *Education Today*, 38, 3, 26–33.

RICHARDS, C. (Ed) (1980) *Primary Education: Issues for the Eighties*. London, A and C Black.

RICHARDS, C. (1989) 'Primary Education in England: An analysis of some recent issues and developments', *Curriculum*, 8, 1, 6–12.

SCHOOLS COUNCIL (1981) *The Practical Curriculum*. London, Schools Council.

SCHOOLS COUNCIL (1983) *Primary Practice*. Schools Council Working Paper 75, London, Methuen.

SCOTTISH CENTRAL COMMITTEE (1976) *The Social Studies in Secondary Schools: Curriculum Paper 15*. London, HMSO.

THOMAS, N. (Ed) (1985) *Improving Secondary Schools*. London, ILEA.

VAN STRAUBENZEE, W. (1987) 'Reflections by the Chairman of the Commons Select Committee on Education', *The Times Educational Supplement*, 12 June.

WHITE, J. *et al.* (1981) *No Minister: A Critique of the DES paper 'The School Curriculum': Bedford Way Paper 4*. London, University of London Institute of Education.

WHITEHEAD, A.N. (1931) *The Aims of Education*. London, Williams and Norgate.

WILLEY, F. (1971) 'Indifference in the DES', *The Times Educational Supplement*, 21 May.

YOUNG, BARONESS (1979) Minister of State for Education quoted in *The Teacher*, 34, 24, 15 June.

Chapter 3

Primary Education: Where Are We Now?

Philip Gammage

Introduction

Visiting primary schools in the late 1980s, there is little observable difference between the activities and organization employed now and in the 1960s. True, the nature table may have become a technology table (wires, batteries, cogs, bits of bicycle and even, recently noticed, parts of a car gearbox). In the other corner, almost invariably, now resides a microcomputer. But Formica-topped tables, that unsung revolution of the early sixties, will be grouped as before, and the walls covered with children's art, writing, collective friezes and joint books. There will, except for the odd phrase in Urdu, be little reference to languages other than English. Generally, few illustrations of our European heritage or of European languages will strike the eye.

The casual visitor to 23,000 small primary schools of England and Wales will, if in the inner city or some midlands conurbation, notice more children of Asian and African orgin than in the 1950s, and be aware of the peculiar cyclic vogue for certain English Christian names as well as their tendency to be associated with socio-economic status. (The Sharons and Waynes of the large council estates are but two examples.) If she stays longer, as one Australian observer remarked recently, 'It may be possible to discern the bones of the English class structure'. By and large, classes will be smaller than twenty years ago, usually in the region of 1:29 (the DES, 1985 figure is 1:25.2, but this includes a proportion of non-teaching heads; I believe my figure is more realistic) and, with luck, parents and other adults will be much more in evidence, especially in the infant school. As the school day develops other differences will manifest themselves to our visitor. The classes will often contain different age cohorts within them, usually about a full two-year range, rarely more. On discussion with the teacher or headteacher, it will become apparent that as many as three-quarters of British primary schools have some form of mixed age groups within them, though the concept of 'redoublement' (repeating a grade or year) is as yet unknown. This vertical grouping of children has, in the past, tended to occur lower down in the age range and, usually as a matter of principle and conviction, planned by teachers and LEA Advisers who believed in 'family grouping' as an appropriate vehicle for socializing and securing children in a new environment. (See especially Education, Science and Arts Committee, 1986, pp. cxvii and cxviii). Now it exists in large numbers of junior schools and departments too, an inevitable consequence of the falling birth-rate of the 1970s, the small size of British schools (average primary school (5–11 years) some 180 children) and the attempts to rationalize the use of that prime scarce resource, the teacher. For Britain, in the 1980s and 1990s, is once more cycling blithely into what promises to be an acute teacher shortage, notably in maths, science, technology and languages at secondary levels (ages 11–16), but also at infant and lower junior levels too.

Walking round our 'average' British schools, the visitor, curiosity now fully aroused, has decided to stay, to find out, to delve, to ask questions. What is British primary education like now? What are its principal problems, constraints, its achievements and needs?

Infants

Many of the hundred plus Local Education authorities now admit four-year-olds to primary school. (The statutory requirements are that the child is engaged in appropriate full-time education after attaining the age of five. In a minority of LEAs (about 10 per cent, 1987 figures) children were only admitted to school in the term following their fifth birthday. In about another third they are admitted at the beginning of the term before their fifth birthday. The rest of the LEAs have various practices of early admission and in some cases (about 15 per cent) they have general assistants or assistants (sometimes unqualified) to help the teacher as well as a markedly lower pupil:teacher ratio.

Many parents appear quite content with this haphazard, somewhat piecemeal provision. In some parts of England and Wales (1988) children started primary school before attaining the age of four. In other parts, they may have waited up to four months after their fifth birthday, especially if admission is less frequent than termly. This 'early attendance' may well make it necessary for the technically pre-school age child to fit into a regime designed for older children. Certainly, some of the problems noted by our visitor will be that the infant teachers are unlikely to have been trained for what in the UK is referred to as 'nursery age' children. The Pre-school Playgroups Association and the British Association for Early Childhood Education (who are not the only groups concerned, but still the principal ones in the UK) claim that, 'Most four-year old children are not ready to be confined to overcrowded classrooms without scope for physical and imaginative play' (Wilby and Wilton, 1987). Clark (1988) sums up the position thus:

> The policy of admission of children to reception class below the statutory age for starting school is likely to be one as vulnerable to economic pressure as pre-school education. It is also a policy likely to be particularly vulnerable to rise or fall in the birthrate and demand for places in infant school nationally and in particular areas.

Intrigued by what she discovers, our visitor has now decided to spend the day in the infant's departments of the primary school. Already she has been told that several LEAs have had, in the past, a policy of separating infant and junior schools where possible (e.g. Bristol in the 1960s). She will have discovered, however, from the almost entirely female staff of the infant's school that most primary schools now combine the overall management of infants and juniors in a single unit. She may have found that well over half of all primary schools in the country have male head teachers, whilst almost three-quarters of British primary teachers are female. She will have noted from staff-room conversation that there are still many non-graduate primary school teachers, that very few (less than 10 per cent, contrary to the case in Canada or USA) hold master's degrees and that opportunties for in-service education are few and somewhat narrowly focused.

Typically, in the infant classroom of the late 1980s our perceptive visitor will see classes drawn together regularly for stories, for music and movement, and for specific instructions at the beginning of lessons or topics. She will *not* see, as she might well in other countries, an overly textbook oriented or programmed form of teaching. More commonly, after initial explanations, the class will be broken down into four or five groups, frequently working on carefully graded or checked levels of assignments, manipulation, number or reading tasks. One group of four and five year olds may be matching shapes to puzzles, another perhaps older group wiring a simple circuit of bulbs and batteries to the puppet theatre, yet another two or three reading colour-coded 'real' story books (not primers), several more counting and colouring in sets of objects on a number sheet. Throughout all this there may well be another adult, perhaps a parent, listening to the reading whilst the teacher moves around the classroom helping and talking.

Recording progress will be much more in evidence than it was some twenty or thirty years ago. All LEAs have oracy, literacy and numeracy records. All of these are becoming much more similar, compatible and are used diagnostically with some care. 'Integration' of the curriculum, that catchword of the sixties, will still be idiosyncratic, school-specific and varying in definition and scope. In some schools an integrated curriculum includes all the range of normal subjects and topics. In others integration occurs after the routine work in oracy, numeracy and literacy. Nevertheless, most infant schools still reflect the centrality of language to effective integration and pay considerable attention to pupil choice, interest and motivation. Thus, it will often be difficult for our visitor to define 'subject' boundaries with any accuracy. Moreover, she will note that, as in her later junior observation, the classroom teacher is with the same children day in, day out.

She will, if having experienced French or Scandinavian elementary schools, become acutely aware of how little time is allotted to the teachers for preparation during school hours. Infant and junior school teachers in England and Wales have little in the way of 'free' periods for preparation or observation of others. They are ceaselessly in demand for the whole working day, their preparation time coming before and after school hours. Currently, they teach for about 195 days per year, of which five are allocated as compulsory in-service days, commonly called 'Baker' days, after the then Secretary of State for Education, 1989 (See Chilver, 1988).

Paragraph 14 of the National Curriculum consultation document states that 'the majority of curriculum time at primary level shoud be devoted to the core subjects' (DES, 1987) and that 'Maths, English and Science will form the core of the curriculum, and the first priority will be given to these subjects.' Unlike Holland or Scandinavia, it is now comparatively unlikely to find a foreign language featuring in the infant or junior stages of English primary education while in Wales bilingual education must be available for parents who wish it, even at the primary stage.

As our visitor moves around the infant school she may well note the repeated use of a concept relatively new to infant method and ideology. This will be the term 'attainment targets'. Under the Education Reform Act 1988, and amongst the plethora of sections of the longest British education act in history, all primary schools are required to teach the core and foundation subjects to all pupils 'for a reasonable time' starting September 1989. DES Circular 5/88 set the timetable for the introduction of the National Curriculum and from September 1989 all primary schools are expected, under Section 4 (2) of the Act, to adopt the new attainment targets for *five-year-olds* in respect of maths, science and English. The age of five to seven years is, in the terminology of the Act and subsequent Orders, referred to as the 'first key stage'. The second is age seven to eleven years. 'Orders relating to mathematics and science and probably English and technology will be introduced for seven and eight year olds in the second key stage in 1990' (DES 5/88 Annex B). Much hinges on the development of appropriate Standard Assessment Tasks (SATs) for pupils at the *end* of their first key stage (currently being developed and trialled by various consortia) since:

from 1991 it will be a statutory requirement that all pupils reaching the end of the first key stage of the national curriculum (ie in classes the majority of whose pupils are aged 7) should be given SATs which test their knowledge, skill and understanding across the range of attainment targets which it is envisaged will by then have been determined for the core subjects — maths, science and English. (SEAC, 1988)

In respect of SATs, it is instructive and perhaps salutary to read a footnote to the House of Commons Third Report *Achievement in Primary Schools.* Referring to an arrangement whereby less advanced older children are sometimes placed with younger ones, it notes:

This arrangement has echoes of the system by which children were put into classes according to the standards they have reached, although here the purpose is to equalise class sizes. The 'standards' system was largely abandoned in England early in this century but is still used to some extent in the German Federal Republic and other countries on the European mainland. (Education, Science and Arts Committee, 1986)

Many educationists fear that SATs, to be established as criterion-referenced tests with appropriate levels within them, will by a process of slippage and usage quickly become closer to norm-referenced 'standards' and will be used comparatively and crudely. *Should* such a position be obtained, then it would be little time before 'standards' become used as a basis for an organization of groupings and classes reminiscent of Victorian England. Sensibly, it is acknowledged that the first year's complete testing (1991) will be, to some extent, 'experimental'. We shall learn much from that.

Whilst the core subject groups reported (at the end of 1988) and their expert reports were somewhat crudely simplified by the Secretary of State, most infant schools were, and are, continuing much as described in the earlier pages. The subject working group reports are unlikely to have much impact before late 1989 at the earliest. Many of the teachers, whilst troubled that the emphasis may soon become as much one of 'weighing the pig' as fattening it, continue to emphasize a non-subject-specific, often topic oriented approach to their teaching. The older and more experienced teachers have seen many educationists from other countries who have admired the British Infant School. These teachers' studies and experiences have been based on an admixture of the Plowden Report (CACE, 1967) and a conviction of the extreme variability in human development. They may well remark to our visitor that, far from having failed, Plowden was not sufficiently followed or adhered to, that of all stages of education it is British infant education which has been the most consistently admired internationally. Of course, as Geva Blenkin comments, 'there are teachers who have accepted the force of developmental theories, but have interpreted research findings and the theories on which they are based in an oversimplified manner . . . [and who] have often been encouraged to do so in their professional training. The effect of this has led to inconsistencies in their practice' (Blenkin, 1988). Moreover, as Katz has pointed out, educational ideology is often used as a substitute for theory and this is particularly true of early childhood education with its polymathic and generalist needs (Gammage, 1987).

All this means that our discerning visitor will notice considerable variability in both practice and belief as she visits the various infant classrooms. Nevertheless, the similarities *will* be greater than the differences. In particular, and despite the looming pressures of attainment targets, our visitor may both observe practices and hear the accompanying maxims, somewhat as follows:

> A child does not learn from a passive kaleidoscope of experiences, but from the outcomes of actions that he or she has initiated . . . All forms of play appear to be essential for the intellectual, imaginative and emotional development of the child and may well be necessary steps to a further stage of development. (Brierley, 1987)

The use of Brierley's elegant and clear language to express that which many infant teachers only half-articulate is deliberate. In his book Brierley summarizes much that links child development with education. As a biologist and ex-HMI he is particularly well-placed to encapsulate the 'would-be' theoretical base on which many avow the best of infant school practice has been built. Alongside an ideology which may, at its best and most sophisticated, become amenable to theory and research (as exemplified by Brierley), there are still many large questions which lie close to the surface of much late twentieth century infant school practice. How does one best match work to need and motivation, whilst still systematically developing and linking ideas in a coherent manner? Does group work really result in diminished and undirected learning activity for some (Bennett, *et al.*, 1984)? How can one best 'stage-manage' scientific and technical work for young girls so that they learn certain skills and dimensions too often left to boys? Is subject specialism a proper or sensitive way forward in the teaching of young children? Some senior HMI and, indeed, the Council for the Accreditaion of Teacher Education (CATE) have tried to push both primary teacher-training and school organization in this direction. Arguably, the greater stress on subject-specific approaches that has followed in the wake of the Education Reform Act will likewise militate against generalism. However, one should recall the realities. Our visitor will have noted infant departments with one, two or three teachers, rarely more than four. She will have noted, like the Select Committee from the House of Commons (1986) — the ways in which children have to be grouped by force of circumstance, size of school and locale, as well as principle. Consequently, she will see the impossibility of any speedy abandonment of the generalist basis of primary teaching which was lauded in Plowden. Moreover, our curious visitor will have armed herself with literature as well as observation. She will have noted that careful (and distinguished) psychologists have abandoned neither Piaget nor Vygotsky; they have, in the words of Wood, 'synthesised' insights and placed them in the cold light of reality, saying:

> under certain conditions, children are able to help each other to solve conservation problems and to achieve a better understanding of other people's perspectives and points of view. Where children share similar but 'erroneous' and egocentric views on the world, their perspectives and opinions (being egocentric) lead them naturally to conflicting ideas. Such conflicts, in true Piagetian style, motivate children to reformulate their ideas and may lead them to develop a deeper understanding of the phenomenon under consideration. (Wood, 1988)

Juniors

The transition from 'infants' to 'juniors' is rarely as traumatic as that from primary to secondary school, though disturbance and discontinuity are possible. Much, however, is the same. Our discerning visitor will have already noted that some schools use the term 'transition class' for a class of six- and seven-year-olds overlapping the traditional infant–junior divide. She will be well aware that the problem of *coverage* (used by Pollard and Tann, 1987, to introduce a discussion on reflective professionalism) is as much a dominant concern for the junior teacher as for the infant one. Building on a solid foundation of reading, however, she will also be aware that schools 'do make a difference' (Mortimore *et al.*, 1986) and that, by and large, the junior schools she visits are still happy and enthusiastic places. Indeed, enjoyment of learning is still regarded by most junior school teachers as a fundamental 'plank' in the ideology. Such a view is neither new nor ill-founded. Joffe and Foxman (APU, 1988) noted the central role which favourable attitudes played in approaches to mathematics by age eleven and the rather negative perspective of the American 'Coleman Report' (Coleman, 1966), whilst casting a shadow over academic and political perspectives of schooling, has, I believe, never found much favour with primary teachers. Their day-to-day system maintenance illustrates their dependence on the commitment and enthusiasm of the pre-pubertal child. Whilst variations in class size (between twenty-five and thirty-five) apparently make little difference in terms of pupil achievement (DES, 1978; Gammage, 1986), ethos clearly does (Mortimore, *op. cit.*). But our visitor will have already noted the difficulty of 'fitting the curriculum quart into the classroom pint-pot' (Desforges and Cockburn, 1987) and will gradually see in the junior school much more teacher-directed learning than occurred in the infants' school.

As the Select Committee of the House of Commons noted (1986) streaming in the junior school is now relatively rare while within-class grouping is common. Such heterogeneity means that, even at eleven years of age, the practice of within-class ability grouping is often a necessity in core curriculum areas, though teacher-directed whole class learning also tends to increase through the age range. In the 1978 Primary Report, the HMI noted that primary teachers accorded a relatively high priority to literacy and that national reading standards appeared to have risen. All classes of seven- and nine-years olds made use of graded reading schemes. Moreover, spelling tests, multiplication tables and comprehension exercises were still well in evidence in the mid-1980s (Barker-Lunn, 1984) and, if anything, the much publicized views of the then Secretary of State on the teaching of English coupled with the Kingman Committee's work and the 'run-up' to the Working Group report on English for ages 5 to 11 years (DES, 1988) have all led to intensive reviews and discussions of what were already dominant curriculum concerns by primary teachers. Hearteningly, the section of the report on English in the primary school starts with quotations from two volumes much loved and used by primary teachers, the Plowden Report (1967) and Sybil Marshall's *An Experiment in Education* (1970). Moreover, it emphasizes the importance of speaking and listening, is flexible in its approach to the attainment targets and seems realistic yet sensitive enough to have earned a modest accolade from the National Association for the Teaching of English (NATE) (a concerned and professional group representing fairly wide, some would say progressive, views in the teaching profession).

Nevertheless, our visitor will note the dismay amongst primary teachers which greeted the narrowing revision of maths and science, the two other core subject working group reports. Many primary teachers will have discussed with her the implications of official reports which can 'have it both ways'. For instance, whilst the English report seems to echo Plowden, the Task Group on Assessment and Testing somewhat apologetically suggests that 'assessment lies at the heart of this (learning) process' (DES, 1988). Whilst it then qualifies this remark by making all the appropriate gestures in the direction of differentiation, development and progression, it provides a complex set of test exemplars in its appendices which many primary teachers know (*vide* the earlier comment on coverage) to be impractical in normal circumstances. Thus our visitor, whilst observing the current picture, will begin to notice the ground-swell of anxiety and low morale which seems now to pervade the profession. Additionally, the classrooms, like their infant counterparts, will normally be lively and attractive places, but the buildings will be old and in a poor state of repair:

> Much of the country's school building stock is in a sorry state and getting worse ... the continued neglect of the school building stock is not only storing up potentially enormous bills for the future but is also seriously affecting the quality of work and achievement of many pupils and providing a grim environment for them and their teachers. (1984 HMI Report quoted in Education, Science and Arts Committee, 1986)

Micro-processors will generally be well in evidence and actively used, but our visitor will have noticed the poor levels of maintenance and capitation available to many primary schools. She will reflect on what Thomas (ILEA, 1985) referred to as the increasing need for 'finance around the edges' and perhaps compare the facilities unfavourably with those found in schools of similar size in Alberta or South Australia. Where are the additional resource teachers, the libraries, the specialist music and physical education staff, the counsellors and the school transport? She will be reminded that British primary schools are relatively numerous and small, that though (in 1984) some 40 per cent of their buildings were put up before 1900, they *do* all have access to micro-processors (unlike all Japanese primary schools in 1988), and that there is still a strong 'anti-textbook' approach to much teaching, leading to considerable attempts at matched individual learning and not a little creativity.

Individualized learning is, our astute observer notices, not *that* much in evidence, though there are threads of it running through the whole age range. As Golby remarks,

> The extreme liberal romantic model of children purposefully learning through self-initiated activity breaks down, except possibly in the hands of the exceptionally talented teacher. It entails a high order of adult-child ratio, and therefore quantity as well as quality of interaction if extension rather than repetition is to be gained from the child. (Golby, 1986)

This does not mean that, in the late 1980s, many British primary teachers are not still striving to provide individualized work and the opportunities for individual and group projects. It is simply to remark that, whilst group work exists, topic work is popular and individually matched assignments are by no means unknown, the majority of junior school time (up to 70 per cent) seems to be spent in standard, teacher-originated, whole class teaching. In this respect, however, there are differences discovered by our observer.

> Teachers in the middle and later years of the primary school maintained several behaviours similar to teachers of younger pupils. But they also become more formal and more subject-oriented. (Kutnick, 1983)

During the periods of observation our visitor will have watched and listened. Comparing her perceptions of European, Australian and North American elementary schools she will note much that is common, but some that is different. There is a vigour about the not overly textual and programmed approaches by British teachers which is not always apparent in other systems. It has weaknesses in that: (a) it entails considerable skill and possibly an increased work load; (b) it often involves too much repetition and too little 'stretching' for the most able; (c) at worst, continuity and coherence suffer severely. Our visitor will have become aware of the major political and educational changes that are now 'waiting in the wings'. She may, like many primary teachers, deplore what appears to be increased prescription and blatant centralism in the organization of a provision and stage of education that has been praised (sometimes erroneously) and celebrated throughout the world. She will note that, as in other countries and systems of education, educational 'reforms' are often driven by economic considerations or political expediency, rather than by a careful weighing of the evidence. She will be aware that currently in much of the western world a market-driven view of education prevails and that this seems to be leading to perspectives that

> what is essentially a human process may be assessed on technical grounds . . . [and encourage] evaluations of educational procedures by those who consider themselves consumers. In both instances the human element is sold short on its affective characteristics and inclinations so that the picture becomes distorted. (Friesen, 1987)

In this context, her view of the current state of British primary education may well be sharpened by reflections that the career prospects for British teachers would not be considered rosy or generous. Whilst in 1987 the target intakes for initial teacher training courses (primary) were broadly achieved, the target figures for 1989 'reflect a considerable expansion in primary training, with an increasing emphasis on PGCE courses' (Chilver, 1988) and London and other expensive locations are already finding it difficult to attract new primary teachers, mainly because initial salaries are insufficient to support mortgage or housing rental costs. Moreover, there is evidence from the National Association of Head Teachers and others that stress is the apparent cause of an increasing wastage rate amongst primary headteachers:

> This was particularly high in primary schools. Premature retirement accounted for more than 3 times as much wastage (34 per cent) as either normal or ill-health retirement (about 10 per cent each). Only a very small proportion of wastage relates to teachers leaving to take up other employment — equivalent to about 0.4 per cent of primary teachers and 1 per cent of secondary teachers per annum. (Chilver, 1988)

Conclusions

Our observer has discovered from the teachers and from the vast array of literature, HMI reports, press reports and general opinions that there are conflicts in what is said to exist and what is said to be desirable. DES and HMI have successfully shaped and impressed both B.Ed and PGCE primary training such that it is now more subject-based, less oriented towards child development and less generalist. This is contrary to what appears to be necessary as represented by primary teacher trainers, the teachers, the smallness of the schools themselves, the mixed nature of the classes. From HMI and other sources there have also been suggestions that a certain *narrowness* has tended to pervade the primary curriculum and its organization. At the same time as praising width and integration (a dominant theme of the Plowden Report) many senior HMI appear to see 'specialization' as leading to more consistent and 'balanced' child achievement prior to the normal age of transfer to secondary school. In 1981 HMI wrote that there was no evidence that concentrating only on basic skills (now core curriculum, excluding science) would raise attainment, rather, their observations suggested that such improvement had been observed as more likely to take place in wide programmes of work where language and maths skills were applied in varied contexts which made sense to the children (DES, 1981). The Middle School Report (DES, 1985) commented that both specialization and 'the carrying over of certain skills' were important in the roughly 1200 remaining middle schools in England and Wales. It also noted, like the Select Committee Report, that material resources did seem to affect the quality of school work (p. 75). But our observer has noticed the greatest congruence between her observations and those resulting from the third major survey by Barker-Lunn (1984). Both have registered that a large proportion of time in junior and infant departments is spent on what may best be termed very traditional basic subject work, the rules of number, computation, writing. This may be less whole-class oriented in the infants' classes, but it is still noticeable. Moreover, such observations chime well with the work of Mortimore *et al.* (1986) on the ILEA *Junior School Project*, and tend to confirm the view that what goes on is not that much changed from the mid-1960s. Certainly, there is no shortage of research which confirms such an overall view (see especially Cohen and Cohen (1986) and Richards *et al.* (1985), vols. 2 and 3). Thus, our visitor has now come, inescapably, to the following broad conclusions:

(1) Individualized work, though frequently referred to as important, is in the minority and is not always well-matched to developing the abilities of the high-attaining child.

(2) Group work, whilst commonly employed, is not sufficiently understood or *systematically* developed. Moreover, interaction within the groups is much less marked than the mere physical/spatial disposition in the classroom might indicate.

(3) Topic work (often the vehicle for 1 and 2 above) can be a very important unifier and integrator of the curriculum, especially of the humanities. It clearly attracts high commitment from the children, substantial curriculum time and often considerable imagination from the teacher.

'The combination of basic-skills teaching and imaginative project and topic work common in many primary schools has been a unique preparation for the future' (Wragg, quoted in Conner, 1988).

Nevertheless it frequently suffers from lack of overall clarity in aims, is insufficiently articulated with development and progress in the individual child's scheme of work and is often not sufficiently analyzed and reflected upon.

(4) Clear attention is given to the basics. These clearly *do* matter to the teachers. Perhaps a slight increase in attention to English comprehension and formal grammar may be detected.

(5) Considerable apprehension concerning the likely effects of the introduction of SATs and the near impossibility of meeting the time demands, especially in science.

(6) Substantial classs teaching (approaching 70 per cent of the week), but significant amounts of group work; the latter often being most carefully exploited and understood at the infants stage.

(7) A not very broad, nor overly textbook oriented curriculum.

(8) Apparent DES pressure (and changed forms of initial training) for

more 'specialist' curriculum leadership in those areas deemed critical (core subjects). Noticeable difficulty with the organization of this in view of (a) the small size of schools and (b) the lack of substantial experience in maths and science by many of the teachers.

(9) Fairly wide use of microprocessors, clearly not simply allied to maths. Considerable enthusiasm for and flexibility in their use.

(10) Weaknesses in provision of match or 'differential access' in the curriculum, especially for children at the extremes of ability.

(11) Decline in specialist music approaches; *slight* increase in attention to health education, noticeable absence of attention to European languages (other than English and Welsh).

(12) Little whole class 'streaming' by ability, but a large preponderance of split-age, vertically grouped forms of classroom organization throughout the primary school.

By and large, our visitor is not unhappy with what she has seen. Like many, she sees the long-term goals of a good foundation in primary education (imagination, adaptability and excitement) as important as mere achievement in the core subjects. Moreover, she notes that much good, solid careful work goes on in an atmosphere of enjoyment and trust.

As Alan Blyth says, of primary education,

> the English story has resonances elsewhere, and may be of positive interest to those who may recognise in it issues similar to their own. (Blyth, 1988)

It is Friesen who reminds us that educational reforms usually reflect the standard considerations of money, accountability, child achievement, rarely educational philosophy (1987). English primary education is, mercifully, still fairly strong on the last, in terms of its *beliefs*. It will need to develop and articulate these clearly if it is to remain the system of enlightenment which it has been in the past.

References

ASSESSMENT OF PERFORMANCE UNIT, JOFFE, L. and FOXMAN, D. (1988) *Attitudes and Gender Differences*. Windsor, NFER-Nelson.

BARKER-LUNN, J. (1984) 'Junior school teachers: Their methods and practices', *Educational Research*, 26, 178–188.

BENNETT, N., DESFORGES, C., COCKBURN, A. and WILKINSON, B. (1984) *The Quality of Pupil Learning Experiences*. London, Lawrence Erlbaum.

BLENKIN, GEVA (1988) 'Education and Development: Some Implications for the Curriculum in the Early Years', in BLYTH, ALAN (Ed) *Informal Primary Education Today*. Lewes, Falmer Press.

BLYTH, A. (Ed) (1988) *Informal Primary Education Today*. Lewes, Falmer Press.

BRIERLEY, J. (1987) *Give Me a Child Until He is Seven*. Lewes, Falmer Press.

CACE (1967) *Children and Their Primary Schools*, vol. 1 (The Plowden Report). London, HMSO.

CHILVER, LORD (1988) *Report of the Interim Advisory Committee on School Teachers' Pay and Conditions 31 March 1988*. London, HMSO.

CLARK, MARGARET M. (1988) *Children under Five: Educational Research and Evidence*, London. Gordon and Breach Science Publishers.

COHEN, A. and COHEN, L. (1986) *Primary Education: A Source Book for Teachers*. London, Harper & Row.

CONNER, C. (1988) 'Topic work: Where are we now?' in Cambridge Institute of Education, *Newsletter*, No. 11, 4–5.

DES (1978) *Primary Education in England: A Survey by HM Inspectorate of Schools*. London, HMSO.

DES (1981) *The School Curriculum*. London, HMSO.

DES (1985) *Education 8 to 12 in Combined and Middle Schools*. London, HMSO.

DES WELSH OFFICE (1987) *The National Curriculum 5–16: A consultation document*. London, DES.

DES (1988a) *National Curriculum: Task Group on Assessment and Testing*. London, DES and Welsh Office.

DES (1988b) *Circular 5/88*. London, DES.

DES (1988c) *English for ages 5–11*. London, DES and Welsh Office.

DESFORGES, C. and COCKBURN, A. (1987) *Understanding the Maths Teacher: A Study of Practice in First Schools*. Lewes, Falmer.

EDUCATION, SCIENCE AND ARTS COMMITTEE (1986) Third Report, *Achievement in Primary Schools*, vol. 1. London, HMSO.

FRIESEN, J.W. (1987) *Reforming the Schools for Teachers*. Lanharm, University Press of America.

GAMMAGE, P. (1986) *Primary Education: Structure and Context*. London, Harper & Row.

GAMMAGE, P. (1987) 'Chinese whispers' *Oxford Review of Education*, vol. 13, No. 1.

GOLBY, M. (1986) 'Microcomputers and curriculum change', in DAVIS, R. *et al. The Infant School: Past Present and Future*, Bedford Way Papers No. 27. London, University of London Institute of Education.

ILEA (1985) *Improving Primary Schools*. (Thomas Report) London, ILEA.

KUTNICK, P. (1983) *Relating to Learning*. London, Allen & Unwin.

MARSHALL, S. (1970) *An Experiment in Education*. Oxford, Oxford University Press.

MORTIMORE, P., SAMMONS, P., STOLL, L., LEWIS, D. and ECOB, R. (1986) *The Junior School Project*. London, ILEA.

NATIONAL CURRICULUM COUNCIL (1988) *Mathematics in the National Curriculum*. York, NCC.

NATIONAL CURRICULUM COUNCIL (1988) *Science in the National Curriculum*. York, NCC.

POLLARD, A. and TANN, S. (1987) *Reflective Teaching in the Primary School*. London, Cassell.

RICHARDS, C. with LOFTHOUSE, B. (1985) *The Study of Primary Education: A Source Book*, Vol. 2. Lewes, Falmer Press.

RICHARDS, C. with LOFTHOUSE, B. (1985) *The Study of Primary Education: A Source Book*, Vol. 3. Lewes, Falmer Press.

SCHOOL EXAMINATION and ASSESSMENT COUNCIL (1988) *Development of Standard Assessment Tasks for Pupils at the End of the First Key Stage of the National Curriculum*, October. London, SEAC.

WILBY, P. and WILTON, G. (1987) 'Too young to be taught a lesson', *The Independent*. 29 January.

WOOD, D. (1988) *How Children Think and Learn*. Oxford, Blackwell.

Part 2 Roles and Viewpoints

Introduction

This part of the book considers the roles and viewpoints of those most directly involved in teaching and learning in primary schools: teachers and heads, children and parents. A key concern is whether they all see the purpose of primary education in the same way. Certainly their individual roles and views must be taken into account in any discussion of the aims of primary schools, but I would not argue that the aims should be their exclusive preserve. As Schwab (1973) indicates:

> Defensible educational thought must take account of four commonplaces of equal rank — the learner, the teacher, the milieu and the subject matter. ... Despite the educational bandwagons which bear witness to the contrary, neither child, nor society, nor subject matter, nor teachers is the proper centre of curriculum.

Chapter 4 considers the views of teachers, who have traditionally been reluctant to debate the purpose of schooling, despite their excellence as practitioners. Indeed in a recent speech to the National Union of Teachers annual primary conference, the Senior Chief Inspector spoke of his concern and despair that primary teachers had been so unforthcoming in trying to define the primary curriculum (Bolton, 1984). Teachers who contributed to one survey (TES, 1977) at the start of the Great Education Debate indicated that they had already recognized the need for standardized tests at 8, 11 and 14 and for greater control over the curriculum, though they rejected such things as a common curriculum and parent power. In his chapter on the aims of primary teachers, Andrew Pollard is able to draw on considerable evidence from empirical research, such as Pat Ashton's survey of 1500 primary teachers, but extends this to consider the relationship between teachers' expressed aims, their practice, and how this will be affected by current legislation. He concludes that, despite increased centralization, no amount of legislation can diminish the teachers' power and responsibilities in providing and improving the quality of education in today's primary schools.

In Chapter 5 one headteacher, Mike Sullivan, battles with aims and provides an appraisal of the value of debating them in primary schools. One of his chief difficulties is the fact that there are so many targets at which primary schools aim. Do we go for loose, 'soft' aims emphasizing liberal views about the needs of primary school children, or for more pragmatic everyday management aims, or even for the harder 'official' curricular aims spelt out by DES, HMI and LEAs? This leads automatically to a discussion about the new responsibilities imposed on heads — accountability to parents and local financial management — which will have so much effect on the aims of schools and on the children who attend them.

The views of the children themselves are considered in Chapter 6. With the shift, highlighted in the first part of this book, from a child-centred to a subject-centred view of education, there is a real danger that children and their needs may be ignored when the aims of schools are being considered. Elsewhere, Sockett (1987:36) states:

> . . . the pupil, in *Better Schools* and *Curriculum 5–16* is something of an abstraction, a receptacle for the receipt of objectives, in embryonic skills and attitudes — a developing entrepreneurial organism. Yet somehow children have to become partners in their own education, not merely recipients of it.
> . . . schools must attempt to provide functional responsibilities for children as early as possible. We need to disseminate best practice in these difficult areas as a priority.

In his chapter, Cedric Cullingford presents some of the findings from recent empirical research which shows that the social aspects of schools, the friendship groups and even the sense of competition, are still considered of real importance to the children themselves. Children also see schooling as a type of preparation, however, rather than just an experience in itself. In this, their opinions of the purpose of schools derive largely from parents whose expectations tend to focus upon discipline, qualifications and employment.

Chapter 7 focuses on the roles of parents, either as school governors, classroom participants or as collaborators. In her chapter, Janet Atkins focuses on the growing partnership between teachers and parents, who share common concerns for the children themselves. This partnership will necessitate a new kind of professionalism for teachers, which may result in improved status and self-esteem, but the role of parents will also change. They may find new, challenging responsibilities (as well as rights) and, through increased formal contacts with teachers, some stereotypes and negative attitudes to the profession may be modified. Some strategies for involving parents are described; this should be of real value to primary schools currently reviewing aims and practice, and directly leads into the following part of the book dealing with the challenge of putting curricular aims into practice.

References

BOLTON, E. (1984) Speech to NUT Annual Primary Conference, Stoke Rochford, reported in *Times Educational Supplement*, 2 November 1984.

SCHWAB, J. (1973) 'The practical 3: translation into curriculum', *School Review*, 1, 501–522.

SOCKETT, H. (1987) 'The school curriculum: a basis for partnership', *British Journal of Educational Studies*, 35, 1.

TES (1977) 'Report of a survey of teachers' views on education.' *Times Educational Supplement*, 2 September 1977.

Chapter 4

The Aims of Primary School Teachers

Andrew Pollard

Introduction

I feel slightly impertinent as I begin to write this paper. The last decade has been a time of such anguish for teachers in primary schools that to have directly experienced the pressures of the classroom, and of parents, governors, Secretaries of State and the media is one important qualification for a commentator — particularly one who has been charged with the responsibility of reviewing a topic like 'teachers' aims'. Perhaps, however, there is also a case for a more distanced account. In any event, one might wonder if the topic is, itself, due to become an historical curiosity as the Education Reform Act of 1988 takes effect! In one sense, this is undeniably true, for the legislation imposes a National Curriculum and a framework for its delivery which represents a serious curtailment of teacher autonomy. Will teachers no longer have to think about aims? Are teachers to become mere deskilled functionaries? The legislation certainly provokes such alarmist thoughts but, towards the end of the paper, I want to argue that there is still considerable scope in the new structures if we, as a profession, have the vision and determination to grasp it. The issue of the aims and principles from which teachers' practice is derived is thus likely to continue to be of considerable importance.

The first part of this paper begins with a review and discussion of some of the major quantitative sources of research evidence on teachers' professional aims over the past twenty years. One theme throughout is the ever-present dilemma for teachers of whether to prioritize individual or societal needs — a theme which is then discussed, drawing on more qualitative research findings, with regard to teachers' personal commitments and experience when working with young children. The second part considers the difficult relationship between expressed aims and practice, discussing some of the methods by which the necessary reconciliation is often achieved, while in the third part of the paper, the previous analysis is related to the present context. The growth and character of legislative regulation are traced and the effects on teacher autonomy are considered. In the final part of the paper a possible stance for teachers in the next decade is considered. I argue that, despite the legislation, there are still many opportunities and areas of responsibility which call for the exercise of professional judgement and decision-making. Thus, teachers' values, aims and commitments will remain of great significance.

Empirical Evidence on Aims

I have to declare, from the outset, an unease in writing about aims *per se*. This is commonly done in the abstract — in ways which are decontextualized both from specific situations and from action itself. I shall return to this issue, but for the present, we might simply note that many of the large-scale studies of teachers' aims, conducted by survey, suffer from this problem. In fact, to some extent they compound it, for, not only are the data based on abstracted teacher judgements about priorities, but they are often based on teacher responses to generalized statements constructed by researchers. It would be prudent to bear in mind then, that we are likely to be dealing with 'professional accounts of aims'. These are not necessarily the same as something we might call 'aims-in-action' or even 'priorities-in-private'.

One empirical base-line for work on teachers' aims is Ashton's 1971 study (Ashton *et al.*, 1975). Data were collected by questionnaire from a nationally representative sample of 1500 primary school teachers. The main purpose of the study was 'to discover what practising teachers think are the aims of primary education' (1975:7) — a slight difference, which we should note, from considering the more specific and personal aims of the teachers themselves. The major outcome of the survey was the identification of 'individualistic' and 'societal' tendencies among teachers. For the more individualistic teachers:

> The purpose of primary education is to foster the development of the child's individuality and independence enabling him to discover his own talents and interests, find a full enjoyment of life in his own way and arrive at his own attitudes towards society. (Ashton, 1981:27)

Whilst for more societal teachers:

> The purpose of primary education is to begin to equip the child with the skills and attitudes which will enable him to take his place effectively and competently in society, fitting him to make a choice of an occupational role and to live harmoniously in his community. (Ashton 1981:27)

In 1979, Ashton revisited this topic when she used the same questionnaire with fifty-three of the sixty teachers involved in the first year of the ORACLE project (Galton, Simon and Croll, 1980). This was a far more restricted sample, limited to teachers of eight- to ten-year-olds within only three LEAs. Nevertheless, occurring as it did eight years later, Ashton (1981) felt able to claim that the new survey revealed a move of about 5 per cent from those formally emphasizing 'individualistic' purposes towards 'societal' purposes. Ashton's findings showing percentages of teachers distributing priority points in different ways as part of the two surveys are shown in Table 4.1.

Table 4.1   *Evaluation of the Basic Purposes of Primary Education*

Societal	Individual	Percentage of 1979 sample	Percentage of 1971 sample
0	5	0	2.1
1	4	7.5	10.1
2	3	32.1	29.9
3	2	39.6	42.4
4	1	18.9	12.2
5	0	1.9	3.3
		100.0	100.0

Ashton, 1981:28

Whilst acknowledging the differences between the size and nature of the samples, Ashton nevertheless took the view that '. . . given the educational history of the period, it is difficult to resist the hypothesis that . . . [these findings] . . . reflect a national trend'. (1981:31) She concluded her 1981 paper as follows:

> To sum up the results of this enquiry, it seems that a primary school child in the early 1980s is likely to have a broadly similar but differently focused experience from his older brothers and sisters in school at the beginning of the last decade. He is more likely to meet teachers concerned to equip him with skills and attitudes which they judge society to require. Probably more attention will be given to his mathematical and formal language competence. He is more likely to find science in the curriculum and less likely to have very much religious education. . . . While required to be equally considerate and well behaved, his personal and social development will be tilted more towards a reasoning than a feeling engagement with his physical and social environment. All this is likely to be sought in an atmosphere of greater formality with more overt teacher direction of his activities. (Ashton, 1981:34)

It is interesting to compare Ashton's work with the results of another survey of the early 1970s, that of Taylor *et al.* (1974). This study was concerned with 'purpose, power and constraint' as such factors affected the formulation of the curriculum of primary schools and it started from the proposition that: 'What is taught in our primary schools is not adventitious, accidental or merely fortuitous; neither is it consciously planned' (1974:ix). In fact, it was proposed, the curriculum 'evolves' through the influence of a 'network of interactions and communications with other institutions, and with individuals outside the school, which connect the primary school to society' — a pluralistic model which is grounded in a recognition of a considerable degree of teacher autonomy. Indeed, in the early 1970s, Taylor *et al.* could write that 'in our kind of society persuasion rather than power, influence rather than coercion are the media of social and political action, and it is forces such as these that help to shape what our institutions attempt to achieve' (1974:ix).

The survey drew data from a sample of 120 teachers from twelve urban schools within one LEA and the information on teacher aims was gathered by asking for ratings of 'most emphasis' when considering eight stated aims. The results are given in Table 4.2.

Table 4.2   *Teacher Ratings of Aims of Primary Education*

Aims	Mean rating	Percentage of most emphasis ratings
Spiritual development	1.4	3.3
Aesthetic awareness	1.8	10.2
Intellectual capabilities	2.4	45.8
Practical skills	2.0	20.3
Physical and emotional development	2.3	38.7
Preparation for secondary education	2.1	27.5
Moral awareness	1.9	9.3
Social awareness	2.4	42.4

Source: Adapted from Taylor *et al.*, 1987, figures 3 and 4, pp. 39–40.

No single aim, from among those offered to the teachers for rating, was considered to be outstandingly important, though developing 'children's intellectual capabilities', 'social awareness' and 'physical and emotional needs' clearly stand out and have direct resonances with the 'individualistic' and 'societal' conceptions offered by Ashton.

One of the most interesting of Taylor *et al.*'s findings concerns the degree of consensus about aims among teachers within the same schools. They comment that this was 'lower than one might expect' and that 'as a "professional", each teacher determines his or her own aims independently or other teachers in a school.' As they elaborate:

> Unless teachers share a common professional view (and all the
> evidence is that they are encouraged by training and by belief in

teacher freedom and responsibility to be autonomous in their professional behaviour), there is likely to be little general agreement about the aims to be emphasised in their teaching. (1974:47)

Empirical studies conducted in the 1980s show considerable continuities with this early work.

For instance, Mortimore *et al.* (1988) studied pupil performance in fifty ILEA junior schools in the early part of the decade. They interviewed class-teachers about their aims and purposes and reported the findings using Ashton's categories (1988:53). In very generalized comments, they report that the aims 'most frequently mentioned' were 'intellectual, personal and social' with . . . 'the vast majority of teachers being concerned with a range . . . of aims.'

In a cross-national study, Broadfoot and Osborn (1988) produced useful indicative data on aims as a by-product of their comparative work on the meaning of 'professional responsibility' to French and English teachers. In 1984/5, 360 primary school teachers in each country completed open-ended questionnaires, and these data were later supplemented by some interviews and periods of classroom observation. The highly centralized French system, with (at that time) far tighter control of the curriculum, produced clear contrasts to English teachers' views of their professional objectives. Broadfoot and Osborn characterize this as 'a strong emphasis on the "process" of learning in England and on the "product" of learning in France' (1988:276). As well as placing more emphasis on how children learn, English teachers were more concerned 'with the development of long-term characteristics rather than the acquisition of a particular body of knowledge' (1988:276). English teachers held such relatively diffuse conceptions of their goals as:

> Creating an atmosphere whereby children will learn through experience — moral and social norms, physical skills and aspects of health and hygiene, develop enquiring minds and creativity and generally to develop, progress and fulfill their potential. (English teacher, quoted in Broadfoot and Osborn 1988:277)

Table 4.3 shows the quantitative categorization of data which Broadfoot and Osborn drew on to support their analysis.

Now, one might be forgiven for wondering what such survey data, taken as a whole, really tell us. The findings are couched at such a level of decontextualized generality that it seems very hard to draw meaningful conclusions. On the other hand, whilst there is certainly variation in the types of aims that are prioritized, it is noticeable too that this variation clusters around a theme — that of the struggle to resolve the dilemma of individual versus societal needs. Indeed, the comparison between English and French teachers seems to suggest that diffuse statements of aims are, themselves,

Table 4.3 Responsibility for What: Percentage of Teachers Mentioning Each of the Following Objectives in Relation to Pupils

Objectives	England	France
Development of intelligence	46.0	17.6
'All-round' education	41.4	17.3
Socialization	33.8	25.9
Personal development	31.7	19.1
Desire to learn	21.8	16.6
Physical development	18.3	11.5
Academic knowledge	14.7	55.6
Basic skills, '3 Rs'	13.3	61.2
Moral education	9.8	9.3
Happiness at school	7.5	8.0
Understanding of the world	4.9	3.9
Preparation for adult life	3.6	23.2
Artistic education	3.2	2.3
Leisure activities	1.6	0.0
'Toughen' them for a difficult life/ help them succeed in spite of system	1.3	3.9
Citizenship	0.0	6.8
Total number of teachers mentioning at least one of these objectives	298	260
Proportion of total sample mentioning at least one of these categories	82.7	72.3

Source: From Broadfoot and Osbourne, 1988.

distinctive features of English primary school teachers' thinking. It suggests that, when English teachers have faced the dilemmas posed by attention to social and individual needs (Berlak and Berlak, 1984), they have generally taken a holistic stance. They have recognized both concerns as being legitimate and have tried to encompass them. Of course, we must remember the suggestion, in Ashton's later work, of a greater prominence for societal aims developing through the 1970s. Although her evidence is really rather thin, we can allow that argument and still note that it is particularly striking that there are so many continuities over the period and through to the late 1980s.

One possible reason for such continuities and diffusion may be highlighted if we consider an example of a study with a very different methodological approach to the issue of aims. Instead of survey work, what findings emerge from talking and working at length and over time with individual teachers?

In a unique study, Nias (1989) interviewed 100 teachers several times over a period of years following their initial Post-graduate Certificate of Education training in the early 1970s. She documented their feelings as they came to terms with work in schools and she recorded how, whilst some left the profession, others gradually and variously established their careers. The key theoretical concept which Nias developed is that of 'substantial self'.

This refers to the nature of each individual person — their core personality, values and self-identity. The issue then becomes one of, 'how do people accommodate themselves to the occupation of teaching in general, and to the workplaces of their schools in particular?' For some, teaching provides contacts and experiences which reinforce their sense of self; they feel rewarded and fulfilled by it. For others, the experience is threatening and the prospect of a long-term career is so daunting that they often leave in the early years.

For many long-term primary school teachers then, teaching is more than just another job. It involves daily contact with rapidly developing children who, whilst they certainly have the capacity to tire and annoy, are also able to learn at a prodigious rate. Children can thus provide considerable fulfilment for teachers; they reinforce the individual teacher's sense of self and achievement. They reward each teacher's self-esteem and bind them, almost inextricably (and often despite the personal costs), into a sense of commitment to the children for whom they have responsibility. Commitment to caring for the whole child, an expression of the general and diffuse aims thrown up by the empirical surveys, for many teachers, almost becomes part of caring for themselves. It becomes part of both professional integrity and of personal dignity. I would submit that this is one reason why, when the dilemma between individualistic and societal aims is abstractly posed or is deployed as an analytical device, a continuing, wide-ranging diffuseness is found. Primary school teachers, as people within the culture of schooling for young children in this country, are committed to a holistic view of children and this is reinforced by the nature of their daily experience and interaction with them. Of course, there is much more to it than that. One might identify the continuing power of child-centred ideologies with their modern projection through the Plowden Report (CACE, 1967), or one might look to the circumstances and socialization which undoubtedly influence the women who make up the majority of teachers in primary schools. Whatever arguments are deployed, the point I want to make is that 'caring for the whole child' is an enduring, and deeply rooted part of primary teachers' thinking. It is not just an element of professional rhetoric — it is also a part of the personal beliefs and identities of many teachers.

Aims, Practice and Pragmatism

Of course, commitment to particular overt aims does not necessarily bear a direct relationship to achievements in practice. Over the past twenty years there has been a steady flow of research focused on teachers' classroom practices and pupil achievement. Much of this work can be traced to the controversy of the early 1970s which was associated with 'progressivism'.

The Plowden Report and Piagetian psychology had been taken as legitimation for 'child-centred' forms of pedagogy — including integrated curricular and integrated forms of classroom organization — and had clearly been influential in the articulation of the 'individualist' concern identified by Ashton. However, the results of HMI surveys (DES, 1978, 1985a) and of research (Bassey, 1978; Galton, Simon and Croll, 1980; Barker-Lunn, 1984) has consistently suggested that actual primary school practice has been characterized by a tight, teacher-controlled environment, with most curriculum time being devoted to mathematics and English — activities which are, arguably, significantly 'societally oriented'. Rather than the discovery-led, pupil-centred, idealized image, the more accurate generalization of actual practice is thus one of a heavy preponderance of managerial interaction and the provision of routinized learning tasks. Even in the specific case of infant schools, where one might expect individual attention to pupils to be most developed, a similar situation is reported by researchers. For instance, Bennett *et al.* (1984) found that, in infant classrooms chosen to exemplify 'good practice', there was a preponderance of routinized work and that many of the learning tasks set were only weakly matched to the child's level of attainment. Similarly, Tizard *et al.* (1988), in their study of London infant schools, reported that less than half of the school day was devoted to learning activities as such and that, of this time, most was spent in individual work on the 'basic' subjects of language or mathematics.

In reflecting on these perhaps surprising findings, one cannot ignore the resourcing which has been made available to teachers over this period. On this, HMI have been consistent in pointing out the inadequacies of funding for repairs, capitation and non-contact time; the inequalities of resourcing between the primary, secondary, FE and HE sectors is also well-documented. Indeed, such arguments were strongly reinforced by the House of Commons Select Committee Report on primary education (House of Commons, 1986). Primary school teachers have thus, in a sense, been 'caught in a trap', torn between the aims which they espouse and the means to bring them about. Thus the forms of practice which commitment to individual children generates, have consistently been found to be very difficult to achieve on a large scale. In these circumstances, the professional's caring, committed ambitions have proved to be very susceptible to being interpreted as 'ideological' (Alexander, 1984), whilst in the media and elsewhere they have often been regarded as a rhetorical smokescreen for a defensive and complacent profession.

Some of my own work has a bearing here. As part of a number of detailed participatory case-studies of primary schools (Pollard, 1985) I produced an analysis of teachers's 'interests-at-hand' — the immediate concerns which inform classroom decision-making. These concerns are not 'aims' as such but rather describe issues which are likely to be considered when such ideals have to be put into action in the real situations and pressures of everyday classroom life. I suggested that, reflecting a basic human attribute, teachers are concerned fundamentally about maintaining their self-image, dignity and integrity, and that they have to act strategically within their classrooms in order to achieve this goal. Immediate concerns, 'interests-at-hand', at that level were identified as seeking enjoyment, controlling workload, managing stress and retaining autonomy. These concerns are achieved through ensuring that the class is reasonably ordered and that the children are kept busy on learning tasks.

In a sense, this analysis describes the sort of creative pragmatism which has been found to be necessary if teachers are to cope with the demands of their workplace. It may help to explain some of the gaps between the abstract statements of intention and the documented nature of actual practice.

There is no doubt too, that teachers' practical knowledge is highly sophisticated at the point of use. This has been clearly demonstrated by detailed studies of teacher thinking, such as those by Elbaz (1983), Clandinin (1986), Calderhead (1988) and Smyth (1987). Such work shows the complexity of the judgements and actions which are required to teach effectively, the need for trade-offs of one priority against another and the need for a detailed knowledge both of children and the curriculum. Teachers may find it hard to achieve the idealized aims to which, in the abstract, they may aspire, but they show considerable determination and creativity in attempting to reconcile such ideals with the practical realities within which they must work.

Summary

To summarize the argument of the paper so far, I would say that, over many years, primary school teachers' statements of aims have articulated a diffuse concern for the 'whole child' — a concern that children should both fulfil their individual potential and should become worthwhile members of society. I have suggested too that the centrality of this wide-ranging, holistic concern reflects its strong linkage to the personal values and identities of many teachers.

Such commitments have been found to be hard to enact in practice and a good deal of strategic pragmatism is evident. Researchers are also beginning to understand and document the detailed and sophisticated thinking of teachers concerning such pedagogic issues and the sorts of judgements which have to be made in classroom action.

I will now take these arguments into the context of public debates on education and with regard to recent changes in policy and legislation.

The Growth of Regulation

In this part, I want to consider how the autonomy of teachers has been increasingly circumscribed so that, irrespective of their personal aims and values, to occupy the role of 'teacher' is now to accept that certain requirements and expectations will apply.

In a wide-ranging analysis of education policy, Dale (1979) has argued that the education system has been developed to a situation where the relative autonomy of schools is being 'regulated' rather than 'licensed', as in the past. Since the 1920s, he argues, an implicit licence has been issued to teachers which entrusted them with responsibility for the curriculum and well-being of pupils. This licence

> . . . was renewable on the meeting of certain conditions, [but] the educational expansion of the decade from the early sixties to the early seventies stretched the terms of the education system's license to new limits. (1979:100)

The result of this was to bring about a new type of regulated autonomy in which

> . . . control over the education system is to become tighter, largely through the codification and monitoring of processes and practices previously left to teachers' professional judgment, taken on trust or hallowed by tradition. (1979:104)

The introduction of greater regulation has arisen as a result of a fundamental change in political values over the last decade. The 'social democratic' post-war consensus, on which the welfare state was based, has been gradually dismantled. Regarding education, this process gathered considerable momentum after the 1976 Ruskin Speech made by the Labour Prime Minister, James Callaghan, in which it was suggested, among other things, that schools paid too little attention to the needs of industry. Whilst continuing the theme, Conservative governments since 1979 have also argued that too much power was in the hands of the professionals, 'the producers', and too little in the hands of public 'consumers' such as parents and industrialists. Such are the underlying ideological forces which have produced the growth of regulation in education, helped greatly by the relative inability of the profession both to coordinate and to explain itself, and to justify the discrepancies between stated educational aspirations (aims) and the actual practice as experienced by many children and parents.

Two of the major educational themes of the past decade will serve to illustrate this point and Dale's thesis — the 'need' for more curriculum coordination and more attention to the assessment of learning. Both issues are traceable to the 1978 HMI survey, *Primary Education in England* (DES, 1978), through to the 1986 House of Commons Select Committee Report, and on to the Education Reform Act 1988.

There has been, since the early 1970s, a steady critique of the degree of curriculum autonomy enjoyed by primary school teachers. The seemingly uncoordinated choice of different 'topics' through each child's career in primary school was highlighted but the criticism was not quelled by the protestation that the process of the development of transferable skills was more important than just 'acquiring knowledge'. In the light of the pressure, new concepts for the analysis of the curriculum gradually emerged, were legitimated by HMI (DES, 1984), and began to pass into the language of the profession: progression, coherence, breadth, balance, differentiation. These have now been reinforced through legislative requirements, so that school staffs must coordinate their curriculum provision in the light of the attainment targets and programmes of study for the core and foundation subjects of the National Curriculum. Such developments are to be guided and monitored by a new body, the National Curriculum Council (NCC).

The issue of assessment expresses two aspects of critique. The first one concerned the quality of teaching itself, for it was suggested that the match of classroom learning tasks to the needs of children has often been inappropriate (DES, 1978). Many children are thus insufficiently challenged in school and do not learn as much as they could. The second issue concerns reporting children's progress to parents and rendering teachers more accountable — a direct intention to curb some of the autonomy of teachers. The proposals of the Task Group on Assessment and Testing (DES, 1987) were an attempt to respond to these concerns. They placed assessment at the centre of the teaching/learning process and required teachers to engage in formative assessment, so that their daily practice can be directly informed. In addition, teachers must now conduct summative forms of assessment through Standard Assessment Tasks (SATs), the results of which are to be used at the reporting point to parents for each key stage. These proposals are now being taken forward by a second national body, the School Examination and Assessment Council (SEAC).

There is thus to be a considerable change in the degree of autonomy of teachers. To a great extent, the content of the curriculum which they teach will be prescribed and they will be required to monitor pupil achievement much more closely, precisely, and publicly than in the past.

Other provisions of the Education Reform Act 1988 and of the Education

Act 1986 are also being implemented and will provide a very significant context in which teachers must work in the future. Such changes include increasing the public accountability of headteachers through strengthening the powers of parents and governors, providing more distinctive management structures in schools backed by procedures for teacher appraisal, and developing school-based decision-making through the introduction of 'local management of schools'. A policy of open enrolment will give material effect to parental views of overall school performance and is likely to lead to changes in the sizes of schools.

There has been considerable discussion of these innovations and their likely effects in primary schools. Some feel that the legislation will, as ostensibly intended, lead to higher standards of pupil attainment and to more cost-effective and efficient schools. Others see it as socially divisive, as constraining teachers and as threatening the quality of pupil learning experiences. There is agreement, however, that the proposals represent the most radical restructuring of educational provision this century. There is little doubt too, that teachers will have far less autonomy and choice in deciding on the aims towards which they will work. Dale's central thesis, about the introduction of regulation, seems proven.

A Professional Stance for the 1990s?

In this part of the paper, I want to project the issue of teachers' aims into the future, for in my view, it is not the case that the growth of regulation has made it impossible for teachers to act creatively and in principled ways. Nevertheless, in staffrooms up and down the country, away from the centralized committees of the DES, NCC and SEAC, teachers are certainly concerned about how they will cope with the new legislation. The scale of the changes is immense, for almost all the 'taken-for-granteds' in the system are being shaken up at once. Indeed, the principles underpinning the legislation are very different from the social democratic, egalitarian and child-centred ideas to which most primary school teachers have subscribed in the past.

Clearly one response is simply to get out if one can, to leave the profession, retire or take up a different job. Another way is to accept the situation, the management, the relative loss of autonomy and simply to comply with it as easily as one can; hard-pressed headteachers may even feel tempted to introduce timetables and more publishers' schemes. The first of these options is very hard on the children of the future who will continue to need the best possible teachers. The second option wholly negates the idea of professional judgement and years of accumulated experience.

The idea which I want to rehearse is that teachers should aim to develop a new level of professionalism in which aims, values and commitments will still play a part. The analysis which underlies this proposal takes us back to my earlier argument about the personal values and commitments of primary teachers and ties it into academic work on 'coping strategies' (Hargreaves, 1978; Pollard, 1982).

I begin with the proposition that, if the teaching profession is to cope with the new situation, it can, and must, be active and creative in the process of change so that a degree of 'control' is taken and maintained. The reasoning behind this is that, beyond the question of 'what is it that we have to cope with?', there is another question which each individual must ask. It is, 'what does *coping* mean to me personally?' Coping, in this sense, is to do with personal dignity, integrity, values and aims. Thus coping is linked to preserving and developing the attributes which individuals identify as being part of themselves. To 'survive' as a professional group then, teachers have to have the self-confidence to stand up for what they believe in and to develop actively into the future.

Two judgements suggest that this is possible. The first is that times of upheaval are also times of opportunity and, as we have seen, there are plenty of areas where improvements in the quality of what is offered in primary schools are possible. For example, it is certainly the case that some parts of the 1988 Act, for instance, provision for local management of schools, could mean an actual increase in some forms of autonomy. Other aspects of the Act, for instance, the measures on accountability, could lead, over time, through 'partnership', towards 'alliance'. Can teachers really collaborate with parents and thus broaden the base of constructive public concern about primary education? The second, more fundamental, judgement is of the depth of the basic commitment of teachers, for despite the dispiriting political and media critique of the past decade, the daily relationship with young children ensures that teachers still have enormous goodwill and feelings of responsibility towards pupils and their education.

The challenge of the proposed strategy comes, very directly, from the time and energy which it will take over the next decade to build the necessary forms of professional practice which are necessary. Teachers will need to think honestly and reflectively about the strengths and weaknesses of present provision, to analyze what the new demands require of them, to think reflectively, to plan strategically and, by no means least, to act sensitively and appropriately on many fronts.

Some may say that teachers are too powerless to think about exercising 'control' of the sort which is suggested above, but this idea can be challenged. Despite the structures which are being imposed, only those in schools are in a position to take face-to-face action with children and parents. We should not underestimate the degree of power which is conveyed by that fact. Thus the ways in which the legislation is interpreted and enacted will depend on professional judgement, on aims and values at the point of delivery, but this can only be influential if teachers have the self-confidence and sense of perspective to use their remaining autonomy and responsibility. Power can be created and enacted by individuals. There are many responsibilities which remain, squarely, with the teaching profession.

Conclusion

Education is fundamentally about the future and the qualities and skills of the people who will go on to create our society in the next century. It inevitably raises issues about values, beliefs and aims. However much certain structures or curricular are centrally prescribed, there are no legislative procedures which can circumscribe the power and quality of face-to-face interaction between people. Primary school teachers will thus continue to exercise enormous responsibilities in their dealing with children, parents, governors and others. The soundness of their judgements will continue to be tested, and will no doubt be refined in the future, but there are good grounds for suggesting that their commitment to children *per se* is unlikely to falter.

References

ASHTON, P.M. (1981) 'Primary Teachers' Aims 1969–1977', in SIMON, R. and WILLCOCKS, J. (Eds) *Research and Practice in the Primary Classroom.* London, Routledge and Kegan Paul.

AHSTON, P.M., KNEEN, P., DAVIS, E. and HOLLEY, B.J. (1975) *The Aims of Primary Education.* London, Macmillan.

BARKER-LUNN, J.C. (1982) 'Junior Schools and their organisational policies', *Educational Research*, 24, 4.

BASSEY, M. (1978) *900 Primary Teachers.* Slough, NFER.

BENNETT, N., DESFORGES, C., COCKBURN, A. and WILKINSON, B. (1984) *The Quality of Pupil Learning Experiences.* London, Lawrence Erlbaum.

BROADFOOT, P. and OSBORN, M. (1988) 'What professional responsibility means to teachers: National contexts and classroom constants', *British Journal of Sociology of Education*, 9, 3, 265–288.

CALDERHEAD, J. (Ed) (1988) *Teachers' Professional Learning.* Lewes, Falmer Press.

CENTRAL ADVISORY COUNCIL FOR EDUCATION (1967) *Children and their Primary Schools: The Plowden Report.* London, HMSO.

CLANDININ, D.J. (1986) *Classroom Practice: Teachers Images in Action.* Lewes, Falmer Press.

DALE, R. (1979) 'The politicisation of school deviance: Reactions to William Tyndale', BARTON, L. and MEIGHAN, R. (Eds). in *Schools, Pupils and Deviance*, Diffield, Nafferton.

DES (1978) *Primary Education in England: A Survey by HM Inspectors of Schools*. London, HMSO.

DES (1984) *The Organisation and Content of the 5–16 Curriculum*. London, HMSO.

DES (1985) *Education 8–12 in Combined and Middle School Schools: An HMI Survey*. London, HMSO.

DES (1987) *Task Group on Assessment and Testing*. London, DES.

ELBAZ, F. (1983) *Teacher Thinking: A Study of Practical Knowledge*. London, Croon Helm.

GALTON, M., SIMON, B. and CROLL, P. (1980) *Inside the Primary Classroom*. London, Routledge and Kegan Paul.

HARGREAVES, A. (1978) 'The significance of classroom coping strategies', in BARTON, L. and MEIGHAN, R. (Eds), *Sociological Interpretations of Schooling and Classrooms*. Driffield, Nafferton.

HOUSE OF COMMONS (1986) *Achievement in Primary Schools: Third report of the Education, Science and Arts Committee*. London, HMSO.

MORTIMORE, P. *et al.* (1988) *School Matters*. London, Open Books.

NIAS, J. (1989) *Primary Teachers Talking*. London, Routledge and Kegan Paul.

POLLARD, A. (1982) 'A model of coping strategies', *British Journal of Sociology of Education*, 3, 1, 19–37.

POLLARD, A. (1985) *The Social World of the Primary School*. London, Holt, Rinehart and Winston.

SMYTH, J. (1987) *Educating Teachers*. Lewes, Falmer Press.

TAYLOR, P.H., REID, W.A., HOLLY, B.J. and EXON, G. (1974) *Purpose, Power and Constraint in the Primary School Curriculum*. London, Macmillan.

TIZARD, B. *et al.* (1988) *Young Children at School in the Inner City*. London, Lawrence Erlbaum.

Chapter 5

A Headteacher's Battle with Aims

Mike Sullivan

Introduction

Our language ripples with military metaphors. They conjure up pictures of strength, power, heroicism, decisiveness but most of all of action. The Dunkirk spirit, turning a blind eye, the two edged sword, conflict, strategy, sabre rattling, bombardment, strategy, tactics, aims and targets give muscle to public language. Those who exert power from the power of words have adopted the language of war to inspire and to lead even when the language seems to contradict the underlying sentiments — 'Onward Christian Soldiers' and 'When a Knight Won His Spurs' still bring volume from my singing and a sparkle to my eye. The language of church, industry and education is enriched and enlivened by this tradition. The strength, and the weakness, of the language that we use is the way in which it enhances but also restricts our vision. Even in my wildest fantasies I can't quite equate my job as a headteacher of a landlocked, embattled, medium sized Midlands primary school with that of an intrepid warrior!

Though rousing, the terminology of wartime and weaponry seems to me often inappropriate and confusing when applied out of context. The most insidious example is of the word 'aim'. This common, simple, seemingly straightforward little word creates havoc for all who teach as almost by implication those teachers who do not play the aims game are perceived as aimless, but this is a theme to which I will return. I am not going to suggest that we should not state our intentions as teachers or that planning is a waste of time, though, in my experience, this process of prediction has the accuracy but not quite the entertainment level of a Russell Grant horoscope.

As a student I hated drawing up lesson plans. Aims, objectives, introduction, lesson development and conclusions had only slight relationship with the reality of classroom interaction. There was no wilful intention on my part to mislead tutors, no conspiracy on the part of children to divert me from my goals but things never quite happened as planned. Meanderings, the exploration of rich by-ways, interesting distractions, even inspiration and serendipity led to outcomes that I had not planned. As a classroom teacher I equally hated drawing up forecasts of work, listing topics to be covered in maths, language and project work as these would only loosely describe some of the things that I would attempt to teach and had very little to do with what children would learn.

As a headteacher I find that I am even more engaged in the business of stating intentions and making forecasts. The plans that I draw up for my own school follow the general consensus of what primary education should be about and are wide, warm, and wet. Basically we do the morning things in the morning — the maths and the language work — and we do the afternoon things in the afternoon — the music, drama, science, project work and games. We do these things as best we can and with kindness and love. We are not dogmatic and will occasionally do the morning things in the afternoon and vice versa. The audience of staff, parents, governors and LEA officers have all given approving nods to such sentiments. I suppose that all the writing that I have done as a student, classroom teacher and head both on intentions and planning had something to do with evidence — not necessarily evidence of practice but evidence of being an industrious and a fairly rational person. Certainly when we now have students at school, an examination of written comments by tutors in the students' teaching practice files show a focus on delivery through classroom management and self-appraisal, being busy and keeping children busy rather than on planning and content. As a classroom teacher I found that my forecasts of work rarely brought forth comment from heads. My aims and intentions have rarely been put to the test, since I suppose I create the impression of being both industrious and a reasonably rational human being.

Aims and Reality

Let's go back to my battle with the military metaphor and in particular my struggle with the weasel word 'aim'. To have an 'aim' implies that you have a target, something at which you are aiming, either on your own initiative or at the behest of others. The target has been perceived, identified and the appropriate course of action set in motion. The problem with teaching and learning is that there are multiple targets; perceptions are not always shared about the respective value of individual targets and often there is no single course of action to take that is appropriate to achieving an aim.

At the time of Plowden (CACE, 1967) and still later at the time of Ashton (1975) heads and other teachers in primary schools had difficulty in articulating specific aims for primary education. This was seen as curious and rather improper but there was no real suggestion then that primary schools were 'aimless'. Most of us knew where we were going and were responsive and responsible individuals. Even though most of us in classrooms may have been unaware of Dearden's (1968) work we would have agreed with his view that there are no aims for primary education but education. Southworth (1988) has taken this further, arguing that if this is so, then there are no terminal points for primary education and there is no time or stage at which teachers can say they have achieved their aims.

The publication of HMI inspections of schools shows that with few exceptions a common sentiment and belief reside in each individual primary school. There is a shared view of content and delivery of the curriculum. The consensus also extends to methods of classroom management within each school. It is no great revelation in that primary schools are small, finely tuned institutions where the exchange of ideas and attitudes are transmitted by action and response rather than by written or even oral statement. The process of education is a highly complex and individualistic activity at all ages and stages. That we teachers had difficulty in articulating our aims in simple 'one liners' reflects the complexity of the real world of teaching and learning and the self-contradictions, compromises and inprecision which surround us. The individuality of children through the mix of environmental, social, economic and physical factors is patently obvious yet is frequently and conveniently ignored by those who are outside schools. Talk in global terms of intent and policy cuts little ice with those who are seriously attempting the task of differentiating the curriculum to meet the needs of individual children. That we in schools have not taken too seriously the task of writing or adhering to aims is an indication of flexibility and pragmatism rather than a lack of direction or purpose.

Talk of aims has a positive firm feel, but is it appropriate to describe in terms of certainty our work that is, in many ways, uncertain? Other writers in this volume trace the politicization of the 'aims' movement. Whatever the intended outcome of the movement, the practical result has been the reinforcement of a popular view that primary education is a simple process of inculcating the 'basic skills' and that the aims of teaching the 'basics' are self-evident. The evidence in the Primary Survey (DES, 1978) indicated that a broad curriculum produced the most effective education even in 'the basics' but this evidence seems to have been brushed aside by the hard core who advocate a more formal, restricted 'core curriculum'.

Soft Aims

Writing aims in global 'hooray' terms is easy. For instance, Schools Council

Working Paper 70 : The Practical Curriculum suggests that schools have the capacity to help their pupils in at least six ways:

(1) to acquire knowledge, skills and practical abilities, and the will to use them;

(2) to develop qualities of mind, body, spirit, feeling and imagination;

(3) to appreciate human achievements in art, music, science, technology and literature;

(4) to acquire understanding of the social, economic and political order, and a reasoned set of attitudes, values and beliefs;

(5) to prepare for their adult lives at home, at work, at leisure, and at large, as consumers and citizens;

(6) to develop a sense of self-respect, the capacity to live as independent, self-motivated adults and the ability to function as contributing members of cooperative groups.

These aims follow the liberal and humane views that characterize the purpose and practice of primary education. The aims are soft, the means of delivery bound up with the intangibles of ethos and tone, there is no imperative to match the rosy rhetoric with rugged reality. The framework is loose enough to accommodate the general expectations of teachers, parents, governors, children and the local community. There is no hard-nosed way of isolating specific fine grain curriculum or school organization factors that bring about the achievement of these aims. The targets are so large, the shots many and the time scale vast. Ashton's (1975) research on teachers' aims indicated that six out of the eight highest rated aims were concerned with children's social behaviour rather than with academic progress. Those in classrooms know that unless a good social environment is established within the school where children listen, are well mannered, treat others and property with respect and are also happy, then the more intellectual aims cannot be pursued effectively and efficiently. Aims follow a hierarchical structure based on social behaviour and are by no means of equal value. It is important occasionally to consider children's needs as opposed to adults' aims. Maslow's (1943) needs hierarchy clearly identifies the structure and relationship that must be established in classroom and school for effective learning (see Figure 5.1). Once lower levels are satisfied higher needs dominate children's activities.

The role of the headteacher has traditionally been to satisfy reasonably the sometime conflicting expectations of very demanding and different audiences and, unless the head has been particularly clumsy or awkward, this is achieved with little fuss or bother. Where aims are soft, the evidence required to indicate achievement is even softer.

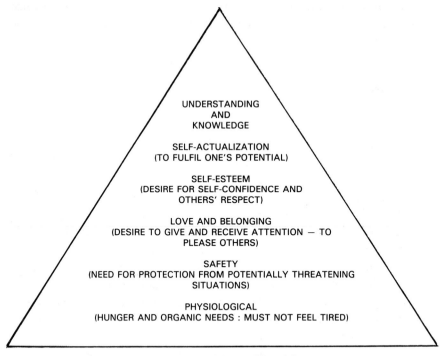

Figure 5.1   A Needs Hierarchy
Source: Maslow, 1943.

Management Aims

There are further sets of aims pursued within schools; not only are the aims of individual members of staff concerned with those things that they wish to teach the children but there are aims which are based on personal career development. The aims of the staff as a group are often concerned with the internal management of resources, equipment and the curriculum stretching from the development of children's conceptual knowledge to keeping the playground tidy. School is as much about finding lost coats, sorting out squabbles in the playground and collecting the money for school photographs as it is for the publicly declared aims. Indeed most of the planning time and monitoring within schools is usually taken up with routine but urgent house-keeping issues and not with wrestling with the content of the curriculum and the way that this should be delivered.

Much has been written to show that in most schools, the curriculum and methods of delivery have remained fairly constant over time and that primary teachers tend to be traditionalists. Where curriculum decision-making is no more than the choice of a commercial scheme for language, or maths, handwriting or history, geography or reading, then these decisions can only be made on an infrequent basis. The discussions that follow these choices are concerned with policy of implementation and management of the schemes rather than debates over content.

Official Aims

We in primary schools have not been short of advice on aims and the focus of that advice has been on curriculum. The HMI 'Curriculum Matters' series (DES, 1985) has spelt out in no uncertain terms the direction that primary, as well as secondary education, should be taking and the belief that at the heart of the educational process should lie the curriculum. HMI reports on individual schools have also emphasized the values that HMI hold dear — language and science work in schools come under the closest scrutiny — yet the social context of the school and efforts to integrate the school within the community, including work with parents, barely receive mention. Though HMI might think that this is unfair, in that they have no ways in which they can inspect the social aspects in which the school operates, it is yet another case of looking where the light is brightest and ignoring the realities in which schools operate.

Parallel to these HMI reports and DES directives, local authorities have also made statements about the direction that primary education should take. The Inner London Education Authority, for example, not only produced *Improving Primary Schools* (ILEA, 1985), the report of a committee of enquiry chaired by Norman Thomas, but also commissioned the 'Junior School Project' and a variety of curriculum documents. These reports, projects and documents are all well-intentioned but frequently ineffective in bringing about change in primary schools. The curse is that much is sensible when taken in isolation, but unfortunately the sheer weight of this good advice is unbearable. Reading the reports and booklets can become in itself a full-time occupation, attempting to put the advice into practice, an impossibility.

What are schools to do? The five Baker days each year provide a little elbow room to consider and revise some aspects of the curriculum but many LEAs see this time as an opportunity to pull large numbers of teachers together for conferences and in-service training where yet more ideas and suggestions are pushed forward, long before schools have had time to assimilate and act on the last batch. Good ideas on what to include in the curriculum are plentiful. What is scarce is the opportunity to view these ideas systematically and reflectively, noting what is no longer relevant and no longer worth pursuing. Those who attempt to assist us in schools through their words and yet more words, exert pull in so many directions that in the extreme we switch off or, as in Robert Graves' words, we 'lurch here and here by guess and God and hope and hopelessness'.

An example of well intentioned but unhelpful advice is that given by Joan Dean, Chief Inspector for Surrey (Dean, 1987):

> spontaneity is valuable but requires very good long term planning if teachers are to be clear what learning should come out of unexpected happenings.

Leicestershire LEA in their *Handbook for Curriculum Review* (1988) ends the brief section on aims with the advice that:

> The search for aims which provide a sense for unity, and at the same time respect cultural diversity, is central to the task of curriculum management.

Both are neat tricks if you can manage them!

Accountability and the Role of Parents

Alongside the movement encouraging headteachers to reveal our aims and intentions has been a parallel growth for us to become accountable for our actions. There has always been direct accountability. I can't remember a time when an irate mum has not felt able to confront me or an unfortunate colleague over a real or imaginary failure to carry out a professional duty. Many heads have suffered through not recognizing a school gate lynch mob of parents when they saw one. The new version of accountability that is flourishing is one that is less open and honest; it has more to do with the exercising of power and control than anything else. Many of us share Golby's suspicion that:

> The emphasis on written statements of aims (with the assumption that the curriculum is the means taken to achieve those aims) places teachers in a contractual and instrumental relationships to those who regard themselves as clients, whether parents, governors, local education authorities or central government.

When the attempt to add a system to appraise teachers is also taken into consideration then the threat to devalue teachers' and a schools' professional independence is clear.

The National Curriculum also devalues the teacher's judgement about what should be taught and the ways in which progress should be monitored. What is left to the teacher are the problems of delivering a curriculum mix conceived by others. The purpose of attainment targets is to 'reflect what pupils must achieve to progress in their education and to become thinking and informed people' (DES, 1987). Also 'Parents will be able to judge their children's progress against agreed national targets for attainment and will also be able to judge the effectiveness of their schools' (DES, 1987).

The development of the aims model in part stems from a general drive to sharpen up the management of public services through the adoption of management techniques developed in commerce and industry. Unlike commercial firms, schools do not express aims in terms of profit, expectation of increased effectiveness, efficiency, productivity and value for money. With 'Local Management of Schools' we may soon be into the profit and loss game that has little to do with children and their learning.

Until recently, schools were given advice and recommendations on aims but, like all advice, it could either be taken or rejected; there was no compulsion. If schools acted unwisely or headteachers indulged their personal preferences in moulding the school in an unacceptable way, then the head and the staff of the school lived with the consequences. In the current climate there is no room for failure nor is there reward for risky innovation. It seems to me that much of the control of the direction that schools should take has been wrenched from the professionals by central government. The government sets parameters through the National Curriculum and has devolved the remaining powers to the local community represented by schools' governing bodies, although recent personal experience has shown that in many cases governing bodies have been hijacked by a narrow band of articulate professional parents with particular sectional interests in mind. The power of one group of professionals, the teachers, is being replaced by the group of professional parents. I do not argue that the only ones who should have a stake in setting aims are those who have to implement them but it does seem that many who have taken up this absorbing hobby have little comprehension of the realities of the classroom. The fun really begins when attempts are made to turn aims into objectives and goals which can be seen to be achieved. HMI in *Curriculum Matters: 1* (DES, 1984) certainly showed that even those who ought to have known better involved themselves in offering primary schools advice on objectives for teaching English that were completely unworkable.

Financial Management

As a response to the 1981 Act, primary schools accepted the aim of providing places for children with special educational needs wherever possible. This was a development greatly encouraged by LEAs but their motives may have been influenced by more than the best interests of children, as Lewis (1988) notes:

Recent DES statistics [DES, 1985] show that the net recurrent institutional expenditure per full-time pupil for 1982–83 was £730 for each primary school pupil and £3265 for each special school pupil.

What use has been made of the money that has been saved by retaining children with serious special educational needs in mainstream schools? Has it funded extra resources, more staff or staff training in the primary schools genuinely to support the aim of integration of special needs children, or have schools been left to aim at yet another impossible target? Those who are good at aiming for educational goals need to be even better at ducking and weaving. Turning the seemingly straightforward and obvious aim of providing 'equal opportunities for all' into effective action can lead to a set of bone crunching tackles and professional fouls from some parents, governors and even administrators. When schools come out of the closet and begin to make this aim explicit, deeply held popular public prejudices can make the school a political battleground. To deliver this aim, the issues of anti-racist education, multi-culturalism, the integration of those with physical or intellectual handicaps and anti-sexist education have to be faced with children, staff, parents and governors. It's far easier to attempt to implement 'equal opportunities for all' and similar aims of stealth rather than by direct confrontation.

Where priorities and directions are decided elsewhere then converting aims into practice becomes increasingly difficult. External incentives designed to change school practices are too small; a computer in every primary school is an example where intention has hardly influenced the learning experience of children except in the field of frustrated expectation. Incentives provided to improve the quality and quantity of science and maths teaching through Educational Support Grant schemes also seem to have had a very limited success in altering the direction and the order of priorities of most primary schools. This may in fact be due to the vast majority of ESG money being earmarked for mid-day supervision of pupils rather than curriculum reform.

The use of the stick to impose external sets of aims on schools is being employed with increasing frequency and openness. The publication of HMI reports on individual schools showed not only how the schools inspected met their internally generated aims but also examined the breadth and relevance of those aims. Getting a HMI general inspection is as likely as winning a major prize with a single Premium Bond; either prospect would have equal effect on the expectations and way of life of most schools.

The aim of Local Financial Management presents a greater threat to schools. Those primaries in prosperous areas will benefit through the division of resources by LEAs into equal portions. Those schools in less advantaged communities will find that the additional resource support provided through special funds and sympathetic LEA officers will no longer be available. A major aim of headteachers will be to keep the books straight and the schools financially solvent. If the accounts don't balance then the auditor is called in and the head is almost invariably shown the door — a case of load, aim and fire!

At this time the National Curriculum is beginning to shape up; politicians believe that they have taken the control of the curriculum from the professionals and placed it under political and consumer control. A system imposed by government and monitored by parents puts schools in an iron grip but, as with most things, the tighter the grip, the more it is likely to slip through the fingers.

Whatever the aims, the strength and the power for delivery rest with those with everyday contact with children in classrooms. Unless those who deliver are convinced that the aim is true, there is absolutely no chance of turning aims into practice.

Leadership

Headteachers have a notion of what a good school should be and the sorts of things that children should learn. We all have a set of yardsticks and perceptions which we apply to schools, teachers and pupils. A mixture of common sense, theory and tradition creates these expectations.

Converting aims into practice is no easy task. Turning staff room rhetoric into classroom action depends, among other characteristics, on leadership, conviction and forcefulness. Developing commitment, generating enthusiasm, presenting cogent arguments and carrying them into effect has to be done without hesitation, qualification or sign of indecisiveness, for if policies are not dynamic and strong then there is little chance that they will be implemented.

Those of us who have been autocratic as heads have bullied, blustered and by strength of conviction achieved those things that we have valued. We have, if we have been lucky, mourned our failures in private. Those of us who have been more democratic in our style of leadership have engaged in winning the hearts and minds in the staff room by encouraging professional development through the sharing of responsibility and power. In these circumstances staff jointly accept responsibility for decision-making and an obligation for implementation. In balance with the loss of autonomy in the classroom we have promised an increase in influence in school policy-making. Unless headteachers have opted out of running the schools, then whatever management style is adopted we draw on some dark unpleasant skills to deliver our aims when reluctant, incompetent or awkward members of staff are encountered.

Mike Sullivan

References

ASHTON, P. *et al.* (1975) *A Study of Primary Education* Basingstoke, Schools Council Research Studies.

CENTRAL ADVISORY COUNCIL FOR EDUCATION (1967) *Children and Their Primary Schools: The Plowden Report.* London, HMSO.

DEAN, J. (1987) *Managing the Primary School Curriculum.* London, Croom Helm.

DEARDEN, R. (1968) *Philosophy of Primary Education: An Introduction.* London, Routledge and Kegan Paul.

DES (1978) *Primary Education in England and Wales: The Primary Survey.* London, HMSO.

DES (1984) *English from 5 to 16: Curriculum Matters No. 1.* London, DES.

ILEA, (1985) *Improving Primary Schools: Report of the Committee of Primary Education.* London, ILEA.

LEWIS, A. (1988) 'Children with Special Needs in Primary Schools', in CLARKSON, M. (Ed) *Emerging Issues in Primary Education.* Lewes, Falmer Press.

MASLOW, A.H. (1943) 'A Theory of Human Motivation', *Psychological Review*, 50, 370–396.

SCHOOLS COUNCIL (1981) *The Practical Curriculum: Schools Council Working Paper*, 70. London, Methuen Educational.

SOUTHWORTH, G. (1988) 'Primary Headship and Collegiality', in GLATTER, R. *et al.* (Eds), *Understanding School Management.* Milton Keynes, Open University Press.

Chapter 6

The Views of Primary School Children on the Purpose and Aims of Primary Education

Cedric Cullingford

'Why do you come to school?' 'Because I have to.'

Schools are very distinctive institutions, unlike any other, and they are our first introduction into a world of organized society. The first impressions that they give, half-hidden subsequently, half-forgotten in our later years, remain formative. For children, the purpose that schools have is implicit in their organization, in their decorations, and in the behaviour and expectations of the adults in them. For them there is no crucial distinction between the ostensible and the hidden curriculum. What they learn is what they experience and observe, not what designs the teachers have on them. From the children's point of view the purpose of schooling is rarely discussed, and thus their speculations about the meaning of school are undisturbed by formal adult explanations (Cullingford, 1986).

The impressions that schools give to children are rarely considered, as if the users of schools were the last to be consulted. Yet children form a consistent and elaborate point of view of all the messages they receive about the underlying purposes of school, an opinion formed more by their observation and outside influences than by any direct manipulation by teachers. Children reach an understanding of the relationship between home and school, the way that classes are organized and the way that teachers go about their business. Given all of their experience it would be surprising if children did not form very clear impressions of the schools they are in. What is, perhaps, slightly more surprising is the similarity of their impressions of different schools, in quite different parts of the country.

Children in primary schools are pragmatic about their experience. They do not, after all, choose the schools they are in, and are not given a sense that there are any alternatives. They therefore accept the realities of the circumstances, and are neither negative nor fulsome about their experiences. They appreciate what teachers are trying to do, and accept the need for rules and discipline. It is from this pragmatic acceptance of the everyday realities of school that children conclude what schools are for.

Primary schools are self-contained institutions only up to a point. The particular ethos of the school, expressed in its decorations as well as in internal organization, is also a reflection of all the values that its inhabitants bring from outside, not only teachers and parents, but also children. Some of the outside influences are highlighted in teachers' minds, from the government, through local authorities, to governors, but it is the children who see the schools most clearly as a distinct part of their larger, individual, lives. Whilst the school appears autonomous, and delivers its own set of values and its sometimes arcane traditions, it remains a separate kind of experience for children. Indeed, children are sometimes determined to keep the experience of home and school separate, despite demands on them like recording the events of a weekend in a diary. They can be embarrassed by the presence of parents in the classroom. Yet they are aware both of the connections between home and school and their distinctions.

The Influence of Parents

The very distinction between home and school, between the types of language used, and the types of relationships fostered, as well as the expectations of behaviour, makes the children more aware of the connections between the two. The attitudes of their parents towards the school and its purposes are clearly influential. So are the attitudes of their peer groups, and the culture of friendships both in the school and outside. Children's attitudes towards the curriculum are formed by conversations between each other, like their assessment of teachers. The information they receive from the formal aspects of school are analyzed through their conversations with each other and with people outside the institution. Parents, for example, not only have a clear set of expectations of what schools should ultimately provide for their children but also express, often negatively, their opinions about teaching methods and the curriculum (Cullingford, 1986).

All the measures leading up to the Education Reform Act have encouraged parents in just such opinions. Parents' expectations that schools should impart a fair measure of discipline and qualify their children for employment, are easily absorbed by children. This point of view, through such clear expectations, highlights the actual differences between the outside world and the school as in the case of discipline:

If I was at home I'd miss the breaks and chats and being told off. When your mum and dad tell you off you tend to shout back at them. But you can't shout at the teacher. You'd get yourself a bad reputation. If your mum and dad give you reasons you don't take any notice. It keeps you good mannered and it's discipline and it's enjoyable. I like that. (girl, 10)

Parents' views about the underlying purpose of schools are reinforced the moment that children question whether they need to go to school. Whilst they accept that they go to school because they have to, they also hear the reverberations of the message that schools equip them for jobs, that without qualifications they will not get far in the competitive world. There is a strong pressure of expectation that children bring with them into school, a point of view that is not reciprocated, as if the school accepted its public role, and considered the world outside as a private affair. The analysis of school is the analysis that is borne out of the distinction between the two separate halves of children's lives, and the desire to keep at least part private:

You can't tell people what you've got inside you because you don't want them to know the things you don't want them to know. They could think badly of you. If you talked to teachers about it they might tell your parents. (boy, 10)

The Social Aspects of School

From children's points of view, one of the essential purposes of school is as a place where they meet their friends. It might not be the most signficant aim but it is one of the reasons they go to school. School is a place of entertainment, since the variety of contacts with others is so much greater:

You get bored at home and you've got nothing to do. It's nice here, you get lots to do and friends to play with. (girl, 11)

When teachers talk of the importance of children's social skills they imply that schools exist to foster the ability to relate to others and to work together. This sense of the individual's 'autonomy' in relation to others is depicted in terms of groups and classes and is accepted as one of the semi-official purposes of schooling, as opposed to learning at home. But children see the fostering of relationships not so much as their response to group work and to classes, but in their friendship patterns. They are aware that they learn from each other, and are aware that they are exploring their abilities to make relationships (Davies, 1982).

Children, therefore, see one of the purposes of school as creating a social world in which they can foster and explore relationships. They feel that they might be bored without school, and that seeing their friends is a necessary part of learning. But their view of school, in terms of working with others, is rarely fostered by the school itself. As with other purposes in schools, most of the messages which children receive from teachers are implicit, and somehow based on an assumption that children receive what is given them without scrutiny. But just as children spend much of their time in school waiting for something to happen, and in the gaps between instructions and between lessons, so they are making use of a different interpretation of what school is for. They explore their friendships just as they test the teacher (Goodnow and Burns, 1985). Whilst they assume that every question the teacher asks is a closed one, to which they need to guess the answer, they explore more open answers with each other.

For children schools are public places but private experiences. The fact that they meet other children is one of the essential attributes. Children are not only made to learn certain rules and expectations but are also initiated into the expectations of their peers. Schools include that underlying purpose of relationships:

If you didn't meet anybody else you wouldn't be socialized. (boy, 11)

Children in primary schools are already aware that they are learning to adapt to a world in which they will, like their parents, acquire jobs. They are also aware that they are learning how to cope with other people, and how to deal with large organizations. But they point out that they are learning this from each other, not only in dealing with other children, but in working together, in seeking help as well as giving it.

Children's views of the purpose of schools are formed through their own individual experiences. Each of them interprets the complex experiences in no doubt idiosyncratic ways and yet the aims of school appear to them very consistent. This is either despite the fact, or because of the fact that teachers rarely, if ever, discuss the purpose of schooling. Perhaps teachers do not think that aims need to be shared with children. Perhaps they assume that the children will work things out for themselves anyway. Perhaps the aims of school are so obvious that they do not need discussion. Yet any examination of the purposes of education will take into account the tension of the rights and needs of the individual against the needs of society. In the absence of discussion there is no such tension for children, for the purpose of education serves both them and the state in preparing them for jobs.

Teachers, in interviews, never suggest that primary schools are to prepare children for employment. Indeed, they suggest that the real concern is with the individual for his and for her own sake. But parents have a more single-minded concern for the success of their own children; a success measured in terms of qualifications for entry into better jobs than they have themselves. It is this view which children consistently take.

Preparation for Employment

Schools give to children some ambiguous messages, and create a context all their own, but to children the underlying purpose of schooling is clear, as clear in any primary school as secondary. Whilst there are many different ways of expressing the purpose, and different layers of achievement surrounding it, all children, when pressed to define the aims of schools, say that in the end it is to prepare them for jobs. The significance of organizations, the meeting with friends, and the variety of the different parts of the curriculum, are all seen to be at the service of that central concern:

If I didn't go to school I'd know nothing and wouldn't be able to get a job or nothing. (boy, 10)

If you want to get a job ... It might help me with my job. It's important 'cos it helps to get jobs. (girl, 10)

Really you need to go to school to get a job when you're older. (girl, 11)

This supposed job preparation does not seem to strike girls in primary schools any differently from boys, nor do children express any deviation from the fundamental purpose.

The most important means of being prepared for employment naturally arises from the curriculum that is presented to them, rather than from the other more subtle skills that children acquire from the school as an institution. It is through learning a particular amount of knowledge that children see themselves being helped; a view of the curriculum that includes skills as well as an accumulation of facts:

It's for teaching children how to learn, like maths and sums so when they grow up they won't start going around without any job, and being unemployed. (girl, 10)

Learning is seen in terms of the acquisition of useful skills, especially those 'central' concerns like spelling and mathematics. When children talk of the important parts of the curriculum they sound rather like the employers themselves, without any need for the government to stress the notion of 'training for employment'.

Children's views on the essential purpose of primary schools mean that they see the schools as a type of preparation rather than as an experience in itself, even whilst they analyze the experience they are undergoing. The school remains seen in a larger context. To this end children's views of the curriculum are as focused towards utility as any analysis of the 'core' subject could suggest. Subjects like mathematics and language are seen to be crucial, not only because of their domination of the timetable but because of the practical bearing they are seen to have on later employability. Although children enjoy subjects such as drama, they do not see them as having any relevance to the central purpose of the curriculum. Children enjoy subjects which entail experiments and practical activities but they submit that those subjects which entail unpopular necessities, like 'writing', are far more important.

Although children focus on the significance of certain subjects in schools, a bias which is reflected in the balance of the curriculum as taught (Galton *et al.*, 1980), they still accept that all that is offered to them in school has some relevance. With some subjects it is far easier to see the connection:

> I'm going to be a vet, if I can be a vet and maths will help me with medicines and things . . . maths helps you when you're shopping . . . (boy, 10)

> To get a job you have to know English, science, history, maths and spellings. (girl, 11)

But in primary schools, unlike secondary schools, children do not question the relevance of what they are doing. At that stage, given their interpretation of the school's purpose, they accept that there are reasons for taking nearly all the subjects.

In children's minds certain subjects are more important than others not only because of the length of time spent on them but because there are definite, measurable, outcomes. With certain tasks it is clear what has been achieved: answered questions and finished sums. It is not only parents who question the relevance of what seems like 'play' to them. Children are able to put up with stretches of mechanical routine because they see that is part of the purpose of school. They might not know whether they are learning anything by undergoing comprehension exercises but they do know they are fulfilling what is expected of them. It is partly because children submit to the ethos of schools that they are willing to accept, without question, many of the tasks that, to the outside observer, would appear to be undemanding. After all, there are few occasions when children are expected to question the purpose of what they are doing.

Whilst children accept that the seemingly disconnected topics that they undertake must have some connection with the outcome of schooling, through examinations, they do not always see any relevance to their futures. Those primary school children who are most aware of the world of work, those, in fact, most economically aware as the government would wish them to be, are more sceptical than others about the relevance of the traditional curriculum:

> I think it would be better to go when you've learned enough and get out to work at what you want to do. I'd rather be at work. Some of the things you learn in school might help you working on a farm . . . but history and geography doesn't. (girl, 10)

When children question the relevance of what they are learning they do so in terms of the relationship between the subject and employment. Purpose is taken to mean heading towards a job.

The curriculum is essentially whatever the teachers offer, and the impression that children receive is that certain subjects are more important than others for reasons that children connect with employment. They point out how mathematics and English dominate the primary school curriculum, and long for greater variety. They often find the primary school curriculum both narrow and monotonous. But they accept a certain amount of tedium as a necessary part of their experience of school, as if that, too, were a preparation for their future lives.

If the underlying purpose of schooling is preparation for employment, this manifests itself in many ways. The importance of what children learn in terms of skills might be clear to teachers but is only implicit in children's minds. They accept that the learning of tables, of reading and writing, is geared towards one ultimate end, even if not particularly apparent at the time:

> When you leave school and you're older and you can get a job, you'll know how to read and write and you'll know English and maths and all that lot. (girl, 11)

Some of the tasks of school can be summed up in terms of the traditional curriculum and the rest in terms of skills. Reading and writing are spoken about by those who have been in primary school for a number of years not in terms of the pleasures derived from literature but in terms of 'learning to get a good job', as if there were a utilitarian end in everything that is presented to them. Whilst at school they do not question the connection between the immediate and ultimate purposes.

and ultimate purposes.

Examinations and Qualifications

In the clear connections made between the curriculum and jobs, examinations play a central role. Even in primary schools the subjects presented to them are relevant because they will be part of examinations. Children already understand the significance of qualifications, even if they do not gear their lives to acquiring them, and see the place of examinations in the competition to gain jobs. They assume that they cannot gain employment without qualifications of the traditional sort.

> Learning so that when you grow up you'll learn how to find a job and add up things that are quite hard. It's for exams. (girl, 10)

> It's really for people to learn things you didn't know before and when you are older you'll have so many 'O' levels you can get what you want. If you didn't go to school you wouldn't have no 'O' levels and you wouldn't ever get a job nowhere. (boy, 9)

The skills are learned so they can be tested:

> Exams see how good you are in your tables, English, maths and that. (boy, 10)

Children already anticipate leaving the secondary school, and see their experiences of primary schools in that context.

Primary school children, in their constant reiteration of the underlying purpose of education, suggest that there is a natural progression towards the leaving qualification and that therefore school becomes more and more serious the older they become. In this context primary schools are not as important as secondary:

> I think comp. is a little bit more important ... it's getting closer and closer to your job. (girl, 10)

Schools are seen not only to prepare them for jobs and examinations but as having a more complex role in both assessing and forming them for later life. The schools themselves are seen as responsible for reporting on them and making sure they have the skills necessary for the best presentation of themselves. Many children are aware of, and afraid of, being unemployed, and although it might seem a long way away from their immediate experience their awareness of the social context does affect the way they understand schools. All the other aspects of what is to be learned in schools, the social skills, the manifestations of the hidden curriculum, have for children an underlying pragmatic purpose. For them, the preparation for jobs implies not just learning skills in the curriculum but how to present themselves in the best way possible:

> Teaching us what we might need to know when we get a job: how to be neat and have manners and how to behave properly, (girl, 10)

The children see a connection between the different emphases given by teachers and parents, between learning for examinations and proper behaviour. The same purpose unites both.

This understanding of certain codes of behaviour has a major role to play in children's understanding of the purpose of education. They realize that in terms of outcome, in employability and the ability to make their way in the world, *how* they present themselves is as important as what they present. They also know that the skills they acquire are as significant as the facts. The tensions between 'knowing how' and 'knowing that' are always before them. They see the preparation for later life in long-ranging terms, in dimensions that go beyond the possession of knowledge just for their own sakes:

> So that if you have children then you can tell them how to get a job and everything. To know things if anyone asks you. (boy, 9)

Whilst children agree that the prime motivation of schooling is the acquisition of qualifications they also suggest that not having a job is not only disappointing but also embarrassing. They see a connection between the ability to do well in school and the capacity to conduct themselves intelligently outside it. On the one hand there is pressure on them to do well, to please the teachers. On the other hand they wish to do well so that they do not become criticized by people outside school:

> Someone might make fun of you when you're older if you're not good at maths or something. (boy, 10)

Children see primary schools in their wider social context. Whilst the school might seem like a complete world in itself, with its own rules and hierarchies, children are constantly aware of the pressures of the outside world. They know that they have to learn, to accept what is given to them, but they assume that it all has an underlying purpose, at least whilst they are in primary school. The sense of excitement in learning which pervades the first experiences of school is replaced by a more pragmatic attitude when children separate ability and hard work. By the time they are ten they feel the pressure to do well, either driven by determination — 'you've got to do it, or you'll never learn' — or out of fear of the consequences 'so we don't get into trouble and all that'. The one purpose which pervades all their thinking is the practical one that 'if you stick it hard at school you'll get a good job'.

Conclusion

Children find schools to be complex places. In the absence of the school itself presenting its aims and purposes they form their own conclusions from

97

their own observations and from conversations with each other. There is a network of rumour about schools which becomes apparent in the mythologies created about secondary schools (Measor and Woods, 1984). This form of myth-making is not just an exaggeration of particular imagined characteristics, but a shared understanding of the meaning and purpose of schools, both an analysis of schools as institutions and an understanding of schools in context. Some of the obvious purposes of school, the dissemination of knowledge and the control of the environment by teachers, are seen quite clearly. But the underlying facts of school, the waiting and the chance to see friends, the significance of groups and the sense of competition, are also part of the understanding which remains a picture of education that children take with them into later life.

But children also form the view of the purpose of schools in such a way that connects with the views of those outside the education system. It is not only the anecdotes, the highlights, the good moments and the terrible half-hours, that form an impression of school, but a sense of it as a rite of passage, a particular part of children's lives. There is sometimes an assumption by teachers inside the system that the same values are shared, just as we know the difference that is made by different kinds of leadership and relationships between staff (Mortimore *et al.*, 1988). We have to remember, however, that this sense of autonomy of the school is not shared in quite the same way by children who are capable of seeing their own lives in relation to the schools in a far more individual way. That sense of submitting to the facts of schools, to its realities, indeed to its peculiarities, is one which is supported by the network of discussion, both in primary and secondary schools, and of one in relation to the other. The information given from one child to another is obvious in terms of their opinions of teachers, but also creates a distinct impression of the school as an institution, a place of peculiar order, implicit warfare, arbitrary controls and necessary rules. The picture of the school which emerges is of a place almost out of control, a picture very different from the assumption that the school's aims and purposes are clear.

Children analyze the school not only in terms of different teaching and learning styles, but as social centres with a pervasive social purpose. They hold on to the idea that the purpose of schools, even if rarely made explicit, is to prepare them for employment. This concern for job preparation, even in the primary schools, pervades all children's conception of what goes on within schools. It justifies many of the activities that would seem meaningless. It justifies some of the longueurs. Such a clear sense of purpose prevails in the absence of any explicit message from the school itself.

References

CULLINGFORD, C. (1985) *Parents, Teachers and Schools*. London, Royce.

CULLINGFORD, C. (1986) '"I suppose learning your tables could help you get a job" — Children's Views on the Purpose of Schools', *Education 3–13*, 14, 2, 41–46.

DAVIES, B. (1982) *Life in the Classroom and Playground: The Accounts of Primary School Children*. London, Routledge and Kegan Paul.

GALTON, M., SIMON, B. and CROLL, P. (1980) *Inside the Primary Classroom*. London, Routledge and Kegan Paul.

GOODNOW, Y. and BURNS, A. (1985) *Home and School: A Child's Eye View*. Hemel Hempstead, Allen & Unwin.

MEASOR, L. and WOODS, P. (1984) *Changing Schools: Pupil Perspectives on Transfer to a Comprehensive*. Milton Keynes, Open University Press.

MORTIMORE, P., SAMMONS, P., STOLL, L., LEWIS, D. and ECOB, R. (1988) *School Matters: The Junior Years*. Wells, Open Books.

Chapter 7

Parents and Schooling

Janet Atkin

Introduction

When I was a child at primary school shortly after the Second World War, my parents had no choice about which school to send me to. They had no say in what I was taught or how. They never met my teachers and rarely the headteacher, unless there was a very serious problem, and the only information they received was an annual report, which consisted of letter grades and a minimum amount of comment. There was no notice actually saying 'No parents beyond this point', but the relationship between them and the school was marked by psychological distance and formality. They were responsible for rearing me in appropriate ways, while the school was responsible for educating me as it saw fit.

It is by contrasting my parents' experiences, which were probably typical of the time, with those of today's parents that we get an indication of the fundamental changes in the relationships between parents and schools that have taken place in the final decades of the twentieth century. Many parents are now welcomed as active participants in the life and work of a school that they have chosen for their children. They are in regular contact with teachers, who are aware of their needs, interests and expectations. They enrich and extend the curriculum through their interests, skills and knowledge. They give support to their children's learning through help at home, which is positively sought and encouraged by the school; and they share in decision-making about the school's aims and policies, both formally through their elected parent-governors and informally through frequent consultation and discussion. In other words, the aims of primary education are being implemented through a partnership between parents and schools, which characterizes a relationship very different from that experienced by my parents.

What is the context within which such changes have occurred and what are their implications for teachers, parents and children at the primary stage of schooling? What does the word 'partnership' really mean and what steps are necessary to achieve it? Does the rhetoric of partnership obscure some inescapable tensions and underlying problems in the relationship between parents and schooling? These are the issues and questions that will be explored in this chapter.

The Current Context

Home-school relationships embody assumptions about the roles of the teacher and the parent in education that are held by both the individuals concerned and by those responsible for policy-making, such as politicians, civil servants, and local education authorities. Many of these assumptions have their roots in attitudes, beliefs and perspectives that form an ideological framework within which particular policies and practices are located. In my childhood, parents and professionals generally attributed children's attainments to inborn mental characteristics over which neither they nor the school had much control. The curriculum was rooted in the elementary tradition, which was familiar and largely acceptable to everyone. The relationship between schooling and work was unproblematic in the post-war boom economy and parents' rights were restricted to the option to withdraw children from religious education or to educate their children 'otherwise' than at school. In this context, it is hardly surprising that the roles of parent and teacher were seen as separate from one another and that there was little interaction between home and school. However, significant changes in assumptions, albeit for a variety of reasons and at different periods of time, have now occurred amongst those most concerned with education.

For politicians of all persuasions, there has been a growing recognition of parents as an important source of support for changes in the purposes and management of education. Most recently this has focused upon public concern (fuelled by the media) about the quality of teaching and standards of educational attainment in a competitive world economy. A series of Education Acts from 1980 onwards has given parents rights over their choice of schooling, the kind of information they receive, representation on governing bodies and involvement in statementing procedures. New conditions of service and the introduction of 'directed time' have made teachers obliged to report on children's progress to parents — a significant change from the previously somewhat optional nature of such obligations, which were often the first to be abandoned when teachers took industrial action. The 1988 Education Reform Act, with the introduction of a National Curriculum, in conjunction with devolved financial responsibilities, wider powers for governing bodies and even greater representation of parents on these, and the reduction of local authority influence through opting-out to grant-maintained status, was indeed presented by the Conservative Government as a major strategy to increase the power of parents over their children's schooling. By making schools directly accountable to parents for children's performance on a prescribed curriculum, the expectation is that this will act as a lever to raise standards.

Professionals, and in particular teachers, have somewhat different perspectives. As a result of a growing body of evidence, patiently accumulated by both academic researchers and practitioners, there is now an acceptance for the most part that parents have a crucial influence on their children's development, attainment and attitudes towards school. The idea that parents educate in the broadest sense and can also assist in their children's learning in the more narrow sense of aspects of the school curriculum is becoming gradually more widespread. Partly as a result of the political pressures described above, and partly because of their own professional acceptance of its importance, teachers are beginning to take account of the needs and expectations of parents, and to listen more carefully to their viewpoints and perspectives. They are also accepting that parents can be a valuable source of information about their own children and have skills, knowledge and experiences that can enrich and augment the curriculum.

Parents, both as individuals and as groups, have also changed their assumptions about their own role in education. The growth of the playgroup movement, the development of national and local organizations for parents, the experience of increased participation in the life and work of the school, for example, have all contributed to the realization that as parents, they have an important role to play that is not restricted to fund-raising or putting in a dutiful attendance at parents' evenings. Through magazines, books, courses, meetings at schools, and informal adult education in, for example, parent and toddler clubs, family centres, and pre-school clubs, many parents are now aware of ways in which they assist their children's learning, and seek to continue this with their school-aged children. Moreover, as television and the media generally have increased the public profile on education, as schools have begun to involve them in formulating aims, and as the annual meeting and report of the governing body have enlarged their awareness of the school's needs, they now see it as valid, not only to make demands of schools, but also to exert pressure on local and central government for adequate resources for education.

Implications

The significant changes in assumptions I have described have implications for the education service as a whole. Creating and sustaining a partnership between parents and schools is a major task which, as Bastiani (1988) cogently points out, cannot be left to individual schools and families. He draws attention to the need for genuine political and professional support, at both national and local level, through appropriate resourcing, adequate staffing, teacher education at both initial and in-service phases, and the monitoring and evaluation of policy and practice. Whilst recognizing and acknowledging the shared nature of the task, it is the implications for those most intimately concerned, namely teachers, parents and children, that I consider here.

For teachers, a partnership with parents entails:

(1) A recognition that parents are the child's prime educators.
(2) Awareness of the differing values and perspectives held by parents and a willingness to negotiate to find common ground.
(3) Knowledge and understanding of the families, neighbourhoods and cultures which the school serves, based upon active exploration and patient listening and enquiry, rather than stereotyping and staffroom mythology.
(4) The development of a variety of effective skills, techniques and methods for facilitating the sharing of knowledge, understanding, expectations and ideas between parents and themselves.
(5) The creation of honest and open dialogue about children's progress and attainments.

All of these imply a new kind of professionalism for teachers which, while it means giving up some of their autonomy and control over what happens in school (which has in any case already been eroded by central and local government), will ultimately, I believe, result in greater public support for the work they do and more understanding of the complexities of educating the next generation, with a consequent rise in their status and self-respect.

For parents, too, a partnership with their children's school implies new ways of thinking about their role and entails:

(1) An acceptance that they are the child's prime educator and that this implies responsibilities and obligations as well as rights. Shipman (1980), Macbeth (1984) and the National Association of Head Teachers (1988) are amongst those who have suggested the need for a form of formal contract between parents and schools.
(2) A willingness to give and seek information actively, and to enter into dialogue with teachers, which may mean modifying stereotypes and negative attitudes.
(3) A commitment to share the educative task in whatever way their circumstances allow, for example, giving their time to work in or for the school, or through helping their children at home.

Janet Atkin

    (4) Developing an appreciation of the constraints under which teachers work, and being prepared to support efforts to counteract or minimize them.

    (5) Being willing to see the needs of their own children in the context of the needs of all the children in the school.

Just as teachers have things to surrender as well as gain, parents, in gaining more power and influence over their children's education, also become more accountable; like teachers, they may no longer be able to play the 'blame game', described so graphically by Macbeth (1984). However, the growth of self-confidence that comes with commitment, involvement and participation, so well exemplified by the playgroup movement, cannot but strengthen parents' sense of personal autonomy and control over their own lives.

Primary teachers have the same aim for children and need to recognize the paradox if they feel threatened by parents who display the qualities they are seeking to cultivate in children!

Finally, what about the children, who should be the ultimate beneficiaries of a closer partnership between their parents and their teachers? What does this relationship, between the people who together are probably the most important figures in their primary school lives, mean for them? I would suggest they benefit from the following:

    (1) An integrated and complementary experience of education at home and at school, rather than living in two separate worlds.

    (2) Greater self-esteem as they see their parents being respected and valued.

    (3) The potential that the child-parent relationship will be enhanced through shared learning and shared understandings of life in school.

    (4) Learning that is more closely tailored to their needs as teacher and parent diagnose difficulties and plan programmes together.

    (5) A richer curriculum, because it is extended and enriched by parental skills and expertise, and one that is more relevant to the community because parents have shared in formulating its aims.

    (6) The strong likelihood that their levels of attainment will be higher than those that can be achieved by teachers alone.

Are there also losses for children as well as gains? I believe there may be unless both parents and teachers are very sensitive to children's needs. Schooling and education are not synonymous and family life is not and should not be a school at home. Moreover, in the same way that parents and teachers need satisfying lives separate from and independent of children, so children need space and freedom within which to develop their own sense of personal identity and independence. In their concern for children's educational progress, which may be exacerbated by assessment and testing procedures, both parents and teachers may forget the child's need for fun, laughter, relaxation and play for play's sake (not because it is educational!), in other words the need to be a child, with all that implies about freedom from pressure, worry and anxiety.

Implementing Partnership

The term 'parental involvement' has a variety of meanings, ranging from external support (e.g. fund-raising, attending social events, supplying materials), participation (e.g. helping in the classroom, attending workshops), through to complete control (e.g. over staff selection, finance, curriculum). The concept of partnership, on the other hand, implies equality, reciprocity, and shared decision-making (Pugh *et al.*, 1987). As the central purpose of schooling is children's learning, no educational partnership with parents can exist if they are not participants in the process of planning, implementing and evaluating the curriculum. Unfortunately, few writers on the primary curriculum appear to recognize this; for example, a very recent and otherwise excellent book on curriculum planning and the primary school (Morrison and Ridley, 1988) makes no mention of parents or governors, despite the requirements of the 1986 Education No. 2 Act that the latter should draw up the aims of the school. There are, however, many sources in the literature on home and school, which describe and analyze the implementation of particular practices, as well as the problems and difficulties encountered, in developing a partnership with parents in the curriculum, for example, Tizard *et al.* (1981), Davies (1983), Griffiths and Hamilton (1984), Widlake and McLeod (1984) Topping and Wolfendale, (1985), Gilkes (1987), Merttens and Vass (1987) and Bastiani (1989).

Such accounts are very useful as sources of ideas, as well as giving insights into the experiences of other schools; however, because individual schools have different circumstances (size, location, cultural and neighbourhood characteristics, age of children, etc.) and because parents differ from one another, there can be no ideal blueprint for action that will meet the needs of all schools and parents. The key feature of any development towards partnership is the willingness of the individual school to listen to parental perspectives and viewpoints, to acquire a more accurate picture of their needs and wishes, and to use professional skills to evolve a programme that is responsive to its particular situation.

In developing a whole-school policy and programme for partnership in the curriculum there are two themes which need to be considered alongside each other:

(1) The concept of 'key moments' when there are special and particular times to create links or remake relationships. Such moments are, for example, when children start school or change classes, when national testing is occurring, when there are major changes happening in the school, or when the annual meeting of governors and parents is being held.

(2) The regular and continuing home-school programme, which revolves around the life and work of the school, the progress of the pupils and the ways in which parents and teachers help one another.

Figure 7.1 provides a framework for thinking about appropriate strategies in conjunction with these two themes, a process which is described more fully in Atkin and Bastiani (1988). It suggests some categories that teachers can use as tools to examine their existing arrangements and identify strengths, weaknesses and potential areas for improvement. An acid test of the amount of partnership already achieved would be the extent of parental involvement and contribution towards the planning, organization and evaluation of the programme of communication and contact.

I shall take each category in turn and illustrate it with examples drawn from a number of schools, showing the variety of ways in which the aim of involving parents in the curriculum can be realized. Of course, many activities can serve more than one purpose and so the placing of an example in one category does not mean it is exclusively related to that purpose alone. For instance, working with a group of parents to design a new school brochure could be developing an interest in the work of the school, utilizing parental skills (e.g. in graphics), and involving parents in decision-making about the contents.

Sharing information on the progress, performance and problems of individual children

Whether such dialogue is through the written or spoken word, the aim is to make it mutual communication that is personal, informative and honest; interviews, reports, case conferences, etc. are designed with this in mind. Schools have tried such strategies as:

— Home-school diaries with space for the parent and teacher to comment.
— 'Surgery' times for special problems.
— Prepared slips with information about something that has happened at home or school, e.g. illness, a particular event or achievement.

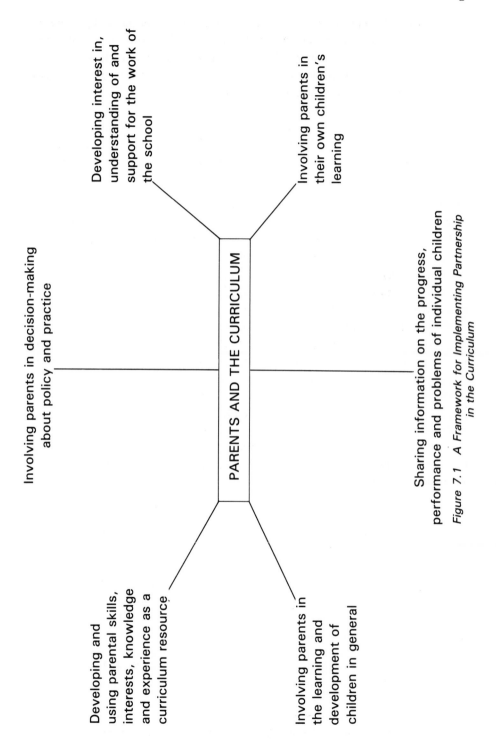

Involving parents in decision-making about policy and practice

Developing interest in, understanding of and support for the work of the school

Involving parents in their own children's learning

PARENTS AND THE CURRICULUM

Developing and using parental skills, interests, knowledge and experience as a curriculum resource

Involving parents in the learning and development of children in general

Sharing information on the progress, performance and problems of individual children

Figure 7.1 A Framework for Implementing Partnership in the Curriculum

— Identifying concerns in advance of regular teacher-parent interviews.
— Involving parents in the design of reports.
— Home visits by the class teacher to all parents (not just those of children with problems).
— Opportunities to observe the child in school.
— Contract-making on particular action.

Involving parents in their own children's learning

The steady increase of home-school reading and mathematics projects demonstrates the gradual acceptance by teachers that parents are coeducators and have a direct role to play in children's learning, both in specific aspects of the curriculum and with more general learning skills and strategies. Ways in which schools have encouraged them include:

— Suggesting follow-up activities to classroom work, e.g. skills to be practised, discussion topics, TV programmes to watch, materials to find.
— Preparing activity packs for children to do at home, before starting school or in the holidays.
— Joint parent-child tasks at school or at home.
— Asking parents to observe particular aspects of their children's development.
— Seeking information on children's interests, behaviour and experiences.
— Workshops and booklets on ways parents can help with learning and assess progress.

Involving parents in the learning and development of children in general

Although the major focus for the individual parent is their own child's schooling, because their child is being educated in the company of other children, a partnership between parents and schools will include the need for shared understanding about the needs of all the children and how they differ from one another. This aspect is particularly important when national testing may lead to crude and simplistic comparisons of children's attainments. Moreover, creating an interest in all children's development not only leads to increased understanding of one's own child but can also help parents to cooperate together to improve community provision for children. Examples here are:

— Class meetings about the aims and purposes of the curriculum in

the coming year or term, together with a regular class newsletter.
— Informal talks on aspects of children's development, such as health, play, nutrition, etc.
— Group work for special difficulties, such as bereavement, abuse, behaviour problems, divorce, etc.
— Collections of pamphlets, books and videos that parents can borrow.
— Inviting parents to special events, such as assemblies, plays, open days, school outings and residential trips.
— Parents running holiday and after-school play schemes and school clubs.
— Resource banks of information about activities for children in the community, such as sporting facilities, clubs and associations, places to visit, etc.
— Collaborating with other agencies, such as health and social services, and the educational support services, to provide information and guidance that is responsive to parents' needs.

Developing and using parental skills, interests, knowledge and experience as a curriculum resource

Underlying this category is the recognition that parents have expertise that can complement that of the teacher and that its use will extend and enrich the curriculum experiences of all the children. For example, schools have:

— Kept an inventory of parents' jobs, hobbies and skills, to be drawn on when planning a programme of work.
— Given information about forthcoming topics and indicated ways in which parents can assist.
— Extended regular invitations for involvement in the classroom, devised a range of activities to suit the individual parent-volunteer and held discussion and feedback sessions for individuals and groups.
— Sought ideas and suggestions, e.g. for recipes from various cultures, places to visit, titles of books children have enjoyed.
— Asked parents to observe and evaluate an aspect of classroom life, e.g. the use of the book corner or computer.
— Had exhibitions in school of parents' work, e.g. art, craft, photography, writing, etc.
— Developed curriculum resources with parents, e.g. tapes of stories, songs, nursery rhymes and music, illustrations, books and other writing, videos, aquaria, environmental studies material, urban trails, etc.

Developing interest in, understanding of and support for the work of the school

Underlying this category is the realization that for parents to be equal partners, their support must be enlisted for the work of the school as a whole, so that parents and teachers are working together for what is seen by both as 'their school'. I would suggest it is only through such an alliance (which also includes shared decision-making) that mutual gain and mutual accountability will be achieved. Genuine support will not come, however, if the school alone determines its aims and purposes. Strategies that schools have used include:

— The development of home-school associations, or parent-teacher organizations, which provide a forum for discussion and debate on school matters, as well as fund-raising and social events.
— Newsletters and magazines produced by joint working parties.
— Induction programmes for new parents, as well as children.
— Making the annual parents' meeting with governors a lively occasion and an opportunity to celebrate the school's achievements, as well as meeting the requirements of the 1986 Education Act.
— Involving parents in the improvement of facilities, such as play areas.
— Invitations to see the school at work.
— Getting the children to demonstrate and explain their work to parents.
— Involving parents in school-based in-service activities.
— Getting parents to participate in publicizing the school's work in local newspapers, shops, libraries, etc. and on radio.

Involving parents in decision-making about policy and practice

Many of the examples that have already been given provide incidental and informal opportunities for parents to share in decision-making but the school also needs to plan deliberate strategies to enable this to happen. The key word here is 'sharing', for partnership implies that control over decision-making does not rest with either the school or the parents, and compromise and adjustment to both points of view are both necessary and inevitable, however difficult to achieve in practice. Some ways that schools have developed are:

— An informal committee with elected or volunteer parents from each class to discuss curriculum matters.
— Arrangements for the parent-governors to meet and consult with other parents on a regular basis.

- The systematic seeking of parental opinion on particular issues, e.g. uniform, school hours, policies on homework, etc.
- Consultation on admission procedures and class groupings.
- Contract-making on an individual child's learning programme.
- A home-school council that regularly evaluates the programme of links.

Rhetoric and Reality

It would be naive to imagine that these changes in attitude towards home-school relationships have been achieved smoothly, have led to changed practices in all schools or transformed all parents into active and positive supporters of their children's education. The shifts in perspectives from those current in my childhood have been gradual and piecemeal, and research, policy and practice have not developed in an integrated way. There are also many pragmatic reasons why, even if they wish to, schools find it difficult to implement change in this area: initial training for teachers has rarely prepared them for work with parents (Atkin and Bastiani, 1984); in-service opportunities are limited and the demands of the National Curriculum have taken precedence; primary school staffing, based on the class teacher role, is quite inadequate for the new demands that such work generates; and financial constraints prevent the development of imaginative and lively support materials. Parents, too, however willing, have constraints, such as domestic pressures, time, or employment, which limit their capacity to be directly involved, while others have still to overcome the negative images they have of schools, often caused by their own experiences as pupils.

For a number of more fundamental reasons, however, there are likely to remain tensions and conflicts between parents and teachers. Many years ago, the sociologist Willard Waller wrote, 'parents and teachers usually live in conditions of mutual mistrust and enmity' (Waller, 1932) and, while few would claim such a state of overt enmity now, the achievement of truly equal partnership and harmonious relationships is unlikely.

First, the essential focus for the parent is their own child whereas teachers must necessarily be concerned with all the children in their care and their induction into a wider society, and even occasionally sacrifice the needs of the individual to the needs of the majority. There may also be competing definitions of the child's needs that are difficult to resolve and these are likely to increase with assessment procedures that emphasize particular aspects of the curriculum. It is not difficult to imagine a situation in which a parent (or teacher) thinks most effort should be directed towards the assessed attainment targets of the core curriculum, whereas the teacher (or parent) values a broader curriculum.

Second, parents themselves have differing beliefs and values about education and child-rearing practices, as do teachers, and any school is likely to have parents who disagree with one another about purposes, policies and practices. Divisions between parents, for example, about opting out, religious and sex education, or the incorporation of race and gender issues into the curriculum, are not resolved by the exercise of a vote and it is simplistic to suggest that parents either will or can simply choose an alternative school as their solution. The management of such conflicts and the mediating role they entail create pressures, particularly on headteachers, but also on parent-governors, who, although not elected to represent parents, are often expected to act on their behalf.

Finally, and this is an argument that many primary teachers find unpalatable, our society distributes rewards unequally. Class, race, and gender are important factors, in addition to learning ability and the quality of schooling, in influencing the kind of success or otherwise children have in school. It is unsurprising, therefore, to find that it is the parents of children who are most successful, namely those who are white and middle-class, that schools find easiest to involve, whether in fund-raising, curriculum meetings, parents' evenings or governing bodies (Bridges, 1981; Tomlinson, 1984; ESCS, 1988). The ways in which some parents become less involved after the earliest stages of schooling reflect the differentiation process that is occurring as children get older. As Sharpe (1980) has shown, parents can influence the ways in which pupil identities are negotiated, but the problem that Batten (1975:4) posed, is probably even more acute in today's climate:

> Advantage is by definition limited and relative, and it is not possible to anticipate that the implementation of a general programme of close parent-teacher contact could significantly affect overall patterns of motivation to attain within the context of an instrumentally orientated education system.

For all these reasons, then, partnership between parents and schools is no simple matter. Politicians, professionals and parents have different and often contradictory motives for advocating it and in any situation where various interest groups are involved in power-sharing there is likely to be tension and conflict.

Conclusion

At the time of writing, the shape and nature of future primary education are unclear. The potential is there for a richer and more balanced curriculum than many children at present experience but so is the danger of a return to an assessment-led curriculum, narrowly focused on specific measurable knowledge and skills, with a payment-by-results ethos which was so damaging to early childhood education in the nineteenth century. However, it is precisely because teachers and parents *do* have at the heart of their shared concerns the children themselves, that together they can form a powerful alliance. In a climate that might be hostile to the needs of children, with shrinking resources, increasing central control over what is taught, and an emphasis on the future usefulness of pupils to the economy, it is possibly only by joining together in partnership that teachers and parents can sustain a wider view of the purposes of primary education and the rights of children to enjoy an education that takes account of their present state of childhood as well as their future as adults. Perhaps we need to remind ourselves of the words of Margaret McMillan written over eighty years ago:

> If the people knew the schools well; were allies and friends of the teacher; understood and loved the methods by which their children were developing; if the school was their place of refreshment or entertainment; the bright spot in every area; a centre of hope and fellowship and sympathy for them, do you think they would yield it up to the control of 'Managers' and 'Committees' to whom they were comparatively indifferent? (McMillan, 1905:17)

Her aspirations were not realized in her own time, nor in my childhood. Are they an ideal to aspire to as schools, parents and children enter the twenty-first century?

References

ATKIN, J. and BASTIANI, J. (1984) *Preparing Teachers to Work With Parents: A Survey of Initial Training*. Nottingham, University of Nottingham School of Education.

ATKIN, J. and BASTIANI, J. with GOODE, J. (1988) *Listening to Parents: An Approach to the Improvement of Home-School Relations*. Beckenham, Croom Helm.

BASTIANI, J. (Ed) (1988) *Parents and Teachers 2: From Policy to Practice*. Windsor, NFER-Nelson.

BASTIANI, J. (Ed) (1989) *Parents and Teachers 3: Developing Practice: A Whole School Approach*. Windsor, NFER-Nelson.

BATTEN, E. (1975) 'Attainment, environment and education', in RUSHTON, J. and TURNER, J.D. (Eds) *Education and Deprivation*. Manchester, Manchester University Press.

BRIDGES, D. (1981) ' "It's the ones who never turn up that you really want to see"; The "problem" of the non-attending parent', in ELLIOT, J. *School Accountability*. London, Blackwell.

DAVIES, E. (1983) 'Parental involvement in school policy-making', *Educ. Manage. Admin.*, 11, 2, 145–148.

ESCS RESEARCH GROUP (1988) *Parents as School Governors: Final Report.* Exeter, University of Exeter School of Education.

GILKES, J. (1987) *Developing Nursery Education.* Milton Keynes, Open University Press.

GRIFFITHS, A. and HAMILTON, D. (1984) *Parent, Teacher, Child: Working Together in Children's Learning.* London, Methuen.

MACBETH, A. (1984) *The Child Between: A Report on School-Family Relations in the Countries of the European Community.* Brussels, Commission of the European Communities. (Available from HMSO).

MCMILLAN, M. (C: 1905) *The Beginnings of Education.* London, ILP pamphlet.

MERTTENS, R. and VASS, J. (1987) 'IMPACT: a learning experience', *Primary Teaching Studies*, 2, 3, 263–272.

MORRISON, K. and RIDLEY, K. (1988) *Curriculum Planning and the Primary School.* London, Paul Chapman Publishing Ltd.

NATIONAL ASSOCIATION OF HEADTEACHERS (1988) 'Home-School Contract of Partnership: A Discussion Paper', Haywards Heath, NAHT.

PUGH, G., APLIN, G., DE'ATH, E. and MOXON, M. (1987) *Partnership in Action: Working with Parents in Pre-school Centres, 2 Vols.* London, National Children's Bureau.

SHARPE, L. (1980) *Home-school Relations: A Reconceptualisation.* Unpublished PhD thesis, University of Sussex.

SHIPMAN, M. (1980) 'The limits of positive discrimination', in MARLAND, M. (Ed) *Education for the Inner City.* London, Heineman.

TIZARD, B., MORTIMORE, J. and BURCHELL, B. (1981) *Involving Parents in Nursery and Infant Schools.* London, Allen and Unwin.

TOMLINSON, S. (1984) *Home and School in Multicultural Britain.* London, Batsford.

TOPPING, K. and WOLFENDALE, S. (1985) *Parental Involvement in Children's Reading*, London, Croom Helm.

WALLER, W. (1932) *The Sociology of Teaching.* 3rd ed. 1967, Chichester, John Wiley and Sons.

WIDLAKE, P. and MCLEOD, F. (1984) *Raising Standards: Part One.* Coventry, Community Education Development Centre.

Part 3 Implementing Curricular Aims

Introduction

While some earlier chapters have considered philosophical aspects of the purpose and aims of primary education in general, this part of the book concerns the question of putting aims into practice in primary schools. The writing of curricular statements has been a requirement since 1981, when the DES (Circular 6/81) requested schools and LEAs to 'develop their curricula, setting out in writing the aims which they pursue through the organisation of the curriculum and teaching programmes'. Most LEAs established working parties to produce guidelines and recommendations for circulation to schools, but the 1988 Education Reform Act now gives school governors the responsibility for ensuring that the curriculum is described and 'delivered' effectively.

All primary schools will therefore have considered their curricular aims and programmes. The worst school will merely collect the various documents and statements in a box-file marked 'Curriculum' — perhaps under five headings — DES, HMI, Schools Council, Local Authority, Others (including press cuttings) — with no further action being considered necessary; the school staff agree with the recommendations produced. The other end of the scale would be where a working party is formed from the school staff to consider all the documents and a school curriculum statement is prepared. More important, all the staff meet to consider how the objectives outlined in the curriculum statement can be implemented, evaluated and justified in each classroom.

If data were to be collected on how the nation's 23,000 primary schools fitted these descriptions, a graph would probably show a 'normal' curve of distribution, with the majority of schools taking some action to replan the curriculum. For instance, the headteacher may have circulated and discussed all the documents with each member of staff, and have written a 'school comment' to be affixed to the LEA statement on the aims, organization and content of the curriculum.

But is this sufficient after the Education Reform Act? To my mind, teachers and governors in these schools should be more than a little concerned about what, for instance, HMI might feel about the statement during a General Inspection. A recent review of published HMI survey reports on 123 primary schools (HMI, 1984) stated about their curriculum statements or guidelines:

> The quality of these documents varies considerably. Moreover, in some cases the guidelines which have been produced appear to have little direct influence on the work being undertaken by most of the pupils for most of their time. Those schools which reach high levels of performance in most areas of the curriculum are, not surprisingly, those which have strong leadership from the head, and where the whole community of the school gives the impression of a clear sense of purpose: their aims and objectives agreed, and the achievement of them monitored and evaluated periodically.

The first priority is, therefore, to write the aims of the school, perhaps adapting for local needs some of the examples included in the first two parts of this book. Primary schools then have to consider a curricular framework which will help them meet the aims. The National Curriculum is, of course, framed around subjects, but this has met with opposition. Summarizing 20,000 responses to the government's proposals, Haviland (1988) concluded: 'I can confirm that the principle [of a National Curriculum] was overwhelmingly approved. I cannot recall one response, however, that endorsed without reservation the structure for the curriculum which the Government was proposing.' This reaction is hardly surprising. At the turn of the century, monumental investigation of Thorndike (1901) convincingly challenged the traditional justification for the subjects in the curriculum. In a UNESCO statement published by the government, Dottrens (1962) showed that, if we use the traditional meanings of 'subjects' in the primary school, say, with English divided into handwriting, spelling, composition, poetry, dictation, comprehension, drama and story, some 352 subjects could be identified. Despite such problems, it is likely that most schools will go through each of the National Curriculum subjects and demonstrate how they will be taught to meet the school's aims and the requirements of national testing. Much of the responsibility for writing these documents will fall on the shoulders of the subject coordinators.

This coordination role is examined in Chapter 8 by Jim Campbell. Even Plowden recognized the need for curriculum leaders, but the role has since been described, and expanded, in a range of documents — the Cockcroft and Bullock reports, the HMI Primary Survey and the NUT Middle Schools Survey, the LEA documents, such as that of ILEA, the House of Commons report and the National Curriculum documents. All of these see curriculum coordination as a key task for the effective implementation of a school's aims. Some examples are provided here of how school coordinators faced up to the task and the conflicts, friction and stress they suffered in the process. Clearly they need some time allowance to carry out these tasks, and this principle has been agreed in a number of DES and HMI statements. When he was Secretary of State, Sir Keith (now Lord) Joseph estimated that 15,000 additional primary school teachers were required just to enable schools to carry out these tasks. A DES survey published in November 1988 showed that primary school teachers get, on average, only eight minutes non-contact time a day. Although the five Baker Days guarantee some time free of teaching for coordinators to tackle their tasks, this is only a beginning; the government must increase the number of teachers if the aims for the National Curriculum are to be achieved through subject coordinators.

Schools also need to consider other curricular frameworks, in addition to National Curriculum subjects, which might help them implement their aims. After reviewing the subject-based framework in one particular DES document, the House of Commons Select Committee (1982) concluded:

> We believe that schools should regard the provisions of 'The School Curriculum' with some scepticism. We hope that in responding to Circular 6/81, schools will take [other] documents into account in framing their curriculum aims. We may add that, in default of a better account, it appears to us that responsible heads and teachers may prove more effective, with a combination of common sense and close consultation with local interests and parents, in producing the most appropriate curriculum framework for their particular children's needs.

The committee, for instance, advised teachers to consider HMI Areas of Experience, a framework which is analyzed in Chapter 2 in this book.

An alternative framework which might help teachers is proposed in Chapter 9, which begins by re-examining what we mean by the 'basics' of primary education. This leads to a consideration of the potential curricular role of our five 'languages' — written, spoken, number, graphic and body language — which are the basis of all learning, in that they are skills used across the curriculum. The cross-curricular roles of three of the languages, literacy, oracy and numeracy, were stressed in the Bullock and Cockcroft reports, and, by having two additional coordinators for the other languages, the workload would be spread more evenly, resulting in a more effective 'whole-school' policy.

A case study of a primary school which has introduced an effective whole-school approach is provided in Chapter 10 by the headteacher, Gordon Wood, and his former deputy, Norma Newell. They demonstrate how aims are put into practice in a large primary school in which staff are involved in decision-making. For instance, the school has developed the use of the computer to such an extent that it is now a pilot school in the Cleveland networking experiment and attracts a constant flow of visitors. The chapter also includes examples of how mathematics, science and language policies have been implemented, and how the review procedures and the policies of shared responsibilities have been adopted. There is plenty of evidence of good practice here.

One of the concerns expressed here focuses on the new assessment targets at 7 and 11. All teachers will recognize the dangers of allowing assessment to dominate their curricular aims, as has happened in the United States. Some of the issues which have emerged over many decades of assessment are evident in the 1988 *Yearbook* (National Society for the Study of Education, 1988). In her introduction, Tanner warns that:

> In the situation which has come to prevail as a result of state-mandated testing programs, teachers spend an enormous amount of time preparing students for tests and neglect curriculum areas not tested. The effect is a reshaping of the curriculum in accord with political not pedagogical interests.

This opinion is endorsed and elaborated in the chapter on 'The Influence of Testing on the Curriculum' in which Madaus states:

> In recent years, it seems that the aims of education, the business of our schools, and the goals of educational reform are addressed not so much in terms of curriculum — the courses of study that are followed — as they are in terms of standardised tests. It is testing, not the 'official' stated curriculum, that is increasingly determining what is taught, how it is taught, what is learned, and how it is learned.

We must take these warnings to heart and ensure that assessment is never allowed to dominate the curricular aims but that the good practice exemplified in Chapter 10 remains the essence of primary education in this country.

References

DOTTRENS, E. (1962) *The Primary School Curriculum*. Paris, UNESCO, and London, HMSO.

HAVILAND, J. (1988) *Take Care, Mr Baker*. London, Fourth Estate.

HMI (1984) *Education Observed 2: A Review of Published Reports*. London, DES.

HOUSE OF COMMONS SELECT COMMITTEE (1982) *The Secondary School Curriculum and Examination*, Paper 116-1, Vol. 1. London, HMSO.

NATIONAL SOCIETY FOR THE STUDY OF EDUCATION (1988) *Critical Issues in Curriculum: 87th Yearbook*. Chicago, University of Chicago Press.

THORNDIKE, E.L. and WOODWORTH, R.S. (1901) 'The influence of improvement in one mental function upon the efficiency of other functions', *Psychological Review*, 8, 247–261.

Chapter 8

Curriculum Coordinators, the National Curriculum and the Aims of Primary Education

Jim Campbell

Introduction

The publication of *Primary Education in England* (DES, 1978) marked the beginning of a decade in which a gradually intensifying interest was focused on teachers with responsibility for an aspect of the curriculum, variously called curriculum postholders, curriculum consultants, subject advisers and curriculum coordinators. I shall standardize on the last term, since the terminology varies, but not the role or specification.

The decade ended with the proposals for a National Curriculum (DES, 1987), identified for primary schools as a list of 'subjects', with attainment targets, programmes of study and assessment arrangements. The curriculum was to be developed in subject categories by advisory committees, called subject working groups. These proposals appeared to reinforce and even to legitimize the role for curriculum coordinators first adumbrated in *Primary Education in England*. This role would be to help their colleagues 'deliver' the National Curriculum in the subject for which they were responsible, even where the school aims, and its curricular organization, were not expressed in subject terms.

Scattered throughout *Primary Education in England* were references to the importance of the curriculum coordinator's role in the quality of pupils' learning, of which the following are significant:

(a) Planning programmes of work.
(b) Helping teachers match work to children's capacities.
(c) Developing and maintaining subject expertise to give a lead in curriculum planning.
(d) Raising the status of the coordinators.

(e) Developing acceptable means of assessing work throughout the school.

(f) The role required time to be allocated for performing the range of duties involved, some of which (keeping up-to-date in a subject, for example) assumed time outside school hours, while others needed to be carried out while the school was in session.

The Inspectors summarized their view of the role as follows:

Teachers in posts of special responsibility need to keep up-to-date in their knowledge of their subject; to be familiar with its main concepts, with the sub-divisions of the subject material, and how they relate to one another. They have to know enough of available teaching materials and teaching approaches to make and advise upon, choices that suit local circumstances. And they should be aware of the ways in which children learn and of any sequences of learning that need to be taken into account. Additionally, these teachers should learn how to lead groups of teachers and to help others teach material which is appropriate to the abilities of the children. They should learn how to establish a programme of work in cooperation with other members of staff and how to judge whether it is being operated successfully. They should also learn how to make the best use of the strengths of teachers of all ages and help them to develop so that they may take on more responsibility . . .

This expanded and elaborated specification of the coordinator's role was presented with the authority of HM Inspectorate. A year after publication of the survey, it appeared to receive the imprimatur of the National Union of Teachers, whose survey of middle schools (NUT, 1979), whatever its ambivalence about the schools themselves, contained illustrative, though not necessarily representative, organizational arrangements from an 8–12 school. It listed the responsibilities of coordinators, now called 'subject area consultants', in a way that reflected the recent changes in their role definition:

(a) to advise on the curriculum and prepare schemes, if necessary, within their particular field of expertise (including books and materials),

(b) to contribute to general curriculum development in the school,

(c) to advise colleagues on any problem of content, background knowledge, sources or method involving their particular field of expertise,

(d) in collaboration with year group leaders to guide probationary teachers, and

(e) whenever appropriate to liaise with colleagues in the first and high schools.

Although this list was perhaps excessively coy about the coordinator's role in visiting colleagues' classes to see work in progress, it implicitly seemed to accept the wide-ranging definition that had already been developed by the Inspectorate. Before that, the Bullock Report (1974) had stressed the importance it attached to language consultants, while the Cockcroft Report (1982), provided a full job specification for mathematics coordinators:

> In our view it should be part of the duties of the mathematics coordinator to:
> Prepare a scheme of work for the school in consultation with the headteacher and staff and, where possible, with schools from which the children come and to which they go (we discuss this further in paragraph 363);
>
> provide guidance and support to other members of staff in implementing the scheme of work, both by means of meetings and by working alongside individual teachers;
>
> organise and be responsible for procuring, within the funds made available, the necessary teaching resources for mathematics, maintain an up-to-date inventory and ensure the members of staff are aware of how to use the resources which are available;
>
> monitor work in mathematics throughout the school, including methods of assessment and record keeping;
>
> assist with the diagnosis of children's learning difficulties and with their remediation;
>
> arrange school-based in-service training for members of staff as appropriate;
>
> maintain liaison with schools from which children come and to which they go, and also with LEA advisory staff.

In the same year we also had the HMI survey on education in first schools (DES, 1982) in which it was proposed that, even for the very youngest children in our school system, curriculum planning and curriculum organization should be influenced by teachers with special expertise: curriculum coordinators.

Further support for the emerging idea that curriculum coordinators should play a central role in developing school-wide curriculum policies came from LEAs' publication of curriculum statements, the best known of which is the report of the enquiry chaired by Thomas into Inner London primary schools (ILEA, 1985). The recommendations of this report included the new proposal that curriculum coordination should not necessarily be associated with above-scale payments, but that what the report called the 'dual role' of class teaching and advising colleagues in an aspect of the curriculum should be part of the expectations for virtually all primary school teachers, and that the schools should be staffed in ways that enabled the coordinating role to be supported and implemented. A year later, a Select Committee report, *Achievement in Primary Schools* (House of Commons, 1986), elaborated on the theme and saw curriculum coordination as a key task in the creation of 'whole school development plans'. It also attempted to clarify the terminology, arguing for the standardization of the term 'coordinator', and describing the role in practice, as follows:

> 9.24 As we have already said, it is too much to expect every teacher to keep up with changes in knowledge and methodology in every field. Each would be helped by having a colleague nearby to turn to for information and help from time to time, and especially so if the roles of adviser and advised could be exchanged on other occasions: i.e. that there was no question of hierarchy.

> 9.25 We envisage that the colleagues giving help should do so in two main ways: by taking the lead in the formulation of a scheme of work; and by helping teachers individually to translate the scheme into classroom practice either through discussion or by helping in the teaching of the children. Much the most frequent method would be discussion. Direct teaching might often take place with the class teacher present, not least so that the class teacher can manage on his or her own next time. But sometimes it might be better to teach the children away from their own teacher because that is easier for the co-ordinator to manage, or because to do so makes it possible to avoid distraction, or because the class teacher could use the time to do something else. If the teaching is done separately, the class teacher should be responsible for ensuring that the work done fits with the rest of the child's programmes. Linkage with the rest of the programme is what matters, not where the teaching takes place. Children near the end of the primary stage are more likely to need access to additional teachers than are those near the beginning.

> 9.26 We believe this scenario represents the highest common factor of what various witnesses have put to us and is consistent with what we have seen and been told by teachers in schools. We consider it to be quite unlike the forms of specialist teaching commonly found in secondary schools, though it does allow the possibility of movement between teachers. The most extreme cases we postulate

are, on the one hand, a class is taught by the class teacher alone; and on the other, a whole class is taught for a minority of subjects by teachers other than the class teacher, who may or may not be present. In between, and most commonly, a class teacher will be advised by another teacher from time to time; or the co-ordinating teacher will help with the teaching of the class or group of children in the presence of the class teacher; or will take a group of children elsewhere for some aspect of their work.

Curriculum Coordination: The Role in Practice

Alongside the official and semi-official sponsorship of an extended role for teachers as curriculum coordinators, a number of small-scale empirical studies (Rodger *et al.*, 1983) of the role in practice began to be published as well as some self-reports (Dodds and Armstong, 1985; Heritage, 1985).

My own study (Campbell, 1985) attempted to analyze the skills required of curriculum coordinators in ten school-based curriculum initiatives, classified as follows:

CLASSIFICATION OF COORDINATION SKILLS

(1) CURRICULAR SKILLS: that is, those skills and qualities involved in knowledge about the curriculum area for which the postholder has responsibility.

    (a) *Knowledge of Subject*: the postholder must keep up-to-date in their subject, must know its conceptual structure and methods, etc.

    (b) *Professional Skills*: the postholder must draw up a programme of work, manage its implementation, maintain it and assess its effectiveness.

    (c) *Professional Judgement*: the postholder must know about, and discriminate between various materials and approaches in their subject, must relate them to children's development stages, manage the school's resources, and achieve a match between the curriculum and the pupils' abilities.

(2) INTERPERSONAL SKILLS: that is, those skills and qualities arising from postholder's relationships with colleagues and other adults.

    (d) *Social Skills*: the postholder must work with colleagues, leading discussion groups, teaching alongside colleagues, help develop their confidence in their subject, advise probationers, etc.

    (e) *External Representation*: the postholder must represent their subject to outsiders (other teachers, advisers, governors, parents, etc.).

A more detailed case by case analysis (Figure 8.1) showed the wide range of skills demanded in practice of curriculum coordinators.

It is worth illustrating by brief versions of case material the nature of the work demands made in particular situations. In Case Study 4, the staff of a multi-ethnic 8–12 middle school followed a school-based programme for a term in which they examined the language of the routine classroom

Figure 8.1   Range of Skills Expected of the Curriculum Coordinators in Ten School-based Curriculum Developments

Skills involved in school-based curriculum development	1	2	3	4	5	6	7	8	9	10
I. CURRICULUM SKILLS										
A. SUBJECT KNOWLEDGE										
1. updating subject knowledge	✓	✓		✓		✓	✓	✓		✓
2. identifying conceptual structure of subject(s)	✓		✓			✓	✓	✓		
3. identifying skills in subject(s)	✓		✓	✓		✓	✓	✓	✓	✓
B. PROFESSIONAL SKILLS										
4. reviewing existing practice	✓	✓	✓	✓	✓	✓	✓	✓	✓	✓
5. constructing scheme/programme	✓	✓	✓	✓	✓	✓	✓	✓	✓	✓
6. implementing scheme/programme		✓	✓	✓	✓	✓	✓	✓	✓	✓
7. assessing scheme/programme		✓	✓	✓	✓			✓		
C. PROFESSIONAL JUDGEMENT										
8. deciding between available resources	✓	✓	✓	✓	✓	✓	✓	✓	✓	✓
9. deciding about methods	✓	✓	✓	✓	✓	✓	✓	✓	✓	✓
10. identifying links between subjects	✓	✓	✓			✓	✓	✓	✓	
11. ordering, maintaining resources	✓	✓	✓		✓	✓	✓	✓	✓	✓
12. relating subject to its form in other schools	✓		✓	✓		✓			✓	
II. INTERPERSONAL SKILLS										
D. WORKING WITH COLLEAGUES										
13. leading workshops/discussions	✓	✓	✓	✓	✓	✓	✓	✓		
14. translating material into comprehensible form	✓	✓	✓	✓	✓	✓	✓			
15. liaising with head and/or senior staff	✓	✓	✓	✓	✓	✓	✓	✓	✓	✓
16. advising colleagues informally	✓	✓	✓	✓	✓	✓	✓	✓	✓	✓
17. teaching alongside colleagues		✓			✓	✓	✓	✓		
18. visiting colleagues' classes to see work in progress		✓	✓						✓	
19. maintaining colleagues' morale, reducing anxiety, etc.		✓		✓		✓	✓			
20. dealing with professional disagreement	✓	✓	✓	✓		✓				
E. EXTERNAL REPRESENTATION										
21. Consulting advisers, university staff, etc.		✓	✓		✓	✓	✓			✓
22. Consulting teachers in other schools	✓				✓		✓			✓
23. Consulting parents, governors										

assignments they set for their pupils, using some Open University materials on language as a basis. The overall aim was to increase staff awareness of the difficulties encountered by pupils when they were attempting to carry out normal learning tasks. Ten staff were involved, with at least one from each of the four year groups. The programme comprised a three stage sequence, as follows:

(i) *Staff planning workshop* led by the coordinator in which an area of classroom language (e.g. the written language on workcards) was identified as worth focusing upon;

(ii) *Teachers observed* the language difficulties by selected pupils in carrying out classroom assignments;

(iii) *Staff evaluation group* led by the coordinator in which the observation activities were discussed and analyzed, children's problems identified, and possible remedies in terms of teaching techniques suggested.

This sequence was repeated three times with three different language topics.

The coordinator's role in this development was crucial. She had had to acquaint herself with some of the recent approaches to language skills (through a post-experience course); she prepared material by rendering it into an easily comprehensible form (the 'idiot's pack' as one of the teachers called it) and organized the agenda of meetings, in a way that convinced the participants that they would not be wasting their time; she explained and justified the approaches she was encouraging; she maintained morale at a time in the programme when the production of a musical and the school-wide administration of achievement tests had tended to drain the teacher's energies and affect participation and she helped maintain an attitude and atmosphere in the meetings which was simultaneously business-like and supportive. In fact the staff involved regarded the discussion sessions as probably the most useful of the activities in the programme. They had helped the staff review their aims. As a participant said:

> They were very useful, you had to think about what you were doing with kids and why . . . it was especially valuable that there was a planning discussion before we did something and then to come back afterwards.

One of the other teachers commented on the atmosphere in which the meetings were conducted, stressing the sense of solidarity amongst staff:

> I think it's worked well here because we don't mind being shown up — you know we don't mind coming in and saying, 'It's been a disaster!' There's no point in doing this kind of thing if you're not

going to be honest with one another — pretending you've got perfect results would be a waste of time.

Above all the teachers valued the expertise and organizational flair of the coordinator:

There would be problems if the discussion sessions had just been started cold. They needed someone who's familiar with the material, who knows that background. The last thing I'd want would be where we'd get to the stage where we'd say, 'What shall we talk about this week?'

Case Study 3 provides a particularly clear image of some aspects of the kinds of conflict brought to the surface by school-based development. In this school, a working group of five staff led by the coordinator had developed a draft language policy that had implications for the classroom practice of every teacher in the school. For example, the policy required that spelling should be taught more from children's mistakes and less from isolated textbook exercises, and that drama should be incorporated regularly into the curriculum of every class. The working group incorporated staff from different years, had been open to other staff and had a written record of its meetings open to inspection. A full staff meeting that concluded the process endorsed the policy as a whole:

There was a lot of discussion and lots of interests. Because of the detailed content of the working party, and the incorporation of amendments as we went along, there was only one further change agreed at this meeting. But the big thing was that the whole staff agreed that this was to be the policy for the school.

Thus the coordinator had helped the staff move to some degree of formal agreement about curricular aims for the school.

Nevertheless, in this programme as in six others studies, the coordinator experienced conflict and strain in her role, especially in the process of implementing the policy. As part of this process she had been allowed about an hour per week free of teaching to work alongside other teachers, to be available to advise them, and to monitor the progress of the policy, throughout the school. As the coordinator saw the last of these aspects of her role, she would be perceived by her colleagues as 'inspecting' the quality of their response to the language policy. The potential for friction, even between staff who normally enjoyed warm friendly relationships, arising from this development was recognized by the coordinator, who preferred to withdraw from actively advising and monitoring work in progress, and settle for the staff taking the initiative in seeking advice. The expectations built into the coordinator's role revealed the critically problematic nature of her status in the school, especially in respect to the perceived autonomy of class teachers.

The empirical studies, despite differences in methodology and problems of representativeness, revealed a number of stresses encountered by coordinators attempting to fulfil the new role expectations. These included:

(i) Ambiguity in relationships with other class teachers, whose view of classroom autonomy clashed with the leadership role of the co-ordinator in whole-school development;

(ii) Conflicting priorities, mainly arising out of inadequate time and facilities for carrying out the coordination action role as well as more normal classroom teaching duties;

(iii) Uncertainty in performing the role of 'educationist', that is in articulating the reasons, justifications and 'theory' of a subject in workshop settings, or in representing the rationale of the subject and its relationship to colleagues, teachers in other schools, and to governors.

Rodger's (1983) study illustrated some of the problems encountered by coordinators not enjoying full support from the headteacher; Goodacre (1984) argued for the coordinators to undertake 'assertiveness training' if they were to fulfil the role adequately; and based on my research, I concluded that the tasks could be effectively carried out only by untypically talented and committed teachers, given the working conditions in most primary schools (Campbell, 1985).

Discussion: Teachers' Work and the Aims of Primary Schools

Acknowledgement of the Resource Needs

What has been experienced in the post-1978 period is a kind of galloping inflation in the coordinator's role. This inflation has been in five areas:

(a) an increase in the significance attached to the role of the curriculum coordinator for raising quality and standards in the curriculum;

(b) increased importance of subject specialization and subject expertise;

(c) increased complexity of the job of curriculum coordination in practice;

(d) increased potential for conflict and strain in the role in practice;

(e) increased importance of what was described earlier as interpersonal skills in implementing change.

Since the early 1980s, the government, HMI and others have begun to face the policy and resource implications of the new role, and to acknowledge some of the problems flowing from current working conditions. Two HMI surveys (DES, 1983; DES, 1985a) on 9–13 and 8–12 middle schools explicitly acknowledged the problem of teacher time as a major obstacle. The report on ILEA primary schools, *Improving Primary Schools* (ILEA, 1985), which recommended the dual role for virtually all teachers, irrespective of position on the salary scales, also recognized the need to improve staffing, probably by about 10 per cent, if the role were to become feasible. In principle moreover, the White Paper, *Better Schools* (DES, 1985b) accepted that primary school teachers 'had the strongest claim for additional time' free from teaching. Perhaps most important of all, the Select Committee (House of Commons, 1986) noted that at least 15,000 extra teachers were needed for coordination tasks, amongst other things, and reported that Sir Keith Joseph, when Secretary of State for Education, had confirmed this figure. Coming at what then seemed like the end of a long period of industrial unrest in the education service, recognition of the importance of resourcing coordination tasks appeared to promise a real chance of realizing the potential in the role, and of developing 'collegiality' in primary schools. Such promise was broken by Kenneth Baker's abrupt dismissal of the Select Committee proposals for resourcing, given in a Parliamentary Memorandum in December 1987.

Teachers' Working Conditions

There is also the impact of the Teachers' Pay and Conditions Act, 1987. From the point of view of curriculum coordination, the new conditions of service seemed supportive, for they made some in-school development possible, by incorporating it into the normal duties and responsibilities of teachers. The five 'Baker Days' per year, although initially perhaps conceived of in a rather mechanistic way, nonetheless provide a significant improvement in teachers' working conditions since they identify time free of teaching contractually assured, that could be used for the development of whole-school curriculum policies. Shortage of time, as the empirical studies revealed, was a major perceived obstacle to such development.

These changes are a start, but only a start. Other aspects of the working conditions of teachers still require attention, including especially the fabric of the buildings and the reprographic and other facilities available to them. And there are still two major problems: of curriculum expertise in the teaching force, especially expertise in science and technology; and of morale in the profession, as yet not recovered from the impact of industrial action and the destruction of its negotiating rights over pay and conditions.

It might be thought that the imposition of a National Curriculum, enforceable in law though the Education Reform Act 1988, and presaged in *The National Curriculum 5–16: A Consultation Document* (DES, 1987), had set all the development activities in schools at nought; that attainment targets, programmes of study and assessment arrangements, specified in considerable detail, would render the role of curriculum coordinators redundant. Even at an early stage in the establishment of the National Curriculum, this would be a dangerous misreading of the political context of primary school teachers' work in the late 1980s and early 1990s. On the contrary, the establishment of the National Curriculum is likely to make the role of curriculum coordinators even more significant.

This is because, first, the National Curriculum, defined in subject terms, will be specified as a *planning* model, not an *implementation* model. There is no intention to specify how the curriculum will be delivered in any particular school and no requirement in law that given proportions of time should be allocated to particular subjects. The organization and implementation of the curriculum will remain a key task for a school's staff. Moreover, it will be impossible, or at least unwise, for curriculum planning to be other than whole-school planning for consistency and continuity. The quality of curriculum leadership by coordinators will be at a premium in such planning. Most important in this respect will be the development of an overall direction to the work of the school, through an agreed statement of aims, perhaps expressed in subject terms.

Second, the skill that has been called external representation (Figure 8.1), i.e., 'representing the subject to outsiders', will become increasingly important. This is because the pressure to account to parents, governors and others for aspects of the curriculum in a school will take on heightened significance as it becomes a legal requirement. Curriculum coordinators will find themselves important contributors to annual meetings, and to governing bodies' meetings, as well as to less formal activities such as workshops for parents and colleagues in the relevant subject area.

In a consumerist climate of open enrolment and effective parental choice, the ability of coordinators to deliver accounts to the school's consumers (or at least to be successful public relations practitioners on the school's behalf) is likely to be a crucial factor in securing or maintaining the confidence of a school's community.

Third, there will be a substantial role for coordinators in helping a school's staff develop systematic approaches to classroom assessment (Burgess, 1987). Although much of the criticism of the proposed National Curriculum has concentrated on the aspect of national 'testing' at ages seven and 11, the Act itself is concerned with 'assessment arrangements'. These will include Standard Assessment Tasks (SATs) from a national bank, but most assessment for most of the primary school pupil's life will be subjective classroom-based assessment, if, as is probable, most of the TGAT proposals (DES, 1988a; 1988b) are accepted. Within an overall and convincingly delivered strategy for pupil assessment, the problems associated with 'testing', and particularly with the public reporting of assessment results, can be mitigated. Once again this will call for effective and informed leadership by curriculum coordinators, if primary schools are to be delivered from the fragmentary, casual and often negligent manner in which pupils' progress is currently assessed in the school curriculum.

None of this will be easy, but, as is often the case, pioneering schools with talented coordinators have led the way. They have revealed some of the potential, and many of the pitfalls of curriculum coordination, but coordinators now have greater opportunities for influencing schools. The National Curriculum will impose greater direction, and bring greater pressure, on primary schools to build upon what has been learned since 1978, rather than to abandon the achievements, admittedly patchily and haltingly created, of individual schools and coordinators. As Richards (1986) has commented, the intention of policies for coordinators in primary schools is to 'support not undermine' class teaching. Such support, which will help a school staff implement its agreed aims, is going to be increasingly needed as schools start to implement the National Curriculum.

References

BULLOCK REPORT (1974) *Committee of Enquiry into Reading and the Use of English: A Language for Life*. London, HMSO.

BURGESS, H. (1987) 'Springing free from formal assessment', *Education 3–13*, 13, 1, 22–27.

CAMPBELL, R.J. (1985) *Developing the Primary School Curriculum*. London, Holt Rinehart and Winston.

COCKCROFT REPORT (1982) *Committee of Enquiry into the Teaching of Mathematics in Schools: Mathematics Counts*. London, HMSO.

DES (1978) *Primary Education in England*. London, HMSO.

DES (1982) *Education 5–9*. London, HMSO.

DES (1983) *9–13 Middle Schools*. London, HMSO.

DES (1985a) *Education 8–12 in Combined and Middle Schools*. London, HMSO.

DES (1985b) *White Paper: Better Schools*. London, HMSO.

DES (1987) *The National Curriculum 5–16: A consultation document*. London, HMSO.

DES (1988a) *Report of the Task Group on Assessment and Testing*. London, DES.

DES (1988b) *Task Group on Assessment and Testing: Three Supplementary Reports*. London, DES.

DODDS, D. and ARMSTRONG, G. (1985) 'Developing a Junior Science Programme', *Education 3–13*, 13, 1, 17–21.

GOODACRE, E. (1984) 'Language Postholders and Assertiveness', *Education 3–13*, 12, 1, 17–21.

HERITAGE, M. (1985) 'Curriculum change: A school-based approach', *Education 3–13*, 13, 1, 22–25.

HOUSE OF COMMONS (1986) *Third Report of the Education Science and Arts Committee: Achievement in Primary Schools.* London, HMSO.

ILEA (1985) *Improving Primary Schools.* London, ILEA.

NUT (1979) *Middle Schools: Deemed or Doomed?* London, Hamilton House.

PRIMARY SCHOOLS RESEARCH AND DEVELOPMENT GROUP (1983) *Curriculum Responsibility and the Use of Teacher Expertise in the Primary School*, University of Birmingham.

RICHARDS, C. (1986) 'The curriculum from 5–16: Implications for primary school teachers', *Education 3–13*, 15, 1, 2–7.

RODGER, I. *et al.* (1983) *Teachers with Posts of Responsibility in Primary Schools.* University of Durham.

Chapter 9

Cross-Curricularity Through Five Basic Skills

Nigel Proctor

Introduction

In a book on the purposes and aims of primary education, some consideration of cross-curricularity is essential. The National Curriculum, as we have seen, comprises a number of separate subjects, but official statements require primary schools to develop a cross-curricular programme to ensure that subjects become part of an integrated 'whole curriculum' for all children. HM Inspectorate (1978) claim that this can best be achieved through a framework comprising Areas of Experience, an approach considered in Chapter 2. The subject coordinators, whose role was described by Jim Campbell in the last chapter, will have to ensure that the National Curriculum is not 'delivered' and assessed as discrete subject packages but is based on integrated, child-centred learning.

The DES guidelines to the National Curriculum (DES, 1989, para 3.8) are quite clear on this principle and state:

> The foundation subjects are certainly *not* a complete curriculum; they are necessary but not sufficient to ensure a curriculum which meets the purposes and covers the elements identified by HMI and others. In particular they will cover fully the acquisition of certain key cross-curricular competences: literacy, numeracy and information technology skills. More will, however, be needed to secure the kind of curriculum required by Section 1 of the Education Reform Act.

Examples of additional requirements are then listed, including careers education, health education, personal and social education, gender and multi-cultural education, environmental education, economic awareness, political and international understanding.

In this chapter, however, we will focus attention on 'certain key cross-curricular competences', in other words, ensuring the acquisition and development by all children of what is popularly described as 'the basics'. The Primary Survey (HMI, 1978, paras 8.16–8.23) referred to the basics as teaching children to read, write and learn mathematics. This emphasis on the three Rs has persisted since Robert Lowe's Revised Code of 1862 introduced 'payment by the results' of children reaching the required 'standards' in reading, writing and arithmetic. We know that mathematics and language today take up two-thirds of the teaching time in primary schools and that these lessons occur mostly in the mornings when children are popularly supposed to be at their most receptive. Teachers recognize their importance; when 1500 teachers were asked by Ashton (1975) to rate seventy-two aims of primary education, reading, oracy, mathematics and writing were pre-eminent (see Chapter 4). This recognition of their importance is reflected in the care taken in planning programmes; the Primary Survey, for instance, showed that 85 per cent of schools had well-structured schemes of work for language and mathematics.

The purpose of this chapter is to suggest that there are other, equally important, 'basics' in primary education and that these together represent a framework for cross-curricular work. But, before demonstrating this, we need to analyze briefly what exactly is meant by the term 'basics'. There are four points we should consider. First, 'the basics' refer not to subjects but to skills. Indeed we usually use the word 'basic' as an adjective, as I have done in the title of this chapter. There is abundant evidence that the learning of these basic skills represents important aims for all primary schools. HMI (1977) have stated that 'No-one disputes the irrefutable case for basic skills and techniques', while the Schools Council's *The Practical Curriculum* (1981) argued that 'knowledge without skill has a long, sad history. We believe schools need to make a conscious effort to ensure that their pupils acquire skills, many of which may prove to have a life-long value. A handful of fundamental skills form the highway to education.'

Second, however, the word 'basic' implies much more than 'fundamental', in the limited sense of 'important'. The inference is surely that 'basics' represent the *basis* of all other work and that, without some grasp of these skills, further knowledge or learning would be difficult. Gagné (1970) has suggested that 'the subjects of school instruction possess hierarchical organisations with respect to required types of learning. Each can be analyzed to reveal pre-requisite learnings. The implications [of this] for the design of instruction are quite clear. If learning at any level is to occur with greatest facility, care and attention must be paid to the pre-requisites of such learning.'

Third, the 'pre-requisite learnings' of the basics are used in teaching all the subjects of the curriculum. They represent skills to be used 'across the curriculum' as advocated in the Bullock and Cockcroft Reports (1975b;

1981) and in subsequent curriculum statements. It will be remembered that the Primary Survey stated that 'the effective application of skills, including their use in practical activities, is important. The teaching of skills in isolation, whether in language or in mathematics, does not produce the best results.'

Fourth, the only common element of the three Rs is that they represent different ways of communicating information. But they cover only two forms of communication. Reading and writing are elements of the same skill, that of literacy, while arithmetic refers to the skill of numeracy. To widen the curriculum we could merely extend 'the basics' to include the other means by which we communicate with one another. Fortunately much of the scientific evidence on which we can build this study has already been assembled, and this possibility is now considered.

Identifying Basic Communication Skills

A television series considered by many to be supreme among documentaries was *Life on Earth* in which David Attenborough (1979) narrated the complex story of evolution. In this series he devoted only one programme to Mankind. This he entitled simply 'The Compulsive Communicators' since 'Man's passion to communicate and to receive communication seems as central to his success as a species as the fin was to the fish or the feather to the birds.' In our uniquely successful evolution, humans have developed five forms of communication and Attenborough visited remote tribes to identify the probable order in which these evolved. Apparently gestures and expression, what is now commonly termed 'body language', must have been pre-eminent in early communication, for there is evidence through fossilized bones that our ancestors' ability to use their voices, which developed into spoken language, was clumsy. Yet today we speak 600 million words in our individual lives! Attenborough went on to argue that 'our complex spoken language seems less special the more we learn about the communications used by chimpanzees and dolphins. But we are the only creatures to have painted representational pictures, and it is this talent which led to developments which ultimately transformed the life of mankind.' This form of communication includes cave paintings some 30,000 years old and apparent map-making and map-reading skills which allowed the construction of architectural megalithic masterpieces in Britain and of pyramids in Egypt; such graphic communication has been termed 'graphicacy' (Balchin and Coleman, 1965). Finally, Attenborough showed the earliest known piece of writing, on a small clay tablet discovered at Uruk in Syria, near the original delta of the Tigris and Euphrates Rivers; it appears to be a record of rations of food and as such suggests the acquisition of skills of literacy and numeracy.

Since then, civilizations such as Babylonians, Mayans and Indians have separately built their own number systems as a written language with similar conventions, using a sequence of digits.

There are, then, only five forms of commuication, all of which are 'languages': literacy (written language), oracy (spoken language), numeracy (number language), graphicacy (graphic language using maps and pictures) and physiognomacy (body language). All these 'languages' have 'productive' and 'receptive' elements, for communication is always between two or more people, one the source, the other the receiver. Figure 9.1 shows this in schematic form.

Figure 9.1   Forms of Communication

Mode of communication	Form of language	Productive element	Receptive element
Literacy	Written language	Writing	Reading
Oracy	Spoken language	Speaking	Listening
Numeracy	Number language	Number manipulation and calculation	Number appreciation
Graphicacy	Graphic language	Sketching and map-making	Map- and picture-reading
Physiognomacy	Body and sign landscape	Movement, dance and expression	Watching and interpreting

The terms for two of the five modes of communication are continually used. 'Literacy' was defined by the Ministry of Education (1959) as the ability to 'read and write for the practical purposes of daily life' thus emphasizing its role as a means of communication. The term 'numeracy' was coined by the Crowther Committee (CACE, 1959) as 'a word to represent the mirror image of literacy' and comprises a practical basis of mathematics which the Assessment of Performance Unit (1980) has described as 'a unique and powerful form of communication.'

'Oracy' is a term used by a team from Birmingham University which began a research programme into speaking and listening in 1965 (Wilkinson, 1974). HMI (1982) state that 'the primacy of the spoken word in human intercourse cannot be too strongly emphasised. Important though the written word is, most communication takes place in speech; and those who do not listen with attention and cannot speak with clarity, articulateness and confidence are at a disadvantage in almost every aspect of their personal, social and working lives.'

Balchin and Coleman (1965) introduced the term 'graphicacy' to define 'the communication of spatial information that cannot be conveyed adequately by verbal or numerical means.' Balchin later described (1979) the academic content of graphicacy, but in school it involves appreciation of, and skills in working with, maps, pictures, diagrams and graphs. The new term 'physiognomacy' (Proctor, 1984a) is derived from 'physiognomy' (defined as the art of judging character from features of face or form of body) but encompasses physical activities. In addition to body language, represented in dance and mime, it includes dexterity and manipulative skills.

Languages as 'Basics' in Child Development

There is no doubt that the five forms of communication are fundamental to all learning; they represent skills which underpin all education in that they allow the transmission of thoughts, facts, concepts, feelings, judgements and instructions. Without these skills a person is disadvantaged practically, emotionally and academically. Communication skills are at the very core of education, as Brook–Smith *et al.* (1976) acknowledged, 'Teaching and learning are mainly language games in which the stakes are high — a true education.' Barnes (1976: 20) expressed a similar view: 'Learning to communicate is at the heart of education.'

Much of the work on language acquisition has, of course, been done by educational psychologists, but they have rarely been consulted about curriculum planning, despite the fact that 'curriculum design is a difficult task, requiring a profound knowledge of psychological principles apart from content knowledge' (Child, 1981: 369). Taylor (1967) deplored the absence of books dealing with 'thinking about the curriculum', arguing that books on the curriculum had their starting point in purely practical considerations, in other words, 'statements of good intentions and gospels of personal practice.' The absence of books or articles on psychological aspects of curriculum design today can be confirmed by referring to the British *Education Index*, which classifies 'curriculum' under such headings as 'development of', but omits reference to psychology. This lack of applicability and relevance of psychology to the school curriculum became an issue for discussion by the Education Section of the British Psychological Society at the 1983 Conference in Glasgow (Proctor, 1985b).

Until recently, the findings of educational psychologists have been too complicated for use in designing a curriculum framework; Guilford's (1967) 'structure of intellect theory', for instance, indicated that there are at least 120 separate kinds of intellectual ability, of which everyone is likely to have at least one developed to a fairly high level. But all that has changed with a recent book by Gardner (1984), an eminent American psychologist, which has received wide acclaim, including support from Jerome Bruner. In his book, *Frames of Mind: The Theory of Multiple Intelligences*, Gardner argues that there are only five 'intelligences' which need to influence curriculum planning. In addition to the obvious verbal and logico-mathematical intelligences, he includes a musical intelligence, a spatial intelligence and a bodily-kinesthetic intelligence, the last of which is well developed in dancers and gymnasts. These 'intelligences' are similar to the five basic 'languages', apart from the 'musical intelligence', which, as a means of communication in the form of a musical score, may be thought of as part of literacy, while the making of music, and the appreciation of it, may be thought of as an aspect of oracy. Spatial intelligence, which Gardner shows is well developed in, for instance, Eskimos and artists, is very closely linked to graphicacy (Proctor, 1984b).

Gardner's main finding of value to curriculum planners is, however, his condemnation of school practice in which the verbal and mathematical intelligences are over-emphasized, thereby handicapping the full development of children. Isaac Asimov, reviewing the American edition of the book, considered that Gardner's framework opened a door onto a new way of looking at individuals and that, where implemented in schools, it would enable children to acquire and develop a wider range of skills and abilities. Certainly, in Britain, there is strong evidence (Lorac and Weiss, 1981: 173) that preference is given to children with high levels of ability in numeracy and literacy, and that, where children are alienated from these two areas, they find it difficult to display their intelligence and creativity.

Gardner's classification, and indeed the curriculum framework comprising the five languages, is particularly applicable for children with special needs, for whom 'planning the curriculum with special relation to basic skills is particularly relevant . . . because the pupils so often have to be taught in school skills which other children acquire naturally in the family situation' (Wilson, 1981: 15). The Warnock Committee's report on special education (DES, 1978: paras 11–13) stated that the development of language was 'the major requirement of the curriculum' and this was confirmed in another report on multi-handicapped children needing special care (Bromley Teachers, 1983: 69). A fairly narrow definition of 'language' was probably intended, but I would argue that the five-language framework would be more useful, for it resembles the five curriculum areas listed in the pioneering work on special needs by Tansley and Gulliford (1980): oral and written language, number, creative and practical work and physical education. When one considers the range of specific difficulties or disabilities, including children with physical handicap, hearing- and sight-impairment, dyslexia or autism, one cannot but recognize that virtually all special needs *are* communication needs. The focus of curriculum planning for special needs must therefore be on enabling children to acquire or improve the specific 'language' skills they lack and to develop those in which they are more proficient (Proctor, 1987a). Acquisition of 'the basics' is clearly essential for all children.

The Five Languages and the Expressive Arts

Although emphasis has so far been placed on language skills as 'basics', it should be remembered that they continue to provide a challenge for the most gifted of children. Indeed, the great achievement of the so-called 'masters' is that they developed their skills to an extraordinary level; they could 'express' themselves supremely in a 'language', whether through writing, oratory, painting or movement and dance. Genius is not only about knowledge, ideas and imagination in one area. It is also about the ability or skill to communicate these to others. Many geniuses, such as Einstein, master only one language. Others, such as Leonardo da Vinci, have transcended normal boundaries, but the all-round genius has perhaps never emerged.

Communication skills are clearly not just 'basics'. By definition, the so-called *expressive* arts must emphasize communication (Proctor, 1985a). Any dictionary will list, under 'expression', communicative qualities, wording or phrase in literature, intonation of voice, symbols together expressing algebraical quality, mode of expressing character in painting and aspects of facial expression or physical performance expressing feeling. These are, in essence, our five languages. But the languages also represent the constituent parts of all aesthetic education: literature (literacy), drama and music (oracy), visual arts (graphicacy) and dance (physiognomacy). This focus on communication in the arts is not new. John Dewey in *Art and Experience* (1934) stated:

> Works of art are the only media of complete and uninhibited communication between man and man that can occur in a world full of gulfs and walls that limit community of experience. Because objects of art are expressive they are a language. Rather they are many languages. For each art has its own medium and that medium is especially fitted for one kind of communication. Each medium says something that cannot be uttered as well and as completely in any other language.

The only form of communication not to have a 'popular' aesthetic or expressive quality is numeracy, yet Pythagoras argued that 'nature is commanded by numbers. There is a harmony in nature, a unity in her variety, and it has a language; numbers are the language of nature.' Bronowski (1973) maintained that mathematics, reasoning with numbers, had become the most elaborated and sophisticated of the sciences, with much aesthetic appeal.

The great advantage of using the five languages as a framework for the primary school curriculum is that it focuses attention on all the expressive arts, and also on both productive (performing) and receptive (appreciative) elements. Certainly our skills change over the years; for instance, our performance in dance and movement will deteriorate, while our skills in interpretation and appreciation will tend to improve. In primary schools, children whose productive or creative skills in all five languages are limited should be encouraged to develop them, while at the same time, their receptive or appreciative responses must be considered. Examples of some of these skills are included in Figure 9.2 which also includes more utilitarian aspects of the five languages, to which we now turn our attention.

The Five Languages and the World of Work

Some primary school teachers may question why space is provided for a brief discussion of a curriculum for the world of work when their pupils are at least six years away from the time they seek employment. Certainly the main responsibility for vocational preparation lies with secondary schools. However, it must be remembered that the only aim stated in the consultative book *The National Curriculum* (DES, 1987), and this is left to the annex, is that the curriculum should 'equip every pupil with the knowledge, skills, understanding and aptitudes to meet the responsibilities of adult life and employment,' though this aim was fortunately changed in the Education Reform Act to a curriculum which 'prepares pupils for the opportunities, responsibilities and experiences of adult life.'

It follows then that even primary schools are expected to consider how their curricula meet this aim, but any thought of restricting the work to specific, narrow technical skills must be rejected. Even in vocational preparation courses the DES specialists argue that a much broader programme is essential: 'This is important at present when high unemployment and technical changes mean many young people face a working life in which they may have to make several changes of employment' (FEU, 1982).

A recent survey of the requirements for employment suggested by industrialists, the CBI, trade unions, HMI and the DES (Proctor, 1987b) stressed the importance attached to basic skills in communication, and this was mirrored in the syllabi of vocational examinations. The five languages represent a cross-curricular framework for the development of these skills, some of which are included in Figure 9.2. Many of the skills can be enhanced through work on the computer and it should be remembered that the DES guidelines *From Policy to Practice* (1989) state that 'In particular [the curriculum] will cover fully the acquisition of certain key cross-curricular competences, literacy, numeracy and information technology skills.' The inter-linking of these three is not accidental; I would argue that learning the 'basics' may now be difficult to achieve without their application on the computer. I should also add that the use of terms like 'computer literacy' and 'computer

Figure 9.2 Some Communication Skills for Work and Leisure

	Basic language skills for work (utilitarian focus)		Extended language skills for leisure (aesthetic focus)	
	Productive	Receptive	Productive	Receptive
	An ability to:	An understanding of:	A proficiency in:	An appreciation of:
Literacy	write a report of an accident	instructions in a work manual	writing in prose or verse	some great literary works
Oracy	formulate questions and requests for a specific purpose	relevant points from telephone messages	debating or singing	skills of musicians and composers
Numeracy	complete tax returns	wage slips and bank statements	computing	the 'language of nature'
Graphicacy	design a replacement part	a street map to deliver goods	painting, sketching or designing	'masterpieces' in art and design
Physiognomacy	type a message	hand signals	sports and dance	choreography and ballet performance

language' does not invalidate the five-fold 'language' classification since work on the computer involves 'traditional' languages — words, numbers, graphics and, of course, dexterity skills — and work in each of these areas needs to include their application on the computer.

The Five Languages Across the Curriculum

The main advantage of the five-language framework is that it builds on skills to be developed across the curriculum, rather than within any one subject. It will be remembered that the Bullock Report (DES, 1975b) advocated a 'language (literacy and oracy) across the curriculum' policy by which work in *all* subjects should develop children's language, and the Cockcroft Report (DES, 1981) recommended a similar approach to numeracy. I have argued elsewhere (Proctor, 1987c) that the recommendations have not always been implemented because too much work and responsibility were expected of only two coordinators. If the two other languages, graphicacy and physiognomacy, were added it would spread the workload and involve all the staff in decision-making. Instead of requiring ten consultants for each of the National Curriculum subjects, which is an improbability given the small size of most primary schools, the scheme should require only five coordinators, perhaps drawn from teachers qualified or interested in English or history (literacy), music or religious education (oracy), mathematics or science (numeracy), art or geography (graphicacy) and physical education or drama (physiognomacy).

Inclusion of physical education is important, for it is one of the foundation subjects of the National Curriculum; additionally one of only two aims of schools identified in the Education Reform Act included 'the promotion of the physical development of pupils at the school.' In primary schools, physical education is commonly taught as 'movement' and the productive and receptive elements of this activity have been identified in another curriculum paper (Scottish Education Department, 1972):

> The language of movement is learned as verbal language . . . As with verbal language, non-verbal language has a receptive as well as an expressive side; it includes not only the ability to express and to communicate ideas and feelings but also the ability to identify and recognize the significance of the behaviour of other people or of changes in the environment and the ability to transform experience into symbols and use these in thinking. The quality of life is diminished when potentials for the language of movement are unrealized.

Another curriculum paper on *Movement* (DES, 1972) advocated integration, suggesting that there might be special value 'in combining subjects such as literature, drama, music and science that have a natural link with some aspects of physical education.' However, the fundamental problem here is trying to integrate a subject which is essentially concerned with acquisition and development of physical skills with subjects which emphasize intellectual skills and knowledge. It may be more appropriate and realistic to recognize movement as a communication skill which can be integrated with the four other languages.

Graphicacy can also be integrated with other languages, as is demonstrated in Figure 9.3. But separate skills within graphicacy itself can be developed, such as inter-relating a map, sketch and aerial photograph of the same locality (perhaps the primary school and its immediate environs).

Figure 9.3   Integrating Other 'Languages' with Graphicacy

Language	Productive graphicate skill	Other productive skill derived from graphicate understanding
Literacy	draw a sketch from a descriptive text	write an essay about a picture
Oracy	draw a map from telephoned route description	describe orally what a painting illustrates
Numeracy	draw population density map from statistics	convert graphs to statistics
Physiognomacy	draw a sketch of football action	dance routine using the choreographer's 'map'

It is perhaps easiest to demonstrate this approach to integration by using a sketch, such as Figure 9.4, of what is a frequently taught topic in primary school. This might illustrate just how powerful a form of communication any visual material can be. For instance, using this sketch, children would quickly discover the details of the physical environment of the Amazon Basin, including the vast extent of relatively flat, low-lying land, the forest, the river and the wet climate, and could also ascertain the sources of food and the uses of timber. But the sketch can also develop conceptual understanding of traditional Amazon Indian life, based upon a communal existence, self-sufficiency using subsistence crops, and shifting cultivation. More important, children's values and attitudes might change from a consideration of the Indians as 'primitive' people to a recognition of their skills in living in total harmony with their environment. Empathy could also be developed by asking them how *they* would feel if a highway were to be built by 'aliens' through *their* homes, or if the burning of the forest added to the 'greenhouse effect' of the atmosphere thereby affecting the quality of their own lives. Apart

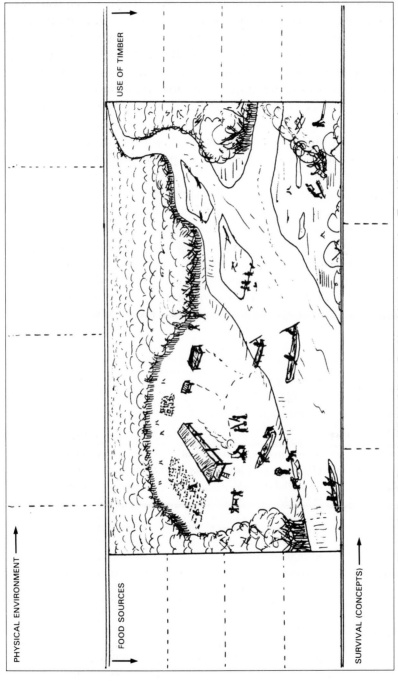

Figure 9.4 A Sketch Which Might Be Used in an Integrative Teaching Approach

from its value in communicating information and helping to develop values and attitudes, the sketch may also illustrate how the five 'language' skills are interrelated and even interdependent. One exercise for primary school teachers, used on initial and in-service courses, is to assemble checklists of classroom activities, derived from the picture, under the five headings of the communication skills. Normally twenty–five to forty activities are collected, always including imaginative writing under the heading literacy, role-play under oracy, 'tribal dance' under physiognomacy and drawing a map from the sketch under graphicacy. Similar checklists could be drawn up from virtually any other graphic material, whether this is presented as aerial photographs, paintings, graphs or maps; the possibilities are endless (Proctor, 1985c).

The five-language framework could influence many of the other ways we teach in classrooms, for it focuses attention on children acquiring skills in the two elements of communication, productive or performing and receptive or appreciative, and on teachers planning programmes of work accordingly. Teachers could also use the framework to organize their own professional work, not only planning work to develop their children's skills, but also developing their own competence and mastery of the skills and techniques they use in everyday teaching (see Figure 9.5).

Figure 9.5   Some Professional Applications of Communication Skills

	Planning skills An appreciation of:	Practical skills A proficiency in:
Literacy	children's reading and writing difficulties; schemes of reading and reading tests; children's literature	writing on blackboards; selecting reading books (readability); marking children's work
Oracy	language acquisition and potential in children; pupil discussion; oral testing	questioning; story-telling; using records and tape recorders
Numeracy	children's difficulties with numeracy; children's mathematical growth; tests of numeracy	analyzing (statistically) pupil performance; using calculators; using computers
Graphicacy	children's spatial difficulties; children's preference for visual material; spatial tests	using projectors (film and slide); using camera, banda, television; using pictures and maps.
Physiognomacy	children's physical development; problems of physically handicapped; physical/dexterity tests	organizing children's play; organizing games and activities; developing children's skills in movement and dance

Source: Proctor, 1984c

The Five Languages: Assessment and Profiling

Good primary schools have always ensured that assessment is an integral part of the curriculum, and many teachers would agree with the Task Group on Assessment and Testing (1988) that 'assessment is at the heart of the process of promoting children's learning.' Moreover, they will go along with the introduction of an assessment system which does not focus on obtaining external qualifications or provides a basis for selection.

Primary school teachers, however, may well be concerned that the assessment system of the National Curriculum is to be based on the foundation subjects, for they will be aware of the dangers of abandoning some existing good practice in order to teach subject knowledge which they may feel needs to be covered for assessment purposes. The guidance from the DES (1989) on assessment targets and programmes of study contains some reassurance, for it concludes by stating: 'It must always be borne in mind that at all stages attainment targets have to be placed within a whole curriculum context and one in which regard is paid to ways in which cross-curricular issues are handled.'

Some teachers may also be concerned about displaying their own lack of subject knowledge when it comes to the whole process of moderation across a range of schools. It would be better if this exercise focused on children's developing skills, across all the foundation subjects; teachers would then be able to discuss and compare children's skills in, for instance, reading and writing, talking and listening about a project they had done and which might also include numeracy and skills in drawing and presenting ideas graphically. Children's developing physical performance can also be discussed. When it comes to recording for reporting, it should be remembered that attainment targets for each subject will be grouped into a small number of profile components. English, for instance, will have only three profile components: reading, writing, and speaking and listening. The guidelines seem to enhance the role of the basic languages.

Much of the preparatory work on assessment was done in the lead–up to the Great Debate. For instance, in the year following the formation of the Assessment of Performance Unit (APU) its Staff Inspector Director, Brian Kay (1975) wrote a paper on 'Monitoring Pupils' Performance'. In this, he suggested that the curriculum should be seen not in terms of subjects but in terms of skills and knowledge; he went on to argue that, in order to monitor pupil performance across the curriculum, six 'kinds of development' were possible. These were in:

  (i) verbal — reading, writing, listening and speaking,
 (ii) mathematical — 'communication through number',
(iii) scientific,

(iv) ethical — later modified to 'social and personal',

(v) aesthetic — including an appreciation of form, colour, texture,

(vi) physical — the pupil's developing muscular control and his ability to use his body efficiently and expressively. This progressed from dexterity in using a pencil to 'movement and dance in communication'.

These 'kinds of development' include most of the five forms of communication; language, literacy, oracy and numeracy were the first to be monitored by the APU and discussion documents were later published on 'Physical Development' and 'Understanding Design and Technology.'

Children's skills in the five languages may be included in the forthcoming standardized pupil profile or record of achievement. At the time of writing, a common format for recording and reporting the most essential information is being considered (DES, 1989) and this is likely to be influenced by the numerous pilot schemes and projects in secondary schools. The policy document (DES, 1984) states that the record and achievement processes in the secondary school should begin with a summary of achievement in the primary school, and there is an intention to extend primary school record-keeping in a way that would provide more complete information about pupils at the point of transfer.

The DES evaluation report (Broadfoot *et al*, 1988) considered the many attempts to assess and record cross-curricular skills used by schools, with such a wide variation in content and interpretation that collection of assessments even for nominally the same skills was impossible; 'It seems fair to conclude that no project has yet devised a wholly satisfactory scheme for the assessment of cross-curricular skills.'

Some of the earliest examples of records of achievement were, of course, from the FEU and were adopted by the Youth Training Scheme (YTS) reporting procedures (Proctor, 1987b); in all of these 'communication skills' represented a major component. The development of children's skills in each of the five 'languages' could represent an essential element in assessment, monitoring and profiling in the primary school.

Conclusion

My design for a whole-school curriculum framework built around the five languages was conceived before the announcement of a National Curriculum based upon subjects. The new regulations could have meant ossification of the curriculum. However, with the appearance of more detailed guidance from the DES on implementing the National Curriculum I am convinced that the development of the skills children use to study the various subjects will remain of paramount importance in primary schools.

Moreover, the cross curricular framework of oracy, literacy, numeracy and graphicacy has been adopted by the NCC in Circular Number 6: *The National Curriculum and Whole Curriculum Planning*, October 1989.

I am not suggesting that the five-language framework represents a panacea for all the problems of the primary school curriculum. Schwab (1969) recognized the difficulties involved, 'What is fatally theoretic is the dispatch, the sweeping appearance of success, the vast simplicity which grounds the purported solution to the problems of the curriculum.' What I am saying is that I believe that the framework could help teachers, in a practical way, to ensure that they continue to emphasize, in their teaching and assessment programme, the development of children's skills, at a time when too much emphasis could be placed on extending children's subject knowledge. It could also influence pedagogy, since the framework focuses attention on the two quite separate elements of communication — productive or performing and receptive or appreciative — which need to be balanced in any school day if children are to be given a fair chance to develop a range of skills necessary for their future lives. This must remain a fundamental aim of primary education, arguably best achieved through a 'five languages' curriculum framework.

References

ASHTON, P. (1975) *Aims of Primary Education*. Research Studies Series London, Schools Council.

ASSESSMENT OF PERFORMANCE UNIT (1980) *Mathematics: A Monitoring Pamphlet*. London, DES.

ATTENBOROUGH, D. (1979) *Life on Earth*. London, BBC/Collins.

BALCHIN, W.G.V. (1979) quoted in Barrett, M. *Art Education: A Strategy for Course Design*. London, Heinemann.

BALCHIN, W.G.V. and COLEMAN, A.M. (1965) 'Graphicacy should be the fourth ace in the pack' *The Times Educational Supplement*, 5 November.

BARNES, D. (1976) *From Communication to Curriculum*. London, Penguin.

BROADFOOT, P. *et al.* (1988) *Records of Achievement*: A report to the DES by the Pilot Records of Achievement in Schools Evaluation (PRAISE) Team.

BROMLEY TEACHERS (at Rectory Paddock School) (1983) *In Search of a Curriculum: Notes on the Education of M.H. children*. Sidcup, Robin Wren Publications.

BRONOWSKI, J. (1973) *The Ascent of Man*. London, BBC.

BROOK-SMITH, E. *et al.* (1976) *Learning and Thinking in the Elementary School*. Eastbourne, Holt, Rinehart and Winston.

CENTRAL ADVISORY COUNCIL FOR EDUCATION (CACE) (1959) *15 to 18: The Crowther Report*. London, HMSO.

CHILD, D. (1981) *Psychology and the Teacher*. Eastbourne, Holt, Rinehart and Winston.

DES (1972) *Movement: Physical Education in the Primary Years*. London, HMSO.

DES (1975a) *Special Education Needs: The Warnock Report*. London, HMSO.

DES (1975b) *A Language for Life: The Bullock Report*. London, HMSO.

DES (1981) *Mathematics Counts: The Cockcroft Report*. London, HMSO.

DES (1984) *Records of Achievement: A Statement of Policy*. London, DES.

DES (1987) *The National Curriculum 5–16: A Consultation Document*. London, DES.

DES (1989) *National Curriculum: From Policy to Practice*. London, DES.

DEWEY, J. (1934) reprint 1980. *Art and Experience*. Pedigree Books.

FURTHER EDUCATION UNIT (1982) *Basic Skills*. London, DES.

GAGNÉ, R.M. (1970) *The Conditions of Learning*. Eastbourne, Holt, Rinehart and Winston.

GARDNER, H. (1984) *Frames of Mind: The Theory of Multiple Intelligences*. London, Heinemann.

GUILFORD, J.P. (1967) *The Nature of Human Intelligence*. London, McGraw-Hill.

HMI (1977) *Curriculum 11–16: The Red Book*. London, HMSO.

HMI (1978) *Primary Education in England: The Primary Survey*. London, HMSO.

HMI (1982) *Bullock Revisited: A Discussion Paper*. London, DES.

KAY, B. (1975) 'Monitoring pupils' performance', *Trends in Education*, 2, 11–18.

LORAC, C. and WEISS, M. (1981) *Communication and Social Skills*, Schools Council Project Report, London, Wheaton.

MINISTRY OF EDUCATION (1959) *Reading Ability*. London, HMSO.

PROCTOR, N. (1984a) 'Physical Education in the revised school curriculum', *PE Review*, 7, 2, 106–112.

PROCTOR, N. (1984b) 'Art as graphicacy in the common curriculum', *Journal of Art and Design Education*, 2, 203–214.

PROCTOR, N. (1984c) 'Professional Studies and the QTS review', *Journal of Education for Teaching*, 10, 1, 61–72.

PROCTOR, N. (1985a) 'From basics to aesthetics in the curriculum', *British Journal of Aesthetics*, 25, 1, 57–65.

PROCTOR, N. (1985b) 'Educational psychology and curriculum design: a child-centred approach', *Educational Studies*, 11, 2, 151–158.

PROCTOR, N. (1985c) 'Redefining the basics of primary education', *Education 3–13*, 13, 5–8.

PROCTOR, N. (1987a) 'Writing a special needs curriculum statement', *Education Today*, 37, 2, 10–17.

PROCTOR, N. (1987b) 'Towards a vocational curriculum', *Educational Studies*, 13, 2, 149–159.

PROCTOR, N. (1987c) 'Bullock refreshed: The five languages of life', *Reading*, 21, 2, 80–91.

SCHOOLS COUNCIL (1981) *The Practical Curriculum*. London, Schools Council.

SCHWAB, J.J. (1969) 'The practical: a language for curriculum', *School Review*, 7–8 November.

SCOTTISH EDUCATION DEPARTMENT (1972) *Physical Education in Secondary Schools, Curriculum Paper 12*, London, HMSO.

TANSLEY, A.E. and GULLIFORD, R. (1980) *The Education of Slow-learning Children*. London, Routledge and Kegan Paul.

TASK GROUP ON ASSESSMENT AND TESTING (1988) *Report*, London, DES.

TAYLOR, P.H. (1967) 'Purpose and Structure in the Curriculum', reprinted in Child, D. (Ed) (1977), *Readings in Psychology for the Teacher*, Eastbourne, Holt, Rinehart and Winston.

WILKINSON, A. *et al.* (1974) *The Quality of Listening*, Schools Council Oracy Project, London, Macmillan.

WILSON, M.D. (1981) *The Curriculum in Special Schools: Schools Council Programme 4: Individual Pupils*. London, Schools Council.

Chapter 10

Putting 'Whole School' Aims into Practice

Norma Newell and Gordon Wood

Introduction

Primary schools are currently undergoing rapid change. The idealism and aspirations of the late sixties and early seventies seem to have been replaced by uncertainty about the future. Teachers' sanctions, imposition of directed time, detailed job profiles, pressure from certain quarters to put the clock back in educational philosophies have made schools into a battleground of conflicting ideologies and interests. With the introduction of the National Curriculum and the associated monitoring and assessment procedures, further change is inevitable and inescapable. How will schools react? Will they become helpless slaves to the chain of events or assume control and be responsible for their own destinies?

We present the view that, with imaginative and yet realistic plannning, a school can remain firmly in control, providing that those within share a view of the future that anticipates and accepts change with positive insight and action. We further suggest that, when a school has developed and continues to nurture successful mechanisms for agreeing aims which permeate the very fabric of school life, then that school has an inbuilt capacity to face change with confidence and optimism.

The emphasis placed upon establishing clear and reliable communication channels and negotiation opportunities has been fundamental to developing a common philosophy amongst individual teachers at Acklam Whin Primary School, Middlesbrough. The school evolved extensive consultative procedures whereby staff at all levels participate in policy and decision-making processes. The four rate 'B' postholders and the deputy-headteacher have acted as team leaders for the year and form a senior management team which meets regularly with the headteacher to discuss curricular and administrative matters affecting the school. In addition, the staff as a whole is divided into a variety of curriculum working parties which meet periodically as the need arises. Underpinning the whole communication network is one very basic premise, that the staff that is given responsibility, made to feel valued, and encouraged to make personal contributions will feel that it controls the philosophy of the school. Only out of shared 'ownership' of the school's ethos can clear and acceptable curricular aims and objectives develop and be achieved.

What follows is a short case study of the school's development over recent years seen through the eyes of the present headteacher. It traces the development of the school as it labours to sort out and to implement its aims in response to the events and statutory requirements since the headteacher's appointment in January 1982.

Initial Considerations

There are times and situations when an experienced practitioner walks into a school and it is evident that the time for change is imminent. This statement is not to suggest stagnation or to imply any previous mismanagement. In the case of this school, the complete reverse was true. The school had a high reputation for innovation and good practice, but an unusual approach to child-grouping by colour, and core curriculum ability was found to be time-consuming and disruptive.

Guidelines prepared by the headteacher and staff groups to cover all curricular and social responsibilities of the school were readily available but dated and in need of revision. An articulate staff owned the literature but suggested that updating and some re-organization were desirable.

At the first staff meeting attended by the new headteacher in January 1982, an appraisal of this situation and suggestions for development were expressed. Even through the natural reserve of such an occasion there was an audible sigh of relief and an immediately supportive response. This positive reaction to the appraisal resulted in the establishment of a weekly staff communication file for all events and administrative essentials; it abolished disruptive acknowledgment of the headteacher's arrival in classrooms, sought to identify the teacher's image, commitment and essential contribution within realistic resources and requirements. The proposals formulated staff responsibilities and expectations in a cooperative, delegative climate embracing the whole staff from probationer to headteacher, and showed a determination to provide a productive and healthy teaching and learning environment throughout the school. It established the total staff meeting as an in-service, organizational, policy-making forum. Within this context, the essential authority of the headteacher was respected but the contribution of every member was heard, valued and acted upon.

The demands of the Department of Education Circular 6/81 had been met locally through a county initiative. Over 300 teachers, advisers and administrators had met over eighteen months to compile phase and subject guidelines. They covered every aspect of curricular and organizational need and had been distributed throughout the county with the requirement that all schools reviewed their own curriculum. They were then presented with examples and justifications to their governing and parent bodies. (One should recall that this was still only 1982.)

To the new headteacher this was a heaven-sent directive but an unnecessary one because a very professional and committed attitude had already been adopted by the staff. The county guidelines were read and accepted for their real intent. They were in turn translated into those needed by the school at that time and within the resources available.

Subject working parties for mathematics, language and environmental sciences were formed on a qualification, responsibility, interest in and enthusiasm for basis. They purposely included teachers of children through-out the primary years and of all responsibility levels. Their task was to look at the literature, consider the recently available materials and draw up suggestions of content and process to meet the educational needs of individual children in our school. It took a considerable time and there were many skirmishes before the guidelines were resolved; the cost implications were notable and change was extensive. The process of involvement had brought ownership, identification, unity and a product which could be transformed into practical activity and a sound teaching and learning environment for our teachers and children alike.

It would have been a serious mistake to be complacent about this, but the very nature of the school would not allow that to happen. After the first term both deputies had moved on to local headships. Several other colleagues followed them on promotion and into other schools during the year. To date and for the same reasons, there has been a constant procession of new faces at the beginning of most terms. They have brought new ideas, skills, attitudes and approaches to enliven and update our practice. These departures could have ruptured continuity and development but the school climate does seem to have provided an environment which has enabled newcomers to find their feet and make their contribution immediately.

There have been several structural adjustments and industrial disputes which could also have disrupted progression. Staff involvement and commitment have swept those aside or simply ignored them in the interests of children. It would be unrealistic to deny periods of limited success and progress but equally wrong not to identify memorable occasions and achievements.

Change which has occurred must be seen to have been both legislative and chosen, but always with cooperation, commitment and planning. The seeds of a school development plan were sown in that initial staff meeting and the first fruits were related to use of computers in the school. The newly appointed second deputy was a computer buff and colleagues in adjacent schools possessed similar interests and skills. A spirit of shared need brought three school staffs together to examine the computing philosophies held and to discuss the practices exercised. Some of these policies are now examined.

The Value of the Computer

A pattern of meetings evolved which sought to give teachers, whether enthusiastic, reluctant, sceptical or intimidated, hands-on experience and confidence. The meetings quickly developed from the level of considering software content to identifying the better educational uses and strategies through which the computer could be applied as a teaching-learning tool across the curriculum. Expertise has been brought in from various county agencies to advance this. Teachers have attended and contributed to short and award-bearing courses. The aims and planning have matured to a stage where, within the normal weekly practice, children are involved in adventure games, word-processing activities, problem-solving situations, data collection functions and electronic mail.

We feel that the process by which computer-assisted learning developed at Acklam Whin as an additional teaching tool clearly demonstrates the extent to which the school faced change in a very controlled and considered way. We went on to develop the new technology as a means of enhancing children's learning experiences. Through the very process of sorting out its aims in this direction, the school became increasingly committed to using computers in education.

The growing enthusiasm of various staff members for computers led to the purchase of a BBC computer in 1982. The number of computers increased later that year when primary schools were included in the 'Micros in Schools' scheme established by Kenneth Baker, then Minister for Information Technology at the Department of Industry. The £9,000,000 subsidy scheme enabled primary schools to obtain a microcomputer at half price. Although one might question the wisdom of spending large sums of public money on providing the hardware without prior training for teachers to use it effectively, the initiative had profound effects upon Acklam Whin. Teachers' convictions about the computer's potential benefits and versatility as a piece of equipment, combined with a sound and enlightened resourcing policy on the part of the school and the LEA, led in 1985 to even wider provision, comprising five BBC Model B computers, three disc drives and two cassette drives. The headteacher approached the LEA computing adviser for two additional disc drives to replace the time-consuming cassettes. As an alternative, it was suggested that the school should be networked, so discarding both disc and cassette drives. This meant replacing them with a terminal outstation in each classroom. It was agreed that the LEA would fund the installation costing approximately £5000. Acklam Whin was destined to become a pilot primary school in the county networking experiment. By 1985 the computer provision consisted of a central Econet file server driven from a Winchester hard disc and twenty-four terminal outstations located in nineteen classrooms and resource areas. As a result, the whole menu of library files could be instantly browsed, loaded within seconds from any computer connected to a terminal outstation.

The school's commitment to developing computers in education was underlined when two senior members of staff enrolled for part-time MA courses in which their research focused on computing in primary schools. The school also acquired four more computers (making nine in total) and a new teacher was appointed for computing. The primary responsibility of this person was as 'systems manager' and as such the job profile included ensuring the availability of files and programs for users, as well as offering informed advice in educational computing to staff and children. An in-school computing curriculum working party was established and this led to a series of in-service staff meetings aimed at promoting an even more effective use of computers in the classroom.

It would be an exaggeration to suggest that computers have transformed schooling at Acklam Whin. Clearly teachers vary considerably in attitudes to, and uses made of, the computers in their classrooms. But many changes have occurred as a direct result of using computers and more change is inevitable, for as Wellington (1985) points out:

> In general, in this field as in most areas of education, problems arise, inadequacies occur, opportunities are lost, not only through bad practice but also, and more often, through bad theory, or rather through bad practice which results from bad theory, from a failure to provide an adequate, theoretical underpinning for practical decisions and action.

Developing the use of microcomputers at Acklam Whin brought into sharp focus the need for a sound overall organizational structure and a clear policy regarding management of the curriculum as a whole, not just computers. Such changes offered the staff an opportunity to take a good look at what was happening in classrooms in general, so that the best, and not the worst, methods were extended so that new possibilities offered by the machine were not missed. Evaluation of the educational worth of the tasks being assigned to computers has been an ongoing process involving staff at all levels. Reviewing the teaching with computers has helped to improve the teaching away from the computer.

Over the past few years the school has received a steady stream of visitors including HMI, local teachers and educationists from abroad, all interested in observing good computer practice in the classroom. Although there is still recognition of the need for improvement and development, we would argue that the right conditions have been created for open, honest discussion amongst staff about the school's philosophy, thus ensuring that the school possesses an inbuilt capacity to face change realistically and confidently. The stage has now been reached where class teachers use computers and information technology across most of the primary curriculum areas and activities.

It must be stressed, however, that computing has never been permitted to dominate the curricular planning and development of the school; the school development plan always maintained a much wider perspective. It has, however, brought together a cluster of local schools in the selection, purchase and shared use of expensive programs and materials. We have reaped the benefit of shared philosophies and classroom experience of teachers within that wider environment. It has enabled the school to make a contribution to the LEA's information technology policy document and various other activities of the Computer Centre. But most important of all, the computer has been used as a tool to motivate and assist children in the learning process.

Mathematics and Science in the Curriculum

One of our original curriculum working parties addressed the fundamentals of teaching mathematics in the school. Sound guidelines existed in 1982 but the published scheme used was limited to the junior years and the language was very difficult. Change was inevitable, so the group obtained examples of every book and card scheme then published. During the following eighteen months they analyzed the materials to establish the suitability of suggested mathematical content, process and activity. The schemes were used by children and staff to check that they were appropriate for our needs; deficient or unsuitable schemes were eliminated, though only after heated discussion focusing on the identification of priorities.

To formalize our aims, the scheme was demonstrated to the Governing and Parent Bodies. That strategy has been continued with the reception group parents annually in order to make them conscious of the appropriate and applied nature of our work in mathematics. It also serves to emphasize the versatility of the scheme from initial steps to the final appraisal process. Using the scheme has shown the need for additional complementary platform materials, particularly for the new nursery class.

Similar developments have taken place in science. The arrival of the Educational Support Grant-funded Science Advisory Teachers in 1985 opened new channels of curriculum planning and practice. Natural science had always been a timetabled feature throughout the school but there were also tentative adventures into wider science teaching by colleagues with training or personal interest in the subject. A group of teachers in our receiving comprehensive school and four feeder primaries revived a science working party to determine what science should be taught through the primary years and into the transition secondary period. This document and the relevant LEA curriculum guidelines which were a response to the DES Circular 6/81 were adapted to our own needs within the school in-service staff meetings. The problems of resourcing were confronted and overcome by a central provision which enabled child or teacher to take a theme box, 'Heat', for example, into a teaching or individual learning situation and use it as required.

Using this thematic technique, the county advisory teachers again led cluster school staff courses, teaching alongside teachers in the classroom in order to increase their confidence in instructing science to show the essential scientific concepts. Using their newly refreshed talents, the staff compiled a record of the children's scientific experiences and progress. Also one member of the staff spent a term at Edge Hill College completing an Otto course; his scientific expertise and experience have been useful in our own and in other local schools.

Language Across the Curriculum

Because of its essential importance across the curriculum, language teaching has been featured in the school's in-service programme over the last seven years. It will continue to do so in our efforts to update our techniques and strategies, as well as meet the demands of new legislation.

One newly appointed teacher possessed some passionately held and original approaches to language teaching, relying on the use of children's literature to heighten her pupils' enthusiasm through sheer enjoyment. Her enthusiasm was infectious and teachers who had previously shown commendable interest and skill found new stimulus and example. Others, lacking confidence or experience, were encouraged to try different approaches. Local and national experts were invited to share ideas and practices, and authors visited and worked with children throughout the school. Pupils in the middle years participated in the National Writing Project and made contact with children as far away as Australia. The walls and ceilings were full of children's language work. Project visitors found the children willing, able and enthusiastic in discussing their work and ideas.

Review Procedures

We are sure that the establishment of aims must not exclude innovation in the determination to attain objectives. This was taken into consideration in two review procedures introduced into the school.

Circular 8/83 (DES, 1983) required the LEA to provide the Secretary of State with a summary of the steps being taken:

> To seek to ensure that the curriculum is planned as a whole; that for each pupil it is balanced, coherent and suited to his or her ability and aptitude; and that the needs of pupils across the full range of ability (including the most able) are met in both primary and secondary schools.

The same circular made similar demands on the schools themselves:

> The Secretary of State would also be grateful to have a summary of the steps which have been taken by primary and secondary schools to set out their aims and to assess regularly how far the education they provide matches those aims.

We all recognize, of course, that schools develop and change according to different circumstances. One such event significantly affecting Acklam Whin's growth was the unfolding of the LEA's plans for monitoring the effectiveness of school and staff development in 1984.

The LEA was realistic in recognizing that schools would only go on improving if they were given the right conditions for growth, i.e. if evaluation were closely linked with development; if the climate and conditions in the LEA as a whole were conducive to honest self-evaluation; and if staff 'owned' their own school development plan indicating 'where the school is now', 'where they want it to go' and 'the means of getting it there'.

To this end, senior headteachers were invited to a residential conference to meet with advisers and LEA representatives. What emerged became known in Cleveland as the School and Staff Development Programme (SSDP), a strategy which schools could adopt (not a set county plan) for profiling itself. This self-evaluation strategy owned by the primary school itself is helped and monitored by the 'Six-Term Review' process, a day put aside every sixth term for whole-school review by the LEA adviser and teachers.

The advisory visit programme is, however, seen only as a small part of a much wider process based on the developmental work of the school and its staff, with emphasis being placed very much on development rather than formal evaluation. Achievement of this necessitates that the staff and school adviser identify and address a subject or organizational aspect of current concern locally or nationally.

The review process got under way at Acklam Whin with a series of staff meetings devoted to drawing up an agenda for the adviser's day-long visit. The staff felt strongly that the review should be based on previously identified school-wide needs, so that it would be firmly founded in the reality of school life and not seen as a 'bolt-on' extra. Science and technology as a problem-solving strategy across the curriculum were identified as areas of the curriculum which required close examination. As these were the school adviser's own speciality, a potentially significantly valuable contribution was available. At the 'negotiation of the agenda' stage with the adviser, the pattern and programme for the day were left very much to the staff. This was very satisfying to us as we felt the review was tailored to our school needs and priorities and not something imposed. A timetable for the day was drawn up involving all staff. Although the review was to be informal, the level of preparation and concern it generated was an indication of the status and importance the staff felt it warranted.

Working parties and teams met together on several occasions to plan constructive discussion with the adviser, again serving to build valuable in-service opportunities for development into the review process itself. All groups hung their thoughts around similar questions:

Where were we?
Where are we now?
Where do we want to be?
How will we get there?

There was great emphasis placed throughout the review on development by building on identifiable positives. Staff felt 'good' about the review and suggestions for future development possibilities put forward by the adviser were acknowledged and discussed prior to the official reporting-back session on a date negotiated in advance for the production of a joint developmental summary.

The review's real value to the school lay not in the day itself, worthwhile though it was, but in the planning and follow-up discussions and activities which it generated. The day served to give professional recognition and credibility to what was already happening. It promoted clear thinking and a corporate sharing of ideas amongst the staff as a whole, adding rigour and yet security to the change process. The six-term review process itself served as an additional and successful mechanism for nurturing 'shared ownership' of the school's ethos; only out of this can clear curricular aims and objectives be achieved. The event also caused a wider assessment and even revision of aims when the staff met with the adviser to discuss observations and recommendations emerging from the exercise. This was again supported by other members of the county advisory team who organized course activities for staff and neighbouring colleagues to develop personal skills and clarify aims.

The second review process has been taking place in the school for some years now. It developed from suggestions made at a county management course and the Durham University Self-Evaluation Conference attended by the headteacher and several senior staff in 1983. It was thought that individual and whole-school development could be gauged and assisted if a programme of negotiated questions could be addressed periodically by the headteacher and each individual member of staff. This did not of course exclude the wider and long-established staff meeting consultative process. In fact, through the closer relationships established, it could be described as productive and complementary.

Space does not allow the chance to describe the process by which the working parties drew up curriculum and process guidelines for all other areas of the curriculum. It is enough to confirm that they exist, are used and were formulated in the same cooperative and consultative manner adopted for those documented in this paper.

We would also stress the value and importance of other documents which have been used in the school. These include the two long-established parental brochures which seek to prepare parents prior to school entry and fully involve them in the event; there is rarely a time when parents are not assisting teachers throughout the school in a wide variety of tasks and activities. The staff handbook documents all decisions and policies established by the staff to regulate and facilitate our day-to-day activities. This serves to remind us of the decisions we have made and is invaluable to temporary or new teachers in the school.

Responsibilities Inside and Outside School

The consultative nature of the staffing policy requires a commensurate responsibility structure. All staff have a class and curricular discipline responsibility within the area of the school in which they currently teach, though this changes when the teacher moves to another phase. These changes maintain a fresh approach and cultivate appreciation of the whole school's organization, working practice, problems and needs.

Teachers on 'incentives' additionally undertake several organizational responsibilities according to interests and qualifications, including sporting, extra-mural or day-to-day necessities such as television and broadcasting arrangements. They also have wider pastoral duties and are actively involved in inter-school activities and intra-school functions like the special needs group. They are expected to know if children exhibit any level of special need and to consult with other collegues before bringing to the group a suggested strategy to support or overcome the need. Paramedics and education social workers are invited to take part in these activities and a community constable is in the school weekly.

The deputy headteacher is expected to work with, or deputize for, the head at any time, so he needs to be familiar with all documentation (including LEA and DES regulations) and with forthcoming events. He also fulfils a teaching programme, supporting all phases throughout the school, thereby appreciating the various needs and activities.

Despite the strong suspicion, and anxiety, felt generally by the profession, against the Grant Related In-service Training regulations, we feel that they have one advantage. They have laid responsibility for in-service requirements firmly at our own doorstep and we have been free to establish and work at our own priorities or those evident in new legislation. For instance, we were able to visit well-established local nurseries and to arrange a teacher's day alongside nine other schools with similar interests and concerns for nursery education prior to the opening of our own nursery.

The staff negotiated training days to address the problems of educational continuity involving our secondary and four other feeder primary school staffs. Trans-school curriculum working parties have evolved from this. We have put ourselves in the place of our pupils within language and CDT workshops to gain skills and appreciation of the demands commonly made. We have rationalized whole-school resources and examined the organization and potential of the library in the primary school. Contribution to the LEA's Policy Document on School Libraries was made through participation by the whole staff in various related activities. After a very careful look at the 'Kidscape' materials about child abuse by the teaching group, and with the agreement of parents, our P4 (7–8-year-old) children followed the programme. The funding has enabled long and short course attendance by many teachers such as the visit to the London science museum, which is designed as much to cement staff relationships as it is to make them aware of the value and intent of the visit and work undertaken by our P7 (10–11-year-old) pupils. Along with the two review procedures, we feel that it has enabled us to identify and meet individual and school priorities within the overall school development plan.

Conclusion

At the time of writing, several curriculum groups evolving from the primary to secondary continuity and liaison conference mentioned earlier have already convened. It is hoped that these groups will share their communal school and personal ideas for the implementation of the change necessitated by the National Curriculum and improve the process of transition and continuity.

We are conveniently at the stage when we must decide the focus for our next six-term review, and a request to look at mathematics again was voiced at the latest whole-staff meeting. It is clearly time for a reconvening of the working parties responsible for the development of mathematics, science and language in the school. We must determine that our aims at least match those contained within the legislation and that our practices will leave our children well-equipped to face the assessment process which is an integral part of the National Curriculum.

For instance, any review of our mathematics programme must examine deficiencies or anomalies and eradicate them. The diagnostic testing procedures must be adjusted to correct previous omissions, and additional essential teaching resources obtained. The total school staff will need to examine the final recommendations for flaws and, only when staff are reasonably satisfied that the diet is reliable and valid, will it be offered to our children. Even then, we shall be alert to consumer comment and reaction and carry out further formative communal review and appraisal at a later date. All this in the light of the National Curriculum.

We are well aware that this review of the teaching of mathematics, now embarked upon, and redefining of aims at the school seeks to satisfy staff anxiety, the LEA requirement and the DES legislation all within a single strategy. We suggest that it ensures an esssential degree of continuity and consistency. It also recognizes the need for staff to address priorities and aims at a time when schools are being inundated with directives. Each of the core and foundation subjects will be analyzed in a similar manner to ensure that our children are presented with programmes designed to help them attain individual potential, possibly beyond the attainment targets stipulated.

Our aims will certainly hinge on the intention to continue planning those programmes together so that our teachers are proud to own corporately what the school stands for and is achieving. We will be equally intent on retaining a positive approach which respects and uses the children's own contributions. We seek these aims in an applied, informed, humorous, colourful and lively climate which rouses and retains their enthusiastic and enjoyable involvement in a developing environment. Only then will our curriculum continue to respond to the DES requirements of breadth, balance, relevance and differentiation within this contemporary innovative educational climate.

Note

Grant Related Inservice Training (GRIST) was renamed Local Education Authority Training Grant Scheme (LEATGS) in 1989.

References

DES (1983) *The School Curriculum, Circular 8/83*, London, HMSO.
KELLY, A.V. (1984) *Microcomputers and the Curriculum*, London, Harper and Row.
WELLINGTON, J.J. (1985) *Children, Computers and the Curriculum*, London, Harper Educational Series.

Part 4 Wider Aims: Childhood, Environment and Society

Introduction

The aims of education commonly reflect the aims of society. In the nineteenth century, for instance, the elementary school system was never intended to have any cultural value, but was predominantly and unmistakably utilitarian (Mannheim and Stewart, 1962). That period was, of course, one of tremendous industrial growth, but it was matched by the post-1945 period when a different type of education prevailed. Maclure (1984: ix) describes it thus:

> The period was one of unparalleled expansion in England and Wales. For a quarter of a century after the end of the Second World War, the social, economic and demographic conditions were uniquely favourable for educational development. It began with a strong political consensus behind the new Education Act which raised expectations and promised wider opportunities for everyone. On this basis, the education system was reconstructed and modernised . . . the consensus did not last: it crumbled in the 1960s, about the time the demographic trend turned down. The optimism and the expectations faded with the on-set of a recession which ended the longest period of sustained prosperity the modern world has known.

Many of today's primary school teachers shared the excitement of this period of growth, prosperity and optimism, and later brought to the classroom a commitment to a set of aims which reflected the values of that society. But what a change today. The growth of primary education has been halted, with the primary school population dropping by 20 per cent from almost 4 million in 1980 to only 3.3 million in 1985, and with only a slow rise since (Richards, 1987). Society has also changed. Differing employment prospects, advances in science and technology, increasing leisure opportunities, greater influences of other cultures, less stable family relationships, shifting sex roles, and dangers of alcohol, drugs and AIDS are all bound to influence our views on the whole purpose of education.

Education is very much a social process (Downey and Kelly, 1979) and schools need to focus attention on aspects of welfare: they commonly include in their curriculum statements an aim such as the maintenance of 'a friendly, caring and well-ordered environment which allows pupils to develop to the full.'

In Chapter 11, Nancy Elliott takes up some of these issues and considers the type of environment that can help to motivate children. She contends that the neighbourhood environment of the 1950s, focusing upon community spirit, probably offered better facilities for children's play than it does at present, with restrictions caused by increasing traffic and violence and shrinking areas of open space. In these circumstances, the role of fieldwork and of investigation into the environment around school takes on new purpose and meaning, as does the role of parents, their attitudes and cooperation. Examples are provided of the boundless opportunities which exist for changing the fabric of, and developing attitudes to, the environment both inside and outside school, though recognition is made of the support which teachers need to achieve these goals.

Alan Blyth, in Chapter 12, revisits some of his earlier research into the social demands on schools and teachers, and their responses to these demands. Some of the original demands, still with us today, concerned the curriculum, particularly the role of language and number, but today demographic change, including mobility and the ethnic composition of the population; economic change, exemplified by the role of women and the world of work; technological change, particularly the use of the computer; and cultural change, such as fashion, adults' impressions of children, leisure and beliefs, all place additional demands on teachers. They respond to these complex dilemmas in different ways, depending upon their own views and aims, though it is clear that the requirements of the National Curriculum and assessment place fresh demands on *all* teachers which will have to be met, and for which additional support will be needed.

> Philip Taylor provides an international perspective in Chapter 13, concluding that increasingly, the world is becoming a global village.

References

DOWNEY, M. and KELLY, A.V. (1979) *Theory and Practice of Education.* London, Harper and Row.

MACLURE, S. (1984) *Educational Development and School Building: Aspects of Public Policy, 1945–1973.* London, Longman.

MANNHEIM, K. and STEWART, W.A.C. (1962) *An Introduction to the Sociology of Education.* London, Routledge and Kegan Paul.

RICHARDS, C. (1987) 'Primary education in England: An analysis of some recent issues and developments', *Curriculum* 8, 1, 6–12.

Chapter 11

The Life of Childhood:
Environment and Experience

Nancy Elliott

Introduction

Reference is made in the House of Commons Select Committee Report, *Achievement in Primary Schools* (1986) to the aims of education summarized by Lady Warnock in her brief guide (1978). They were primarily to increase both the child's knowledge and understanding of the world he lives in and then to foster to the full this independence and self-sufficiency. In the USA, Public Law 94142, similarly introduced for children with special educational needs, called for them to be educated in 'the least restrictive environment'.

English primary education has always acknowledged the influence of the environment upon children's learning, though this commonly expressed belief has not always resulted in a school looking analytically enough at what actually is provided for children throughout their total experience of schooling. Were we to draw up a list of what children need and should experience throughout primary education we would probably include the following:

— a comfortable, friendly, unthreatening and supportive environment;
— an interesting environment with opportunities for all-round development and challenge;
— a child-centred approach, with individual needs recognized and understood;
— good provision across the curriculum;
— recognition of achievement and talents;
— opportunities to take responsibility;
— good assessment procedures;
— opportunity to encounter success and overcome failure.

(Were we to draw up a list of what teachers need in a primary school there might be a remarkable similarity in the lists.) Further definition of what children need and ought to experience in school might include:

- a sense of their own worth, through shared perceptions of progress and contribution;
- some in put into their surroundngs;
- opportunity to work as an individual as well as a member of a class or group;
- opportunity to lead, to be a member of a team, to be led;
- to share in decision-making;
- to have fun; to share celebrations and treats;
- to meet interesting people, go to interesting places;
- to be encouraged to offer ideas.

There is nothing original about such a list, but it is worth noting the similarity between the needs and expectations of both children and adults. A list by itself is of small value. What is necessary is the will and the means by which the staff of a primary school sets about providing the kind of environment in which children are more likely to gain a sense of their own worth and, in the hackneyed phrase, 'reach their full potential'.

It is not possible to undertake any positive major change unless the context of that proposed change is taken into account. There ought to be an addition to the list of children's needs and rights referred to formerly; it is an important addition which applies equally to the needs of staff, namely that of being given time for reflection. A belief persists that by making demands, standards can be raised. Without adequate time for reflection upon the many aspects of imminent change, its successful implementation is threatened. Moreover, if we are to provide the quality of environment to which primary children are entitled, we must not let that issue be subordinate to others.

The Educational Context

The Select Committee Report (1986) began by referring to the social changes and problems in England which schools are expected to take in their stride. They included cultural and ethnic change, differences in attitudes towards moral and social issues, the problems of unemployment and industrial conflict, and the many children and their parents disadvantaged by a variety of circumstances. Statistical evidence substantiated the view that there were other children who had 'much to contend with' because of circumstances beyond their control.

The chapter on 'Aspects of Primary Education Today' considered the effects of falling rolls, reduced resources and the lack of adequate money for capital expenditure on school buildings, in a national overview of schools and local education authorities where considerable diversity of provision exists.

Many primary schools and teachers have been affected greatly by falling rolls. Closures and mergers had immediate and continuing effects upon promotion prospects; the deployment, premature retirement and the inability of many LEAs to take on the newly qualified often resulting in an imbalance of staff expertise either across the curriculum or in the early childhood and junior phases, is still evident today.

Several years on from the publication of the report, there is still a national shortage of teachers with expertise in early childhood teaching. Furthermore, the inequality and unsuitability of much of the educational provision for the four- and five-year-olds in formal schooling have aroused national concern. *The Times Educational Supplement* (October 1988) reports a survey of primary teachers conducted by the Labour Party which stated that 69 per cent of authorities reported a lack of teachers qualified to teach mathematics, science and craft, design and technology.

Fortunately there are positive factors. School INSET initiatives have encouraged a pattern of cooperative planning and discussion amongst staff. Liaison between and amongst schools in clusters and pyramids has proved to be mutually supportive in curricular and pastoral issues. It has led to a sharing of resources, increased knowledge of patterns of organization and greater parental awareness of learning throughout primary and secondary sectors. The positive effect of more teacher-advisers and INSET through ESG grants has led to greater confidence of many teachers in certain curriculum areas. The participation of serving heads and teachers in initial training is making welcome professional demands; not only have they to demonstrate clearly effective practice, there is an academic requirement for clear exposition of that practice underpinned by an educational philosophy.

Nevertheless, the demands upon schools to take on more and more issues, social as well as educational, threaten to push aside the necessary staff consultation on the nature and quality of experience offered by a school to its pupils.

Social Changes and Their Effect upon Children's Play and Experience

For many children the neighbourhood environment in the immediate decade after the Second World War probably offered better facilities for children's social, physical and imaginative play than it does in the eighties.

Several factors militate against children's freedom to use their neighbourhood today: the huge increase in traffic, including stationary vehicles which take up play space; the greater risks from physical violence; and the shrinking amount of available land. Housing has changed, often with detrimental results to children's need to move and explore. Though indoor sanitation, better heating and lighting have brought some physical benefits, poor design and disregard for the immediate environment have resulted in a reduction in the quality of life for many families. High-rise density flats, urban concrete estates with minimal, unimaginative play and recreation space, and council and private estates with tiny gardens or open-grassed communal space, offer few opportunities for children's mental, emotional and intellectual growth. Looking at a recent exercise in a primary classroom on how to improve the neighbourhood it was salutary to see that all the children had offered suggestions from a negative standpoint: 'don't make a noise'; 'don't throw balls about'; 'don't pick flowers'; 'don't chop down trees', were all worthy and public-spirited enough to warrant praise (and may indeed have been suggested as replies that the teacher wanted to hear), but it was revealing to see that children's immediate response was not to proffer positive ideas of planting trees and flowers and setting aside play-space for ball-games, but to propose what they should *not* do.

Considerable changes in patterns of living since the beginning of the sixties have also affected children's neighbourhood play, particularly in the well-established communities surrounding the then traditional industries of coal mining, steel making, ship building and farming.

I began my teaching career in the mining villages and industrial townships of County Durham and the north-east, where the communities themselves offered resources to support children's play and experiential learning. The extended families, established for generations, were well-known to each other, and the tradition, transmitted from the hard days of poverty and unemployment, was one of support for those needing practical help. Children were often cared for, both short- and long-term, by friends and neighbours in the event of a mother's illness; a great deal of leisure and recreation was communal, with different generations sharing domestic and seasonal celebrations.

The streets on summer evenings saw different groupings of people: old, young, male, female, the groups settling, shifting, altering in an exchange of gossip, street game or proffering of opinion. The close social networks supported other leisure activities. Chapel hall, institute or community centre were the venue for local concert or pantomime, traditional entertainments in which all age groups participated. Shows were more often than not followed by light refreshments or even large suppers, at a minimum cost and possibly because of the hard work of women in the community. The food added to the sense of occasion and it was quite common for a show to last a full week. Children could go unaccompanied with little fear of being out alone; the talents of individuals as entertainers, costume-makers, carpenters and electricians were recognized and encouraged. It was not all sweetness and light, however. Such events sometimes promoted rivalries and rows; indeed the communities themselves were not always free from bitterness and violence, where long-standing feuds or sudden quarrels caused great unhappiness. Nevertheless, such communities allowed children to experience play and recreation with peers and adults in a largely supportive environment.

There were other benefits. Most children in mining villages had access to open countryside within a very short distance of home. Fell and waste-land, small plantations or natural woodland were available to all. Draining-ditches, streams and burns were resources for paddling, water-play, fishing, or for the more sophisticated engineering of dams and harbours. Reading *Cider with Rosie*, one is struck by the contrast between Laurie Lee's learning experiences at school and those at home. He described the scullery at home as:

> a mine of all the minerals of living. Here I discovered water — a very different element from the green crawling scum that stank in the garden tub. You could pump it in pure blue gulps out of the ground, you could swing on the pump handle and it came out sparkling like liquid sky. And it broke and ran and shone on the tiled floor, or quivered in a jug, or weighted your clothes with cold. You could drink it, draw with it, froth it with soap, swim beetles across it, or fly it in bubbles in the air. You could put your head in it, and open your eyes, and see the sides of the bucket buckle, and hear your caught breath roar, and work your mouth like a fish, and smell the lime from the ground. Substance of magic — which you could tear or wear, confine or scatter, or send down holes, but never burn or break or destroy.

The houses in the industrial districts may have been cramped and lacking in amenities, but the back-yards, streets, waste-land and open countryside allowed for imaginative as well as exploratory play. Dens and camps could easily be made amongst bushes and trees; an old-fashioned clothes-horse and a sheet provided a tent in the back-yard. Material for lighting fires on waste-land was easily accessible; burnt and half-raw potatoes emerged blackened from the flames to be sampled with enthusiasm or trepidation.

Even were there not the physical dangers from adults in the outdoor environment today, much of that traditional play-space has gone forever. Agricultural development has fenced off many fields and stopped rights of way. Old quarries, haunts of wild-life and lavish in provision for imaginative play, have been filled in by local authorities forever seeking places to bury industrial and domestic waste; parks are too often provided with the usual assortment of swings and see-saws, restricting opportunities for mental, emotional and spiritual growth. School fields and playgrounds are still designed by many with little insight into the importance of that outdoor environment as a source of pleasure and all-round learning. Fortunately, pioneering individuals are now receiving some recognition and support, but there are still too many schools having to fight the battle without the understanding of those who have the power and influence to determine the nature of that resource.

For those children who had access to play in open countryside there was, perhaps, an added joy, i.e. the sense of adventure than can stem from being away from the immediate environment of home. Primarily there was space: room to walk, run, jump and room to engage in vigorous physical activity without restriction. There were trees to climb, Tarzan-like ropes to transport them into imaginary worlds as well as physically from branch to branch. To be with friends and out of reach of adults was a freedom in itself.

As a teacher, taking children on nature or 'interest' walks into this countryside, there was a sense of its being *their* territory, where they knew far more about its topography and resources than I ever would. Frequently, in mining areas, old waggon-ways and other industrial remains could be found. The position of some ruined stone walls showed where once a habitable dwelling might have stood. To use the children's knowledge and experiences to promote more academic learning was not difficult. Ordnance and old survey maps, showing tracks and paths, naming coppices and fields, providing evidence that cottages had indeed existed, proved fascinating to the children. Poems like 'The Listeners' and 'The Way through the Woods' provided language by which their own experiences might be compared and imaginatively extended. Much of this learning is now described as environmental studies and acts as a stimulus for successful integrated learning. Perhaps the children I taught gained more from learning first through their own experiences.

The changes to those communities who depended for their livelihood on the heavy industries have been devastating. Some villages, stubbornly resisting category D^1 classification, refused to die, but factors like the migration of families to find work elsewhere, the increase in the number of women going out to work, the bitterness of those unemployed at a time when advertising for consumer spending assails eyes and ears on every side, have forever altered traditional ways of life.

Re-housing in towns has often separated extended families, whilst amenities for play and recreation are variable. Cheap, frequent public transport, needed in town and country alike, has decreased in many areas, so that parents and children are more dependent on facilities immediately available. Urging parents to share books with children needs good library provision close at hand; the excitement of seeing live theatre is out of the question for many families and the reduction in public spending on the arts in general makes for impoverishment in the quality of life.

Of course there are many children whose home background is not adversely affected by poor housing, unemployment or lack of transport to places of interest. Nevertheless, we cannot assume that all children with advantaged social backgrounds have the opportunity for good play in the sense of learning experience. It is equally wrong to assume that children from homes where money is short, or who live in poor housing conditions, are necessarily not receiving the intellectual and emotional stimulation vital to their growth. Perhaps this classification into background is dangerous; we would do better to determine what all children need to experience in the primary school and set about providing it.

The 'Innocent Years'

The idea that children might talk freely and openly (no matter how erroneously) upon sexual matters would have aroused cries of horror only a few years ago. Yet that is precisely what has happened in the case of AIDS which is fairly common parlance even in infant shools. The recognition of sexual abuse against young children, the need to protect them against violence both within the home and without, have blown away any notion adults might have held that sex should not be referred to until the upper junior age. The influence of the media in the promotion of positive attitudes to sex education is questionable. For example, homosexuality is often the subject of vulgar comment in many so-called 'comedy' shows, establishing stereotypes which children mimic and refer to without having the necessary maturity to consider the emotions and issues involved.

The mass of advertising aimed at stimulating demand for consumer goods does not stop at adults. Children are daily depicted on television as individuals asking for, and expecting to receive, sweets, canned drinks, ice-cream, clothes and toys. The natural rhythms of the seasons, annual festivals and celebrations are destroyed by the manufacturers and retailers stimulating demand for goods weeks — even months — before time. The subtle message being transmitted constantly is an equation of possessions with happiness and contentment.

The insidious effect of regular, transmitted views and propaganda is no less influential in issues of race and gender. Again, there have been expressions of disbelief that very young children could already have prejudiced attitudes to people of other race or culture. Although it is necessary for education to take the issues of equal opportunities into the curriculum, it is equally important that they are incorporated into the hidden curriculum, and that all aspects of the school environment endorse values which emphasize living together in harmony.

There is no way that these 'innocent years' can be ignored as being inappropriate for issues of sex, race, gender and consumerism to be raised. Psychologists and psychiatrists tell us that interest in sex and in all bodily functions is present in normal children. Susan Isaacs (1946) reported this in her study of nursery school children.

There are few children who do not wants sweets, new clothes and toys. It is hardly strange if children repeat the views and attitudes of those with whom they spend the greatest part of their lives. What is important are the ways in which children can be helped towards a knowledge of how people can be manipulated, a very difficult task for teachers to manage on their own. Many people would question whether this is the task of primary schools. Others might feel that it is highly desirable, but that there is not enough time for schools to undertake anything other than the implementation of the National Curriculum. In most cases the question would surely arise as to how it could be done at all.

Parental Understanding

The pressures and demands upon schools, including the changes in society referred to, are to be increased as a result of the Reform Act. Though some educational opinion states that schools need not alter their activity-based learning approach, there may be a need for such schools to describe clearly and more publicly their educational philosophy. Moreover, they may need to substantiate that philosophy by demonstrating good practice, particularly in programmes of study and through continuous assessment. It is, of course, the task of all schools to do this, but there is some evidence to suggest that on the whole teachers use didactic rather than exploratory teaching methods. Those who support the latter approach may feel more pressure to be articulate, particularly with parents. Unless teachers really believe that active learning and a challenging environment support, benefit and improve children's development it is unlikely that priority will be given to their promotion. Moreover, it is one thing to hold that belief as professionals; it is another to gain the full support and understanding of parents.

The vast majority of parents want their children to succeed at school; they also want them to be happy. Some are particularly anxious about the more formal aspects of the curriculum. Their own understanding of their role as educators varies widely and though parental contact and involvement have increased, there are still wide differences in practice. Some of this practice is lacking in sufficient quality or scope for any real understanding of the curriculum to develop. A recent survey (Jowett and Baginsky, 1988) commented that the theme schools commonly used to describe parental involvement was that of a desire to bring together in some ways the separate domains of home and school. A very wide range of activities would fit into this description.

Society requires schools to transmit values of good citizenship, children are expected to behave in an acceptable fashion and 'discipline' is seen as important in inculcating good behaviour. Most parents expect the school to set the rules and the limits within which they operate. A code to which everyone subscribes is more likely to promote self-discipline and to produce an atmosphere and working environment where conflict is minimized. Some primary schools have gone some way towards involving all teachers, non-teaching staff and children in forming a code of behaviour to which all (more or less) subscribe. The agreement and support of parents and governors in this code is essential. Conflict exists in society and schools can be affected by it, yet valuable ways of promoting cooperation have been developed through curriculum work, notably involving world studies (see Schools Council, 1985. Issues of race, gender and the just and fair society were the subject of work undertaken with the four to thirteen age-group in schools (Baker *et al.*, 1987) in which the Centre for Global Education at York University played a considerable part.

Schools need to establish a clear understanding with parents and governors on two fronts: first, the nature of the establishment itself, the values it wishes to transmit and the suitability of the total environment for children's happiness and progress; second, the nature of the education the school offers to pupils, the ways in which children are assessed and the arrangements it makes for informing parents about children's assessment and progress.

The Learning Environment inside the Classroom

When Scale 2 posts proliferated after the Houghton Award, it was fairly common practice for one to be awarded for 'art and display'. The recognition of the value of art in the curriculum is always welcome. So, too, is the recognition given to children by selecting work and giving time and trouble to its display. The notion that primary schools should be bright, attractive and interesting places is one subscribed to by most people. But display in schools can also highlight poorer practice. On occasions too much attention and time are given to mounting work. Display itself may be beautiful, the quality of the work moderate. Not every child has his or her efforts recognized. Too many examples show copies of writing or illustration, rather than original ideas. Display can reveal a lack of progression in certain topics or subject areas throughout the school, and there may be only meagre examples of work in some curriculum areas.

I have not, myself, heard as yet of any teacher with responsibility for 'the learning environment', though advice on resources for subject areas is certainly accepted as part of the task of curriculum leaders and coordinators. Why should it be the responsibility of one person? Surely it is essential that each teacher provides a good learning environment. This is generally the assumption made, though it is one that bears investigation. Perhaps the importance of the environment as a source for learning should take priority through whole-staff discussion. As a means of interesting and challenging children across the curriculum it demands far more attention than it receives. In too many cases children are inadequately assessed because they are functioning in an environment not rich enough to reveal their talents and potential. Even an analysis by the whole staff of the quality of tools and resources available to children as they move from class to class might highlight gaps in provision which hinder progress and continuity.

Although we know enough to accept that no teacher can actually be the sole educator of all the children in the class for every minute of the time allocated, nor can written exercises be set and undertaken so that pupils work at the same rate and complete tasks in unison, a belief persists that somehow this can be achieved and that all teachers are sufficiently able to accomplish these feats of organization. There is a genuine and expressed concern that children should not 'waste time'. But children do not learn solely from teachers; they learn from other adults, from their peers, from their own actions and from the resources of the world around them. The environment of the primary classroom should reflect this belief and children should be given the space, time and materials to enable them to learn both independently and in cooperation with others. This applies even when didactic methods are more commonly used. The definition of 'learning' may need close examination; there are many aspects supportive of children's development which make for achievement in its fullest sense.

The analysis of achievement in the Hargreaves Committee Report (ILEA, 1984) and referred to in the Select Committee Report (1986), while accepted by both committees as having limitations, nevertheless provides us with a useful definition by which we might look at children's progress and the context in which they learn. The four aspects: academic attainment; the capacity to apply knowledge rather than knowledge itself; personal and social skills; motivation and commitment all have implications for the ways classrooms are organized, space and time allocated and support given to children as individuals.

Not all the requirements of the Reform Act are to be deplored; a great deal of the legislation can be seen as positive to activity-based learning, particularly aspects of the TGAT Report (1988). If external tests are to be devised which extend beyond the more formal written tests in English and mathematics, then the need for children to show a wider variety of skills and abilities could result in an opening-out of methods of teaching. Assessment which includes questions which can be presented orally, in writing or through pictures and diagrams, tasks which require mental work, speech, and different forms of practical activity are to be welcomed. A classroom which is more of a workshop, where children are given materials to enjoy as well as to challenge their thinking, could revolutionize the ways in which many teachers approach the curriculum. There is a possibility of further benefit. If parents begin to understand that achievement is not always measured by the more formal tests with which they are familiar, then exploratory methods will be valued and considered worthwhile.

Each classroom needs provision for areas of learning: to promote communication and literacy skills and support the environmental, scientific and information technology areas. The expressive arts need support; materials for practical mathematics, craft and design are essential. The range and practicality of tools available determine the quality of work and experience. An evaluation of instruments for measurement (in all its aspects), and an examination of aids which develop observational skills should be undertaken by all teachers in a school. What provision is there for board games, puzzles of every kind, constructive play? There are many children capable of working with construction kits deemed too difficult for their age-group. Is there a range varied enough for all abilities? Imaginative play is not just a matter of dressing-up boxes, home corners and 'pretend' situations, though these are important. Using imagination is essential in problem-making, innovation and invention.

Classrooms are often very 'age-centred' and include materials levelled at some arbitrary phase. This can be particularly true of infant classrooms where too much is provided for repetitive play and too little to challenge thinking. Children who come from what we deem 'educationally advantaged' backgrounds are constantly surrounded with adult provision. Infant classrooms frequently lack maps and globes; there are no photographs, pictures or aerial views of the district to show where children live, where the school is positioned and where significant physical and natural features are situated. Tools and materials for art are sometimes unsuitable for developing skills. There are too many classrooms with scissors which won't cut, glues which won't stick, paint ready-mixed for children and no fine brushes at all. As a recipe for frustration it has all the right ingredients. This situation can apply equally well in junior classrooms. A recent group of teachers in our city, looking at ways in which we might assess children through their approach to art, listed benefits of art in assisting children's all-round development. They decided that art offers:

- opportunity for achievement;
- creativity outside 'right and wrong' categories;
- opportunities for individual and group expression;
- a means of encouraging aesthetic awareness;
- an opportunity to communicate information;
- other ways of conveying ideas;
- self-development through self-expression;
- choice and discrimination;
- a means of developing a child's self-esteem;
- opportunities for practical maths and science.

Furthermore, art develops skills in observation, organization, cooperation, imagination, manipulation, decision-making, reflection and concentration. It encourages all forms of language; and through art, children can gain emotional satisfaction and solve problems.

It might be thought that teachers do not need to engage in this sort of 'listing'. After all, there are innumerable books on art in the primary school, policy statements abound and all teachers 'do' art. The difference in this group's approach, however, was the emphasis on the value of art in the assessment of children — not as to whether they were 'good' or 'poor' at the subject, but what teachers can learn about children when they are engaged in creative work. It soon became apparent that if they were to assess children fairly they needed to provide an environment that allowed the pupils to show their attitudes and skills. The group then went back to their individual classrooms to consider how that environment might be improved so that attitudes and skills could be better developed. An obvious area for study was concentration. The length of time a child is capable of concentrating might very largely depend on the range and quality of paints, collage materials, tools and space available to him. The group continued the study by listing how they had each altered their organization and provision so that they could better observe how children set about tasks. Three major changes in the approach to art were noted:

(i) Not only had provision to be improved, but the actual care and storing of resources had to be better organized. In junior classes this was seen to be the responsibility of the children and they had to arrive at the decisions themselves.

(It is interesting that in many nursery schools and classes children are given the responsibility of taking out and putting away their own materials and are quite capable of it.)

(ii) Children needed time to work at and complete pictures or models to *their* satisfaction. An art 'lesson' where everything had to be completed or pushed away and perhaps damaged was detrimental and frustrating. Space and further time had to be granted.

(iii) Children were encouraged to talk more about their work, i.e. the thinking and ideas behind it, how it was planned and executed, their observations on the finished product.

It was an interesting project and showed, not surprisingly, that children's attitudes and performance can be markedly different in certain circumstances. Children who were poor readers, or who lacked concentration in written work, revealed different attitudes and abilities when engaged in creative work. A video was made in one school and used for assessment purposes; it was also used with parents to emphasize the many talents and skills that are encouraged by art.

Art is not a 'frill', a relaxation to be indulged in when more important work is completed. The need to retain art as a subject in its own right is essential; too often it is used solely as a vehicle for illustrating other aspects of the curriculum. It is a subject which allows children ownership through their own interpretation and ideas; we must never undervalue its contribution to their development.

The Learning Environment Outside the Classroom

A welcome recommendation in the TGAT Report was that of assessment through 'making and doing'. Design-related activities are worthy of inclusion in assessment. They cross all areas of the curriculum and certainly enable children's achievement in all aspects of the Hargreaves definition. There is hope, therefore, that the value given to practical tasks will encourage teachers to improve their classroom environment so that children can reveal their talents and demonstrate their skills.

Design can offer more than that, however. It can be the means by which children can actually improve their own environment, an experience which may have a profound influence upon their future attitudes and behaviour (Design Council, 1987). Many schools have achieved remarkable results in improving their outdoor environment. In common with others nationwide, several schools in Newcastle have given pupils the opportunity to effect change. The city's primary schools are largely provided with asphalt playgrounds, open-grassed areas (not very practical in the north-east), flower-beds and (perhaps) a playing field on site. To many heads and teachers, this is unacceptable at a time when children are more and more lacking in safe and imaginative places to play. They began by asking the children what they wanted in their outdoor environment, requesting ideas and designs from individuals or groups. The task of translating those into working plans needed the help of professionals, and invaluable support was given by Architecture Workshop and architecture students from the university. This added another dimension to their learning for they were working with professionals, using proper planning techniques and documents, and finding out about site problems and costings.

They discovered that not all their ideas were practicable. The task of financing the project had to be tackled and they learned that a great deal of hard work and time was necessary before their play space was a reality. Disappointments had to be overcome and in some schools the eldest children in the school had left before there was visible sign of change. Success came, finally, however, and there was not one school where a celebration of one sort or another did not take place. The projects had had the support and understanding of parents and governors from the beginning. Exhibitions and regular reporting had shown where the formal aspects of the curriculum had benefited. In many cases there was substantial community involvement. Individuals lent their services, local industries contributed in a variety of ways, neighbourhood organizations gave practical help. Primary schools are often focal points for their immediate community, and mutual interests, pleasure and benefit can result when projects and events are shared. Like parental liaison, community involvement exists at a number of levels, but the potential for learning is certainly there and well-described in many accounts (CSV, 1984; Parker and Davis, 1987).

Developing Attitudes

The positive learning environment does not only consider material provision. It is, and should be, concerned with developing positive attitudes towards global issues which affect people and their environments. Curriculum work in the eighties has shown a marked shift in incorporating positive attitude change as part of the primary programme. This work has the added advantage of asking children for their ideas and opinions. Media studies is not just about learning how to use video; it enables children to study the powerful effect of the media upon our lives.

The teacher's role in enriching children's language and communication skills is well-appreciated. The National Writing Project is changing attitudes about content and approaches to writing; research on the early acquisition of literacy (Hall, 1987) is challenging teachers' assumptions on how young children should be taught. The role of literature (including poetry) in the curriculum must never be undervalued, and teachers need to continue telling and reading stories to children throughout the primary school. The assumptions that children can read for themselves and that story telling should take a small slot in the timetable have dire effects upon children who find reading difficult. Not only do they not encounter more complex text and vocabulary (vital for their future education), they do not even have the opportunity to listen to it in the context of a story where enjoyment is shared. Literature is powerful in developing imagination. It is a resource for life.

Teachers and Children

The relationship between primary teachers and their classes is a special one. Where there is rapport, empathy and humour the bond is very close. Teachers have always had a responsible and difficult job, but the rewards from sharing your day with young children, full of ideas and enthusiasm, are rich. The strategy largely adopted by primary schools in the face of added pressures is that of coping; there comes a point, however, when that may no longer be fair to pupils or themselves. If the new legislation is to be successful, schools will need positive support. Recognition is long overdue.

Feuerstein made the comment that:

> a child's success at solving intellectual problems is as dependent on his feelings of competence as on his actual competence; for if the first is not present, children become so convinced of their likely failure that they do not attempt to solve problems, or do so only half-heartedly and with an expectation of defeat. (Stanton, 1987)

It is essential that we recognize what children bring, and offer them an environment and experiences designed to give them a sense of their own worth.

The professional development through in-service has hitherto supported staff through curriculum and organizational changes, but the Reform Act has massive training implications as yet largely unknown. The schools will need to sustain children through a great deal of disruption; already there is a shortage of supply teachers, particularly those experienced in the teaching of children in the early years.

It is time that primary schools were staffed in ways that enabled them to meet the needs of children fully, without needing to 'cope'. They should be able to enjoy the challenge of change and hold to what is good, without feeling that it is expected of them under any set of circumstances. Several people (no longer teachers themselves) are too easily given to stating that 'the good primary schools will be able to "make it work"; they always have done'. The good primary schools will certainly always try, but should we really make them feel they have failed when the support given them is inadequate? They have the ability to raise the quality of children's experiences and environment both now and for their future. That is too important to lose.

Note

1 Category D villages are those which planners have categorized as not worthy of any future development. They are not considered very desirable in terms of amenities or standards of housing, and are considered unlikely to be places where people would want to live.

References

BAKER, T. *et al.* (1987) *Co-operating for a Change*. Newcastle upon Tyne LEA.

DESIGN COUNCIL (1987) *Design and Primary Education*. Report of the Design Council Primary Education Working Party.

HALL, N. (1987) *The Emergence of Literacy*. London, Arnold in association with UKRA.

HOUSE OF COMMONS (1978) *Report of the Committee of Enquiry into the Education of Handicapped Children and Young People, Special Educational Needs*. London, HMSO.

HOUSE OF COMMONS (1986) *Third Report from the Education, Science and Arts Committee, Achievement in Primary Schools*. London, HMSO.

ILEA (1984) *Report of the Committee on the Curriculum and Organisation of Secondary Schools* (Chaired Dr D.H. Hargreaves) London, ILEA.

ISAACS, S. (1946) *Social Development in Young Children: A Study of Beginnings*. London, Routledge.

JOWETT, S. and BAGINSKY, M. (1988) 'Parents and Education: A survey of their involvement and a discussion of some issues', *Educational Research*, 30, 1.

LEE, L. (1959) *Cider with Rosie*. London, The Hogarth Press.

PARKER, C. and DAVIS, P. (1987) *Open Doors. Elderly People as Volunteers in Primary Schools*. Community Service Volunteers and Health Education Authority.

SCIP: Avon, SCIP: Newcastle (1984) *Opening Doors*. Community Service Volunteers.

SCHOOLS COUNCIL/ROWNTREE TRUST (1985) *World Studies 8–13 Project A Teacher's Handbook*. London, Oliver and Boyd.

STANTON, H. (1987) *Changing Children's Minds, Feuerstein's Revolution in the Teaching of Intelligence*. London, Souvenir Press.

Chapter 12

Social Demands and Schools' Responses

Alan Blyth

Introduction

In my opinion (Blyth, 1984), the needs of society should take third place in primary curriculum policy, after children's development and the ways of understanding and endeavour that are open to them. Yet, nowadays, primary teachers often feel that they are on the point of being overwhelmed by social imperatives and demands. To write about those demands may seem like spelling out the obvious. Some analysis of this seemingly obvious could help towards understanding the nature of those demands, and of the responses that teachers can realistically make. So this chapter will attempt to present a reasonably balanced view of social demands on schools and teachers, and of responses to those demands, twenty-five years or so after my first attempt to do something similar (Blyth, 1965). Inevitably, a survey of so large a subject, when confined to a single chapter, must take the form of a discursive essay rather than of an exhaustive account. It will be based on personal first-hand and others' experiences and perceptions, derived in various ways, and not on the mammoth piece of research that it really calls for. Similarly, the handful of references gives no idea of the immense range of source material that could have been tapped for such a purpose.

Social Demands

Traditional Demands

Earlier chapters in this book trace some of the general changes in the national scene which have, in recent decades, reflected and also engendered social demands (see also Cunningham, 1988). Some of these have a long ancestry; others are of quite recent origin. In general it could be said that some of those earlier demands have dissolved away; we no longer expect rural schools to adjust their year's programme to the potato harvest, nor do we celebrate Empire Day. But other social demands originating in earlier times continue to influence what happens today. Those will be considered first, and then rather more attention will be paid to the interrelated complex of newer demands.

Chief among the more traditional demands is the call for the maintenance and strengthening of the basic disciplines of language and number in the primary curriculum, together with a grounding in acceptable behaviour. As Alexander (1984) has indicated, primary education has never deviated very far from this core curriculum. In most countries, there has been an overt legal mandate for a curriculum of this kind, and the 1988 Education Reform Act aims to bring England and Wales into line, with the significant modification that science, probably with technology, is to be added to the core. Outside this core there has always been a penumbra of other curricular elements, some more established and some more controversial than others. The 1988 Education Reform Act epitomizes this imprecision faithfully, with its amalgam of foundation subjects, cross–curricular themes and peripheral remainders. Within that general framework there is an opportunity, and perhaps an invitation, to foster a pattern for the hidden curriculum of transmitted attitudes, though there is limited agreement about what that pattern should be. But the social demand for something of this kind is unmistakable; and understandably so, for it is difficult to conceive of a society that did not value this basic equipment.

Alongside the official curriculum and its hidden counterpart, another kind of social demand has been regularly recognized, one that I once termed 'classification' (Blyth, 1965). Since then, formal selection has of course become much less prevalent, but assortative processes of various kinds continue within primary schools as the work of Galton and his colleagues (1980) and Pollard (1987) demonstrates. From the children's point of view, such processes are valuable in the construction of distinctive personal identities. From the structural standpoint, they reflect the demands of existing society, though they may also enable a primary school to exercise a limited autonomy in modifying the prospects and destinations of individual children. For example, promise in football or dance, or in language or computer studies or music, may be either fostered or held back or ignored, while reputations for conduct and attitudes can become stereotyped, or can be purposefully modified.

Such are the most obvious traditional demands on the teacher's role, entertained by the public and by many teachers too. But it is the newer social demands, the consequences of more recent social change, that show the higher profile and have received the greater attention. Since these newer demands did not arise in a neat sequence but rather as a part of an interacting matrix of social forces, it is not possible to present them in any clear logical sequence. The classification that follows is one of convenience and should not be regarded as implying a causal chain, so the sequence in which the categories of demand appear should not be regarded as significant.

Recent Demands

First among these newer demands is the outcome of demographic change. With successive peaks and troughs in the live-birth rate, expectations about what primary schools should do have figured differently in different years. When the proportion of primary pupils is high in relation to the total population, there is usually an assumption that desired improvements in staffing and resources must be postponed to make way for the urgent task of accommodating such hordes. When however that proportion becomes low, a different kind of pressure is felt; for now the urge is to transfer resources from the primary to the secondary and further education sectors where the major pressure now is. This in fact becomes a social ratchet mechanism that always seems to operate to the disadvantage of the primary phase.

In addition to these general demographic trends, internal mobility of population also makes an impact on primary education. Three aspects in particular affect schools. First, there is the movement from areas of high to those of low unemployment, and from areas of low to those of high prosperity, mostly towards the south-east, retarded by housing costs. Second, there is an outward movement from cities into suburbs, and beyond into commuter country. Lastly, neutralizing the previous only in part, there is a movement mainly of younger people from rural areas into towns. To predict the consequences of the combination of all three for any one primary school would be very difficult. To note the consequences, when they have been operating for some time, can be sobering. For while some schools have to turn away pupils, and the larger ones at least may be under hitherto unknown managerial pressures, others become relatively uneconomic and face closure. Any closures are traumatic for the schools concerned, wherever they are; but when the axe falls on a village school, the outcry is greater, because this may be the only surviving communal institution that the village has (Bell and Sigsworth, 1987). Moreover, Ward (1988) has recently emphasized a point that already seemed to me important in 1965, namely that the nature of village children's social experience is itself transformed when they have to travel in the closed community of the school bus to a larger, more distant, and more heterogeneous area school. All such changes also tend to unsettle schools as communities; even the threat of possible change can do so, and such threats are perceived as widespread, especially when public rhetoric emphasizes efficiency as an aim and regards community as a sentimental and outmoded slogan.

A particular aspect of demographic change is that of change in the ethnic composition of neighbourhoods. The story of immigration, mainly from Afro-Caribbean lands and from the Indian sub-continent, and of the relationships between these new British and indigenous and the population, is familiar to everyone, if not entirely understood. It has in turn given rise to one of the most strident and controversial forms of social demand, made both on the comparatively limited regions in which minority ethnic groups have become concentrated, for mainly financial and economic reasons, and also on the rest of the country where they are represented by scattered individuals but where the implications of life in a multicultural society are nevertheless important. In the past two decades, such matters have grown into a major social demand: we are all multiculturalists now. Lip-service, at least, is paid on all sides to the 'permeation' of the formal and the hidden curriculum by multicultural considerations, carrying with it the assumption that here, at least, social demands should have precedence over child-centred and subject-centred assumptions alike. More difficulty arises when this issue is more closely scrutinized and the further demand for anti-racist education, itself a contentious term, is encountered, and when the possibility of backlash phenomena is faced. The literature on these issues is clearly too vast to be considered here, especially since that literature has itself become part of the conflict, but the issues and their complexity have become much more evident in recent years.

The link between ethnic distributions and the next kind of changing social demand, the economic, is evident; one does not need to be either a Marxist or a monetarist to appreciate that. Ethnic change was largely a response to twin economic circumstances: impoverishment in homelands during the last days of Empire, and the call for abundant cheap labour in British industry as post-war foreign competition developed. The concentration of ethnic and linguistic minorities, beginning with the Irish, in inner-city and other locations where housing was relatively cheap, constituted the next episode. This coincided broadly with functional transitions in the cities themselves, particularly the transformation of inner-city districts from close-knit working-class communities to something more akin to ethnic ghettoes whose names have, in some cases, become nationally familiar. This development has been accompanied by various problems in inner-city primary schools and a bad press contrived by critics from several directions. Fortunately, writers such as Ward (1978) and Tizard and his colleagues (1988) have provided a better-informed picture, in which the role of teachers is more positively, if more prosaically, portrayed.

Another issue related to both demographic and economic circumstances, but transcending both in terms of social roles, is that of gender. The place of women in full-time employment, with benefits such as maternity leave, has affected primary education in three ways. First, patterns of family life and role relationships in all social groups have been changed. Second, a rather different role model is held up to girls, and in a related sense to boys, in primary schools as well as later. Third, married women primary teachers have themselves come to exemplify this wider social pattern instead of manifesting, as they once did, something of an exception to prevailing practice. On balance, this modification of gender expectations is something that has worked in favour of primary schools, though there are many who remain markedly dissatisfied with the extent of this change.

Meanwhile, there are other aspects of economic change that have placed new demands on primary schools since the 1960s. The link between education and economic viability, rather caustically delineated by Corelli Barnett in *The Audit of War* (Barnett, 1986), was largely concealed from those active in primary education during the years after the Hadow Report of 1931, right down to the time of the Plowden Report of 1967, and after. It was often considered improper to mention such matters for fear of seeming to pervert education for the sake of cheap and docile labour. However, in recent years, the changing climate of opinion has resulted in a new and constructive consensus. Recognition on all sides of the need for fostering economic awareness in primary as well as in secondary education has coincided with an upsurge of interest in industry education and the world of work at primary level (Smith, 1988). This addition to the primary repertoire is welcome, provided that it does not result in disproportionate influence on schools by particular firms or activities, or excessive distortion of balance in the curriculum. One difficulty in encouraging business concerns to make decisions about activities in the public sector is that, while negotiating with schools, they have also to keep one eye on their competitors.

Beyond economic change, though closely linked with it (as is apparent in industry education), there are technological changes that make demands of their own. Their impact in primary education has been quite striking, in two ways. First, they have obviously affected almost every aspect of the primary curriculum itself. Instead of dabbling tentatively with filmstrips or teaching machines, schools have been transformed, first by pocket calculators, and then more radically by word processors and microcomputers. These have been introduced at an early age both at the behest of government and industry as a means of engendering facility in information technology, and also in response to the explosion of personal computers in the home and in entertainment: schools could not afford to lag behind. Moreover, the advent of City Technology Colleges could well increase the competitive pressure on individual primary schools to put themselves up in front in the new technology. Strangely, this development is enthusiastically espoused by those who suspect almost all other kinds of innovation in primary education. It is also very popular with most children, and it is widely believed that they take to it more readily than parents or teachers do, though I consider that the older generation is probably catching up fast. Every area of the curriculum has been affected by this new and stimulating kind of social pressure, though most effort has hitherto been put into what are now to be the core subjects in the National Curriculum, and especially into mathematics and science. Alongside this particular application of technology there are others such as the electronic keyboard and synthesizer, making different impacts on the curriculum. All of these developments are to be welcomed, but that welcome has to be tempered with the age-old reminder that technology cannot claim a monopoly of values.

That observation leads to the question of the changes that have taken place in culture, and to the new social demands that it engenders. One facet of cultural change, that of the acceleration of children's social maturation, is widely recognized. Pre-adolescence is increasingly absorbed into teenage culture, especially in music and (perhaps particularly for girls) dance and fashion, while junior and even infant boys dress like mini-adolescents, much as their forerunners in earlier centuries were attired as mini-adults. In addition, children participate increasingly in the shared adult culture of today. This cultural transformation is often regarded, with some reason, as being further accelerated by advertising and the media generally; for in spite of some apprehensive exaggerations, the media do powerfully influence the matrix of assumptions within which children live. Meanwhile, in reaction against the twee and sentimental images of childhood inherited from middle-class culture in Victorian and Edwardian times, primary-age children seem nowadays to be portrayed as untidy, knowing, pert and intent on having a good time. This generalized impression could have implications for primary education if it represents a collective expectation of what children are and should be like, and of how adults, including long-suffering teachers, ought to behave towards them. It may be a healthier image than the earlier one, partly because it can be shared across social classes and ethnic groups, but that does not necessarily legitimate it totally. Inevitably it makes some impact on children themselves, even though they mock it and modify it among themselves as they think fit, and allow themselves to revert to a much more dependent status when necessary. Sometimes it is considered that this perception of childhood in our current culture reacts unfavourably on social climate in schools and on the status and authority of teachers; but it is not quite so simple as that. Social harmony and social relationships within schools may be affected, but where this occurs, there are usually other reasons too.

In any case, however, the public images of childhood represent a social demand that cannot be ignored.

Leisure patterns are also influential insofar as they harmonize or conflict with what is on offer in school. Thus football is differently perceived from cricket, and both from swimming or snooker. Pop music is not viewed as classical music is, while both are seen as different from the *avant-garde* with is specialized musical culture; parallel distinctions are to be found in drama and to some extent in art. As for holidaying, now much more universal than it used to be, the switch from the traditional seaside to packaged Mediterranean sun has altered perceptions of other countries and indeed of holidays themselves, not always beneficially, while also underlining both the priority of family holiday over school and the oddity of those who cannot afford, or do not choose, to conform to the usual practice. Thus holidaying presents challenges to schools in both the formal and the hidden curriculum.

Although these cultural changes have an element of universality, it is also clear that their impact is not uniform. To the social-class and regional cultural differences that have existed for a long time must now be added the ethnic differences that are interwoven with them. Although the boundaries between social groups and their relative influences in society have been modified, and although the differences between them have changed since the mid-century, the existence of such differences is as clear as ever; indeed it sometimes appears that they are wider than they were, and even that this widening, and the sharper definitions of social status that accompany it, are themselves generally approved. Clearly, these cultural differences, including attitudes to work and behaviour and social organization, are related to the demographic and economic pressures already mentioned, and they powerfully affect primary schools, both in monocultural areas where there is an expectation that the school will reinforce the culture, and in cross-cultural areas where schools may be expected to contain conflict and somehow satisfy everybody (or alternatively to become everybody's scapegoat, with results that occasionally attain notoriety).

As another related component of culture, but much more than that, belief systems also engender social demands. The tension between technological development and ecological balance exemplifies this. So does the evolution of a multicultural society in which there is a greater range of religious and political beliefs than was the case thirty or forty years ago. The denominational disputes and the Christian/Humanist/Marxist conflicts characteristic of the years after the previous major Education Act, that of 1944, have been overtaken by other and less familiar issues, which yield kaleidoscopic permutations of understanding and interest that oblige all of the protagonists to reconsider their assumptions and attitudes, thus rendering the demands on teachers' comprehension much greater. Meanwhile, the rather astringent philosophy that was fashionable in the 1950s and for a while afterwards has given place to a more pluralistic, less positivist stance that chimes better with more recent developments in the social sciences. With these changes both in belief systems themselves and in ways of thinking and feeling about them, the language of primary education itself has been changed, and with it the demands made on primary teachers to understand their own roles.

This is almost part of the final social demand to be mentioned, one that is oddly enough aggravated by fuller professional consciousness among teachers themselves. Instead of following a fairly narrow furrow along a limited field, with a plough brought from college some years ago, as their forerunners in earlier decades were accustomed to do, primary teachers nowadays are more akin to scientific farmers, open to advice and persuasion from a number of professional sources, both in their initial training, itself more intellectual, comprehensive and demanding than the old Certificate in Education, and later in in-service and advanced studies (Delamont, 1987; Nias, 1988). In fact their claims to wider professionality are bombarded with advice, both from lobbies of professionals and from the general public, often by way of the quality press. Philosophers, psychologists, sociologists, paediatricians, curriculum theorists, management specialists, and political and religious spokesmen all pitch in with recommendations and recriminations. Visiting speakers at teachers' conferences, and indeed at other conferences, are often quoted as saying, 'Teachers should . . .' or 'Teachers must understand . . .', a procedure which itself styles teachers as people whose obligation, for all their claims to professional status, is first to learn instructions from other people and then to carry them out.

There is certainly no lack of readiness to prescribe social demands for these well-equipped teachers to implement. Multicultural considerations are only one instance of the obligations designated by others. Smoking, drug-taking, Green Cross Code, cycle safety and healthy diet, and defence against child abusers and sex offenders are only some of the social demands made upon teachers, though others may participate in meeting them. One major consequence of the 1988 Education Reform Act will be a legally enforceable intensification of this process of handing down orders.

As for independent primary schools, they have to meet their own set of social demands, sometimes delicately and sometimes forcefully expressed, but nevertheless cogent in their impact. Some of them are identical with those affecting the public system, some similar and some quite different. For the most part they require a more formal and traditional pattern of education than in the public sector, though there are exceptions in the opposite direction and these will be legally able to continue, being technically exempt from the National Curriculum, though practicalities may dictate otherwise.

To do justice to the whole question of social demands on independent primary schools would require a chapter to itself. Some of course would give pride of place to that chapter. Others, equally of course, would allow it no place at all.

Taken together, the social demands on primary schools, especially on those in the more exposed parts of the public sector, are perhaps greater now than at any earlier time. Moreover, many of those demands have come to be grouped together into coherent ideologies associated respectively with the New Left and the New Right, both convinced of the inadequacies of the older centrist consensus within which primary schools enjoyed more autonomy. To both, primary teachers are part of the problem rather than part of the solution. Part at least of the New Left sees primary teachers as imbued with social and ideological conservatism, middle-class attitudes and unwitting racism, all concealed behind the arras of liberal progressivism. In this analysis, the agenda of teacher education, including in-service education, must include the radicalization of primary teachers.

This view, held by some quite influential people, has in practice played into the hands of those on the New Right who conceive the whole educational 'establishment' as infected by such outlooks and as therefore ripe for disinfestation. They too see liberal progressivism as a cover, but this time for neo-Marxist ideas deliberately foisted on unwilling and unsuspecting primary teachers, who must therefore, for their own as well as society's sake, be urged, and if necessary obliged, to adopt the ideas of an enterprise culture.

According to their situation within the school system, some individual teachers are more open to one pressure, some to the other and a few to both at once. It is not quite true to say that these two ideologies represent more than minority views, or that they are equally strong, for at present there is an asymmetrical bias, in terms of power, in favour of the Right. Meanwhile the Left is prepared to wait; but children are there, and primary teachers, whatever they may think, cannot wait.

Schools' Responses

Faced with all these various demands, primary teachers encounter today a more complex task than ever before, one for which they often receive little more encouragement than was given to their diligent, low-status counterparts a century ago, and this in spite of the thoroughness of their own professional grounding. Some understanding of the dilemmas, transient as well as deep-seated, with which teachers are confronted, is a necessary step towards effective action, both by teachers themselves and by those outside the profession who are genuinely and influentially concerned about what goes on in primary education. This was realized by the Berlaks in their work with British primary teachers (Berlak and Berlak, 1981), though even their (or any other) definition of dilemmas implies a value position. The present brief survey could not constitute as comprehensive an analysis as the Berlaks', though, as will now be apparent, it too embodies values; there is no such thing as a Martian observer of education. It may be worthwhile to make, from this value position, some comments on teachers' potential response to the challenges posed by the social demands reviewed in the earlier part of the chapter.

Basic to any such series of responses is a sense of professional maturity and support, and this, fortunately, is one social feature that has become more obviously marked in recent years. Collegiality of organization within schools (Campbell, 1985) is one means by which a school staff can provide mutual support; opportunity for discussion and reflective thinking on neutral ground, away from the everyday rush of school, is another. Local 'cluster groups' or 'pyramids' of schools, working together with advisory staffs and institutions of higher education, extend the basis of mutual support more widely. Beyond this range again, professional discussions on a national scale, and taking in a range of opinions, about the nature of response to social demands can gain momentum. Some idea of the ways in which a constructive professional eclecticism might develop are suggested in a recent symposium on informal primary education as it is today (Blyth, 1988).

Actual responses must be based on aims as well as on demands, and it is evident that individual teachers will differ about the nature of their own aims and also about the readiness with which they will pursue those aims. Some may hold strong religious or political views. Some may be particularly concerned about working-class children, or girls, or children of one-parent families or members of minority ethnic groups, or those with special needs including dire poverty. It is pointless to hope that teachers in any school will all share the same views and emphases, but it is far from pointless to expect that teachers will be aware of, and tolerate, their colleagues' views and be prepared to help define such consensus as they can achieve among themselves, in mutual respect, and that the school management will promote the establishment of an atmosphere in which this kind of constructive mutuality can be fostered. So much for what might be called the 'structure of response'.

It is necessary to examine the nature of response to the demands themselves and the challenges that they represent. For this purpose it is also important to bear in mind which challenges are likely to be the most difficult to reconcile with the aims that teachers profess. In this perspective, response to the social demands already outlined will be briefly surveyed.

The demands raised by sectors of the teaching profession itself, and by those who claim to give instructions to it, are the ones that are perceived as falling at least partly within the effective purview of primary schools. They should be met with considered dignity. To 'Teachers should . . .' the reply must be 'Teachers consider . . .', their reply being based on substantial professional experience and expertise which expresses not only what schools aspire to do but also what they cannot be expected to do, on the basis of understanding of the functioning of primary education (Marriott, 1985). This also calls for a strategy of communication about the school and its purposes with governors, parents and the adult community, in implementation of the 1986 and 1988 Acts.

Continuing response to the traditional demands is the most conspicuous requirement, and in view of the shape of the National Curriculum and assessment as envisaged in the new legislation, schools are not likely to be allowed to give less than central attention to this kind of demand, both in the overt and in the hidden curriculum. It appears likely that administrative machinery will be developed for just that purpose. The probable effectiveness of that machinery is another question, but there can be no doubt about its purposes. Again, the assessment procedure itself implies an element of classification and some insistence that teachers should exercise that role effectively, though humanely. Schools will respond variously to this demand, but will not be able to sidestep it.

Less attention has hitherto been paid to the ways in which schools are likely to respond to the newer and less tangible social demands outlined earlier in the chapter. One of these concerns reaction to the general pressure for accelerated maturation. If this merely entails nostalgia for a less sophisticated and more dependent style of childhood, it would be difficult to sustain. If, however, it consists of emphasizing that growing up is to be encouraged but that it entails greater choice and greater responsibility and independence, within a relaxed but purposive and supportive community, then it can be enthusiastically recommended, as the best of middle schools clearly show. A jovial yet kindly concern for individual children can do much to combat media stereotypes, and to encourage them to challenge stereotypes for themselves.

Several of the other social demands have implications for the curriculum, and can be considered jointly. Perhaps the easiest in principle are those concerned with technologies within school, for these, buttressed by the National Curriculum, depend on teachers' acquisition of expertise and enthusiasm rather than on changes in aims. As was previously mentioned, the chief caveat has to be that of avoiding devoting too much time and resource to these demands, especially if this is done through mere compliance with external directives. Much the same is true of the introduction of economic awareness into the curriculum, though here there is more scope for controversy, especially over the model of economic life that may be presented: there is and should be room for more than one. But that issue pales into insignificance beside those raised by multicultural and multifaith education. Here schools may themselves be divided; in future their divisions might even come to be concentrated in the governing body which could send out contrary commands.

In some aspects of curriculum, multicultural material presents enrichment that can be welcomed by all teachers, recognizing that it involves new learning. In humanities there can be more problems, for example, in reconciling the claims of different cultures for consideration with those of experiential learning in the local area where the traditional culture is embedded, and indeed, with the sheer bulk of potential subject-matter. It is in moral and religious education, however, that the principal difficulties lie, as was shown in 1988 during the debates on the Education Reform Bill. This is a matter on which teachers should hold views based on their own faith and conscience, and in any school such views will show considerable variety. Moreover, it is often assumed that just because this social demand is so important, and a range of insights into religious and other world views so hard to encompass, it might be sufficient for class teachers in general to respond to this demand with a well-meant sequence of visits and festivals, accompanied by a conscientious avoidance of indoctrination. Yet this may in turn only result in indoctrinating children after all, into the idea that belief systems, instead of being magnificent conceptions by which people live and for which they may die, are rather tiresome and superficial extras that seem to mean something to some rather exotic or old-fashioned folk; a strange outcome for multicultural education. An infectious zest for understanding, combined maybe with a faith deep enough to appreciate and be enriched by others, can be a far more effective approach; but it may be too much to expect from every primary teacher burdened with so many other obligations.

There is in fact a general question here, that of the total burdens laid upon teachers and schools. The definition of a demand or an obligation is of course derived from principle; but the ability to respond to that demand or obligation is a question that can only be empirically estimated. Some needs may be within the response capacity of all schools and teachers; some may be beyond the powers of any, irrespective of their fine quota of curriculum consultants; and between these there lies an intermediate territory in which some schools can meet some of the needs, not always the same ones. Unfortunately, it is widely believed that a school that does not do what is expected of it, 'within existing resources', human and material, must be blamed for failing to do the impossible, rather than supported for trying to move in that direction. This collective whipping-boy role is something that calls for sustained professional resistance.

The remaining sets of demands, those posed by demography and by wider social and technological changes, are something to which schools as such are more palpably unable to respond within their own spheres of action. It may be that the stimulus to enterprise and initiative that will follow under the provisions of the 1988 Education Reform Act, in terms of budgetary control (in the larger primary schools) and of competitive pupil recruitment, will enable schools henceforth to adopt a more initiatory role, but this is likely to be offset, from the teachers' standpoint, by the enhanced powers of governors to determine the schools' aims and how they should be implemented.

For in this, as in many other ways, the new Education Act will alter the established order in English education, as it is intended to do; it will also introduce new areas of overwhelming uncertainty and instability even where its supporters intend an opposite outcome. Yet I believe that in this very situation a new social demand may arise, one which, paradoxically, may help to set the other demands in a more encouraging perspective. Twenty-five years ago I hoped that primary schools might, through their roles as welfare and cultural centres and with particular emphasis on the arts, develop as a source of local creativity that could help break down social and cultural stereotypes and barriers (Blyth, 1965). Now I believe that they should adapt this social function to a less optimistic age by offering, especially in the less affluent and confident communities, a kind of anchor that could be styled as 'creative stability'.

For the fulfilment of this function, a school will need the full support of its governing body and of its parents, and a clear recognition from them of what the school can and cannot be expected to achieve (see Chapter 7). Parents should be fully incorporated into the working of the school, and welcome in its activities, as in many schools they are. Heads and other teachers should in turn make contacts in the communities around schools, as far as is practicable, thus not only enlisting support but also offering the warmth of creative stability that is so often lacking in localities. In this way the extent of the capacity of schools to respond to other social demands can be more deeply understood; the values which they represent can be more fully appreciated; and they can identify purposefully, even prophetically, with the communities that they exist to serve.

References

ALEXANDER, R.J. (1984) *Primary Teaching*. London, Holt, Rinehart and Winston.
BARNETT. C. (1986) *The Audit of War: The Illusion and Reality*. London, Macmillan.
BELL, A. and SIGSWORTH, A. (1987) *The Small Rural Primary School: A Matter of Quality*. Lewes, Falmer Press.

BERLAK, A. and BERLAK, H. (1981) *Dilemmas of Schooling: Teaching and Social Change.* London, Methuen.

BLYTH, W.A.L. (1965) *English Primary Education: A Sociological Description.* 2 vols. Reprinted with postscript, 1967, London, Routledge and Kegan Paul.

BLYTH, W. A. L. (1984) *Development, Experience and Curriculum in Primary Education.* London, Croom Helm.

BLYTH, W.A.L. (Ed) (1988) *Informal Primary Education Today: Essays and Studies.* Lewes, Falmer Press.

CAMPBELL, R.J. (1985) *Developing the Primary Curriculum.* London, Holt, Rinehart and Winston.

CUNNINGHAM, P. (1988) *Curriculum Change in the Primary School Since 1945: Dissemination of the Progressive Ideal.* Lewes, Falmer Press.

DELAMONT, S. (Ed) (1987) *The Primary School Teacher.* Lewes, Falmer Press.

GALTON, M. *et al.* (1980) *Inside the Primary Classroom.* London, Routledge and Kegan Paul.

MARRIOTT, S. (1985) *Primary Education and Society.* Lewes, Falmer Press.

NIAS, J. (1988) *On Becoming and Being a Teacher.* London, Methuen.

POLLARD, A. (1987) *The Social World of the Primary School.* London, Holt, Rinehart and Winston.

SMITH, D. (Ed) (1988) *Industry in the Primary School Curriculum.* Lewes, Falmer Press.

TIZARD, B. *et al.* (1988) *Young Children at School in the Inner City.* London, Lawrence Erlbaum Associates.

WARD, C. (1978) *The Child in the City.* London, Architectural Press.

WARD, C. (1988) *The Child in the Country.* London, Robert Hale.

Chapter 13

The Aims of Primary Education in World Perspective

Philip Taylor

Our counsels go astray because they are not rightly addressed, and have no fixed end. No wind makes for him that hath no intended porte to sail unto.

The First Chapter
Essays of Montaigne, 1603

Introduction

Aims serve primary education in many ways. They indicate what primary education proposes to achieve by interfering in the lives of the young for the better: to make them numerate, literate and sociate. Aims serve to guide the processes of education in desired directions and justify, among other things, the teaching of the 'basics'. They also serve as the criteria in the debates about styles of primary education which from time to time sweep across the educational landscape; debates about 'formal' and 'informal' styles of teaching; about 'teacher-centred' and 'pupil-centred' methods of education. Advocates of each style and each method protagonistically claim that they achieve more or better educational ends than the other. More importantly, aims relate present attempts in education to their future moral, social and economic consequences. In the abstract education may be a millenial pursuit: a concern of great hopes and ideals. In its reality as a system of society the expectations are more mundane. In essence, education is expected to contribute to the maintenance of an informed citizenry which makes a valued material contribution to the well-being of society and to its economic and political progress.

Even a cursory examination of codes, regulations and reports on primary and elementary education now and in times past will confirm the essentially utilitarian aims which are held to be the purposes to be served:

- habits of industry
- respect for duty
- good manners
- self-discipline

— perseverance in difficult times
— devotion to truth

These are but some of the aims which late-Victorian England required elementary schools to set for themselves (BoE, 1905a). For the 'new kind of man' of the twentieth century:

— to master both scientific and practical knowledge
— to be an engineer for raising the level of the people
— to be a citizen armed with irreproachable morals

are all aims to be pursued by the school and in the classroom for the benefit of society.[2] (Tanzania, 1978)

The fact that many, if not most, of the aims of primary and elementary education, as well as first-cycle education, are cast in a utilitarian mould, does not mean that they are beyond contention and controversy. They are not. What are 'irreproachable morals'? What constitutes 'self-discipline'? When is the mastery of scientific knowledge achieved?

Contentious or not, aims serve to provide an orientation for educational systems, a guide to the purposes they are to serve and broad criteria against which their achievements may be judged. More than this, aims provide the template which shapes the design that educational processes are to take, determining in large measure the content of teaching and the substance of educational evaluation.

Aims in primary education, like most means of guidance in social systems, need refurbishing. Some will have served their day and need to be replaced. The meaning to be attached to others will require re-thinking. New, even radically different, aims may emerge, most frequently within complex metaphors which serve either to convey new educational possibilities or to return primary education to earlier purposes (Taylor, 1982). Both have happened within two decades in English primary education, from the acute child-centredness of the Plowden Report, to the work and subject-centredness of recent national surveys (CACE, 1967). To this issue, a return will be made later. It is to the question, 'What are in fact the aims of primary, elementary and first cycle education which are pursued the world over?' that we now turn.

Aims the World Over

In 1980 the *International Yearbook of Education* was devoted to a survey of educational systems throughout the world (IBE, 1980). Included in the survey was a statement of educational aims for ninety countries from the United States to Malawi, from Senegal to China, and from the Soviet Union to Columbia. Countries of North and South America, Africa, Australasia,

Europe (both east and west of the Urals), Asia and the Middle East were included. In fact, countries with highly differentiated education systems and countries with less differentiated systems were included as well as countries whose educational systems were ideologically embedded and those whose were not, or were less so.

In almost all these countries, whatever their level of educational development, compulsory primary education is the norm. In most, it also assumes a duty of the state having constitutional force: it is a right of the individual to receive primary education, in most instances from the age of 6-years-old until the age of 11- or 12-years-old. In only a minority of countries does primary education start earlier. The school week is almost universally five days, with a school year of between 180 and 200 days. The average size of a primary school class is forty, but the range is wide. In many African countries a primary school class will exceed sixty pupils. Only in some parts of the United States of America will a primary school class comprise fewer than twenty pupils.

The aims assigned to primary education in each country tend to be nested within the general aims of education for that country, except where primary or first-cycle education is all that the majority can expect, and such aims are indistinguishable. It is not feasible to do more than provide a flavour and an indication of the scope of the aims for primary and elementary education which are promulgated for each country, though an attempt will be made later both to summarize them in terms of general categories of aims and to analyze them in relation to economic, ideological and other variables.

There are, as one would expect, sharply contrasting educational aspirations from country to country, for example:

Gabon, Africa: Elementary primary schools will guarantee that basic education is provided for all children.

Austria, Europe: Schools will develop talents and capacities in accordance with ethical and religious values.

Bangladesh, Asia: Schools will be responsive to the specific needs of the country, will eradicate illiteracy and contribute to skill training for rural development.

Belgium, Europe: Schools will achieve a child's full potential through self-instruction in the light of daily realities.

Burma, Asia: Schools will eradicate illiteracy and contribute to productive work.

USA, North America: Schools will develop a positive attitude towards learning providing self-confidence through the acquisition of the basic tools of knowledge.

Contrasting or otherwise, there is a considerable consensus throughout the world about the aims that primary and elementary education should pursue, as Table 13.1 indicates.

Table 13.1   Aims of Primary and Elementary Education

Category of aims	Percentage
1. *Basic knowledge and skills* e.g. literacy and numeracy	41
2. *General education leading to intellectual, social and moral development* e.g. development of a child's full potential	38
3. *As a foundation for subsequent education* e.g. education preparatory to the next stage	20
4. *Other* e.g. social integration, pre-vocational skills, patriotism, religious indoctrination	1
	100

Almost 80 per cent of aims are concerned, as one would expect, with basic educational skills and a grounding in the general understanding of a range of subject matter and knowledge codes. This somewhat rough-and-ready categorization, as must be obvious, conceals significant differences in the scope of aims which are embraced country by country. As was suggested earlier, in the contrasting examples given, the educational sights of economically poorer countries are set at more fundamental aims — the eradication of illiteracy, for example — than are the sights of economically richer countries, which aim at more complex educational aims. Table 13.2 is an attempt to explore this as well as other relevant variables.

Even a cursory glance at Table 13.2 suggests that the marked difference between highly industrialized and mainly rural economies resides in the emphasis placed on liberal educational aims, defined for purposes of this comparative analysis as apolitical, secular and wide-ranging, though around 50 per cent of both mixed and mainly rural economies embrace such aims. Rural economies place significantly more emphasis on vocational aims than highly industrialized ones. Rather more than a quarter of mixed economies (27 per cent) emphasize the creation of and support for national unity. Concern to relate aims to multicultural and multifaith values is also more evident in countries with rural economies than with mixed and industrial ones. An emphasis on aims concerned with one or other form of socialism, whether communism, Marxist-Leninism or an adaptation of these, as in Yugoslavia, is about equally common among all countries irrespective of economic status.

Table 13.2 Emphasis on Aims by Country and Economic Status

Markedly industrial

Austria	L	
Australia	L	m/c
Belgium	L	m/f
Canada	L	
Czechoslovakia	C	
Denmark	L	
Finland	L	
France	L	
Germany DR	S	
Germany FR	L	
Italy	L	
Japan	L*	
Netherlands	L	
New Zealand	L	
Norway	L	
Poland	S	
Scotland	L	
Singapore	L	m/c
Spain	L	
Sweden	L	
United Kingdom	L	
USA	L	
USSR	C	

*By decree or occupying powers in 1946

Mixed

Argentina	L	C		
Bahrain	L	voc		
Bulgaria	M/L			
Byelorussia	M/L			
Chile	N/U			
China	C S	m/c	m/f	
Columbia	L			
Costa Rica	L			
Cuba	C			
Dominican Republic	L			
Egypt		voc		
India	L			
Iran	M	i		
Iraq	M	i		
Ireland	L	c		
Israel	L	z		
Ivory Coast	L			
Jordan	L	voc		
Kuwait		i		
Malaysia	N/U	voc	m/c	
Malta	L	voc		
Mauritius	L			
Mexico	L			
Oman	M	i		
Pakistan	M	i		
Peru	L			
Philippines	L			
Romania	S			
Libya	S	i		
Saudi Arabia	M	i		
Turkey	N/U	voc		
Yugoslavia	S	voc		

Markedly rural

Country				
Algeria	M	I		
Bangladesh	L	voc		
Burma	M/L	voc		
Burundi	L	voc		
Central African Republic	N/U	rep		
Chad	L	voc		
Congo	L	voc	m/c	m/f
Cyprus	L			
Ethiopia	S			
Gabon	L	voc		
Gambia	L			
Kenya	N/U			
Laos	S	voc		
Liberia	N/U			
Madagascar	S			
Malawi	L			
Morocco	N/U			
Nigeria	L			
Senegal	L			
Sierra Leone	L	m/c		
Sri Lanka	L			
Sudan	S	m/c	m/f	
Syria	N/U	voc		
Thailand	N/U	b		
Tunisia	N/U	voc		
United Republic of Cameroon	N/U	m/c	m/f	

Key: *Political emphasis*   *Religious emphasis*
L   =liberal educational emphasis   C =Christian
S   =socialist political emphasis   i =Islamic
C   =communist political emphasis   z =Zionist
M/L=Marxist-Leninist political emphasis   Vocational emphasis   =voc
M   =Muslim   Multicultural emphasis=m/c
N/U=emphasis on national unit   Multifaith emphasis   =m/f

A reading of Tables 13.2 and 13.3 indicates that an East–West, North–South divide will associate an aims emphasis in significant ways. The East (i.e. the USSR and its aligned countries) emphasize socialist, political aims in primary education and the West (including Australia and New Zealand) emphasize liberal, apolitical, 'open' and secular aims. As for the South, vocational aims and aims concerned with national unity tend to be emphasized to a greater extent than in countries of the North.

Economic conditions and political and religious interactions, now more

Table 13.3   Emphasis of Aims by Political, Religious and Other Categories

Emphasis	Percentages *		
	Industrial	Mixed	Rural
Political			
Liberal emphasis	79	59	46
Socialist emphasis	22	23	19
National unity	0	10	27
Religious			
Muslim	0	17	8
Christian	4	7	0
Islamic	0	23	4
Other			
Vocational	0	23	38
Multicultural	8	7	15
Multifaith	4	3	11

*Rounded to the nearest whole number

marked than at any time this century., especially in the Middle East and Asia, are bound to influence the values and purposes that a society places on primary education and in some societies to condition and delimit the scope of the aims employed to guide and shape what is taught. Nevertheless, educational aspirations seem difficult to suppress, even in poor countries or countries bounded within rigid political systems. Tanzania, a confirmed socialist country, for example, aims in its primary education:

'to produce a person able to master both scientific and practical knowledge'

an aim quite the educational equal of anything to which most Western democracies aspire. Science and mother-tongue teaching are found to be the concern of primary education as much in Iraq as they are in England, and numeracy as an aim has become almost as universal an aim as literacy. What marks country from country, nation from nation, is not so much the aims which they hold valid for primary education, as the qualitative meaning that they ascribe to them. Literacy in a small, largely rural, African country is not the same as it is in England, France or the USSR — as must be evident.

Aims and Qualities in Primary Education

In a short but seminal book, which addressed the economic and administrative problems of education in developing countries, in particular problems arising from the inertia of educational systems, Beeby (1966) proposed a theory of stages in the development of primary school systems.[6] The stages were:

'Dame School' : Stage 1   A stage characterized by the mechanical teaching of the 3 Rs which aims to inculcate the most rudimentary skills of literacy and numeracy.

Formalism : Stage 2 This is a stage of didactic teaching which aims to teach both the 3 Rs and their use in a variety of contexts but in a routine and formal manner.

Transition : Stage 3 This stage seeks to give currency to a wider concept of education than the previous stage. The 'primariness' (see Taylor, 1986) of this stage incorporates some qualities of pupil participation with the aims of raising motivation and encouraging a degree of curiosity and questioning.

Meaning : Stage 4 The aims of this stage are those which result in understanding rather than just knowing. The 3 Rs and their use in a range of subject-matter are employed to enhance the quality of meaning acquired from learning.

In effect, Beeby charts the evolution of primary schooling from its crude beginnings to the complex and sophisticated form which it takes in many wealthy, Western societies. As primary schooling evolves, it pursues aims the realization of which depends on advances not only in teacher education and sophisticated resources — libraries, visual and audio aids — but also on a concept of education whose texture is both broad and deep. More subjects are called into play, notions of discovery and enquiry displace memorization and rote learning, and the aims in view entail complex intellectual, personal and social understanding, as is demonstrated by Taylor and Holley (1975).

In an analysis of the stated aims of some 500 English primary school teachers of children respectively of 5, 7, 9 and 11 years of age Taylor and Holley showed that seven factors substantially accounted for the structure of the teachers' ratings. Of the seven factors, five were groupings of aims in ascending levels of complexity concerned with cognitive skills, socio-moral skills and skills related to aesthetic-creative dispositions. The remaining three were aims pursued at every level of English primary education at the time of the study.

Intellectual and socio-moral aims were emphasized differently at each age, as were aims related to aesthetic-creative disposition. Intellectual aims were the more significantly emphasized with higher age, as shown in Figure 13.1. Aims concerned with personal and with spiritual development were not. They were emphasized to the same degree throughout the years of primary education.

Taylor and Holley's proposition is that two levels of intellectual and two levels of socio-moral aims, a first and second level in both cases, come sequentially into play with the increasing age of the children. The grouping of aims (or aims factors) was as follows:

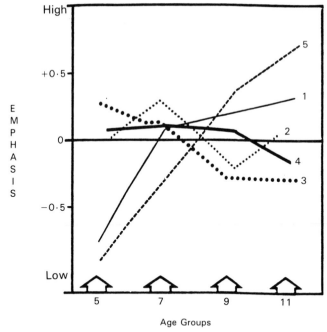

1. Intellectual: First Level Cognitive Skills.
2. Socio-Moral: First Level Affective Skills.
3. Aesthetic-Creative Affective Dispositions.
4. Socio-Moral: Second Level Affective Skills.
5. Intellectual: Second Level Cognitive Skills.

Figure 13.1   Emphasis of Aims by Age Group.
Source: Taylor and Holley, 1975

Intellectual First Level : Cognitive Skills Basic intellectual aims — simple literacy and numeracy with little subject-matter spread.

Intellectual Second Level : Cognitive Skills The deployment of basic intellectual skills in problem-solving and in a range of subject-matter areas are the aims at this level. The ground work of cognitive maturity is the goal.

Socio-Moral First Level : Affective Skills Aims concern the elementary know-how of social relations and the simple moral code that gives them meaning. The basic rules of conduct, which like the rules of basic literacy and numeracy, provide a grounding in 'sociocy'.

Social Moral Second Level : Affective Skills Aims relating to the social world become more complex; they have to do with understanding the 'why' of social interaction and the beginning of moral insight.

Aesthetic-Creative Skills Aims are initially concerned with the progressive unfolding of expressive behaviour and later the child's ability to produce pre-specified outcomes in art and music, drama and dance. Aims in this domain, as Figure 13.1 suggests, tended to be de-emphasized at later stages in primary education at the time of the study.

What this study in fact suggests is that Beeby's stages, discussed earlier, overlap at times; that the aims pursued vary, not only within stages, but also between stages as age and the opportunities that are presented vary. Aims considered as final educational goals may not correspond to the ways in which they function in directing teaching. In fact, it is in the process of teaching that opportunity for the achievement of aims, if only in part, may present itself, although the dynamics through which the achievement of educational ends are pursued is by no means as cut and dried as Beeby's model would suggest. Even so, the model has proved to be, and remains, a useful sensitizing paradigm through which to locate the increasingly complex character which aims take during the evolution of primary education. (Beeby, 1980) What more complexity of aim can there have been than that advocated in the Plowden Report which launched English child-centred primary education into a brave, and as it turned out, a delimited educational future: 'To realise the child's full potential'?

Primary Education the World Over

In an important paper, Meyer (1980), writing about which levels of educational systems have most effect on pupil and student achievement, suggests that a large part is played by those authoritatively defined categories which give meaning to educational systems, namely primary, secondary, further and higher education, as well as the sub-categories of which each is structured.[10] Further, he argues that institutional categories — schools, classrooms, as well as local and national managerial structures — are less relevant than educational categories of meaning in relation to educational achievement.

Having established the distinctions between educational and institutional categories, Meyer goes on to state:

> In the view taken here, what is often taken as rhetoric is in fact educational rationality; what is taken as rational organisational action is likely to be irrelevant decoration. If the rhetorical exoskeleton of education is its central ingredient, effective manipulation should focus there.

Part, and a large part at that, of Meyer's rhetorical exoskeleton, which he asserts is 'educational rationality', is made up of educational aims. The qualities which they signal give form and sense to educational categories. Without such aims as 'to develop basic literacy and numeracy and the beginnings of social and moral understanding', primary and elementary education would not be recognizable educational category; it would not convey that sense of primariness which is essential to those who accord the institutions of primary education their material and moral support. Such is not only true in the United States, which provided the data for Meyer's speculations, but is true wherever primary and elementary education is to be found. Aims are the cement which tie all those involved in primary education together in a common enterprise; an enterprise which knows few boundaries and shares a community of aspiration. As Beeby (1980) has suggested, as primary education evolves, the character of its aims changes to signal the pursuit of evermore complex educational aspirations.

As the world approaches the year 2000 new aims for primary education will merge and old ones will be reinterpreted. Whenever this occurs, in any country, primary education will, in time, be affected. That the world is 'a global village' is becoming more certain with every decade that passes. In primary education, such has been true for a long time. Aims and their entailed metaphors have seen to that. (Lakoff and Johnson, 1980)

At the beginning of this century aims were embodied in the teacher, the example he or she set, the knowledge he or she commanded. (BoE, 1905b) Today new knowledge, new ways of knowing and new situations needing to be understood increase with such rapidity that no teacher can comprehend nor exemplify them all. (Vickers, 1973) At best he or she is able to introduce to the young sufficient modes of thinking and feeling to equip them to cope with the contingent and uncertain. In such circumstances aims take on a markedly rhetorical tone that echoes qualities not previously seen as attainable through primary education — qualities to do with analysis and judgment. It is to these ends that the most recent mathematics curriculum (DES, 1988) and the newly-introduced science in primary schools serve. (NCC, 1988) Such aims as these will, in time, become as commonplace as once were the 3Rs, and as universal.

References

BEEBY, C.E. (1966) *The Quality of Education in Developing Countries*. Cambridge, MA: Harvard University Press.

See Beeby's essay in HEYNEMAN, S.P. (Ed) (1980) *Economic Development and Educational Quality*. Washington, DC: World Bank.

BOARD OF EDUCATION (1905) *Code of Regulations for Public Elementary Schools*. London, HMSO.

BOARD OF EDUCATION (1905) *Handbook of Suggestions for Teachers and Others Concerned in Elementary Education*. London, HMSO. (See title page, 'The most important thing that is taught in the elementary school is the teacher himself'.)

CENTRAL ADVISORY COUNCIL FOR EDUCATION (1967) *The Plowden Report.* **1**, London, HMSO.

DEPARTMENT OF EDUCATION AND SCIENCE (1988) *Mathematics for Ages 5 to 15.* London, HMSO.

INTERNATIONAL BUREAU OF EDUCATION (1980) *International Yearbook of Education.* **32**, Paris, UNESCO.

LAKOFF, G. and JOHNSON, M. (1980) *Metaphors We Live By.* Chicago, Chicago University Press.

MEYER, J. (1980) 'Levels of educational systems and schooling effects' in BIDWELL, C. and WINDHAM, D. (Eds), *The Analysis of Educational Productivity,* **2**, Cambridge, MA: Ballinger.

NATIONAL CURRICULUM COUNCIL (1988) *Science in the National Curriculum.* London, NCC.

TANZANIA (UNITED REPUBLIC OF) (1978) *Major Trends in Education.* Dar es Salaam, National Commission for UNESCO.

TAYLOR, P.H. (1982) 'Metaphor and meaning in the curriculum on opening windows on the not yet seen', *Journal of Curriculum Theorizing:* **4,** 1 pp. 209–16.

For the development of this concept see TAYLOR, P.H. (1986) *Expertise and the Primary School Teacher.* Windsor, NFER-Nelson Pub. Co.

TAYLOR, P.H. and HOLLEY, B. (1975) 'A study of the emphasis given by teachers of different age groups to aims in primary education' in TAYLOR, P.H. (Ed) *Aims, Influence and Change in the Primary School Curriculum.* Windsor, NFER.

VICKERS, G. (1973) 'Educational criteria for times of change', *Journal of Curric. Studies,* **5(1)**, pp. 13–24.

Notes on Contributors

Janet Atkin is a Lecturer in Infant and Pre-school Education in the School of Education, University of Nottingham, where she is engaged in teacher in-service education. Her particular interests are home/school relations and early childhood curricula.

Alan Blyth is a graduate of Cambridge, Nottingham and Manchester Universities and has taught in schools, colleges and universities. For nearly twenty years, he was Sydney Jones Professor of Education at the University of Liverpool, where he is now an Honorary Senior Fellow. His publications have been mainly in the field of primary education, with special reference to curriculum and social context, and he is now completing a study of assessment in primary humanities.

Jim Campbell is Reader in Education, University of Warwick; he is author of *Developing the Primary School Curriculum*, *The Routledge Compendium of Primary Education*, and editor of the journal *Education 3–13*.

Cedric Cullingford is Head of Primary Education at Brighton Polytechnic. His books include *Children and Television*, *Parents, Teachers and Schools* and *The Primary Teacher*. He is at present researching children's attitudes to schools and to politics.

Peter Cunningham was formerly a lecturer at Westminster College, Oxford, and is currently a teacher of infants in Leicestershire. His research interests combine curriculum and educational policy with social and cultural history, and his most recent book, *Curriculum Change in the Primary School Since 1945*, was published by Falmer Press in 1988.

Nancy Elliott has spent all her working life in primary education as teacher, deputy head, head, adviser and inspector. She has worked for the British Council in Botswana on continuous assessment and has a particular interest in community education. She is currently a member of three national primary school committees, and is Senior Inspector (Primary Education) with Newcastle upon Tyne Education Authority.

Philip Gammage was originally trained as a primary school teacher, teaching for ten years in London and eventually reading for a doctorate in psychology whilst on the staff of Bristol University. He divides his research and teaching interests between early childhood education and health education, has taught at all levels in the system, from infants to university in the UK and abroad. Currently, he is a member of the National Curriculum Council (Interim Whole Curriculum Committee) and Professor and head of initial training at the University of Nottingham.

Norma Newell studied initially at the University of Newcastle upon Tyne, took a PGCE at Neville's Cross, Durham, and an MA in applied educational studies at York University. She is now a headteacher in Cleveland and takes a keen interest in the county's in-service provision.

Andrew Pollard has taught across the primary age range and written books on social relationships, child perspectives and 'reflective teaching' in primary schools. He is Director of the Redland Centre for Primary Education at Bristol Polytechnic.

Nigel Proctor studied at the universities of Manchester, London and Leicester and has thirty years' teaching experience in school, college, polytechnic and university. He is now PGCE Tutor and Coordinator of Curriculum Research at Manchester Polytechnic's Didsbury School of Education. He is currently researching into the school curriculum and teacher education, on which he has over thirty publications since 1984.

Mike Sullivan has been headteacher of a Walsall primary school since 1980. He has published widely and is the author of *Parents and Schools* and editor of *Supporting Curriculum Change in Primary Schools*. He is Review Editor for *Education 3–13* and an external examiner for Warwick University's PGCE course.

Philip Taylor is Professor of Education at the University of Birmingham and for some years taught in a primary school in Manchester. Among his interests are the work of the Primary Schools Research and Development Group, its publication *Education 3–13* and the research which it undertakes, the most recent of which is published as *The Primary School Teacher: A Profession in Distress*. Most recently he has been involved in writing *Primary School Science and the National Curriculum*.

Gordon Wood trained as a teacher in York and continued his studies at Teeside Polytechnic, The Open University and York University. He is headteacher at Acklam Whin Primary School, Middlesborough and since 1973 has been involved in Cleveland's in-service programme. He is currently a member of the National Curriculum Council (Interim Advisory Committee for the In-Service Education of Teachers).

Index

WIDENER UNIVERSITY
WOLFGRAM
LIBRARY
CHESTER, PA.